Last Words and the Death Penalty

Voices of the Condemned and their Co-Victims

A book in the series:

Criminal Justice Recent Scholarship
Edited by Marilyn McShane and Frank P. Williams III

Last Words and the Death Penalty

Voices of the Condemned and their Co-Victims

Scott Vollum

LFB Scholarly Publishing LLC
El Paso 2010

First published 2008 by LFB Scholarly Publishing LLC.
First printing in paperback, 2010.

Library of Congress Cataloging-in-Publication Data

Vollum, Scott, 1970-
Last words and the death penalty : voices of the condemned and their co-victims / Scott Vollum.
p. cm. -- (Criminal justice recent scholarship)
Includes bibliographical references and index.
ISBN 978-1-59332-264-9 (alk. paper)
1. Death row inmates--United States--Biography. 2. Victims of crimes--United States--Case studies. 3. Capital punishment--United States--Case studies. I. Title.
HV8699.U5V65 2008
364.660973--dc22
2007043130

ISBN 978-1-59332-264-9 (casebound)
ISBN 978-1-59332-436-0 (paperback)

Printed on acid-free 250-year-life paper.
Manufactured in the United States of America.

Dedication

This book is dedicated to the victims of violence whose voices are represented throughout these pages, and to those whose voices remain unheard.

Table of Contents

Acknowledgements

As I sit here reflecting on what to say about the numerous people who played a role in the completion of this book, I can only conclude that I am extremely fortunate. Over the years, so many individuals have touched my life in such positive ways. I have truly been fortunate to have come in contact with each of you and to have had the opportunity to benefit from your presence in my life.

I owe a very special debt of thanks to Dennis Longmire. There are few people to whom I owe more. Your influence on me cannot be measured or adequately expressed in words. You have been, and will continue to be, a model for me professionally and personally. Your commitment to making the world a better place is a true inspiration.

To my parents, Jay and Mickey, I owe such a debt of gratitude for the support and love you have unconditionally offered me at every turn along the long path of my personal and professional life. I owe so much of who I am to your love and support and would likely not be where I am today without it. Mom, I also thank you for your more practical assistance in this study. You diligently read every page and always provided positive feedback.

I reserve my deepest and most heartfelt gratitude for Jacki—my wife, best friend, and partner in life. I don't even know where to begin. You are such an integral part of my life that it is impossible to imagine how I could have accomplished any of this without you. I quite simply would not be where I am or who I am today without you. You not only provided an essential support system during the writing of this book but also acted as a sounding board and editor. I am more grateful for these things than you know. Throughout the process of writing this book, your patience, understanding and encouragement were immeasurable. But, more importantly, your love and compassion sustained me at each step along the way. You are my love and my life-force and truly make me a better person, both professionally and personally.

Finally, I must thank my "girls," Abby and Beauty. On lonely days and nights at the computer, you were always there devotedly lying nearby. And, you never failed to remind me to lighten up and take a break once in a while.

To all of the individuals identified herein, I am eternally grateful. You have had a great deal to do with the completion of this book and with my professional and personal success more generally. The flaws and failures, however, rest on my shoulders alone.

CHAPTER I:

Introduction

As we begin the 21st century, the death penalty has become a defining institution in American culture. It has also become a political and emotional hot button and polarizing point of debate. The last decade has seen rapidly growing death row populations and record numbers of executions in the United States. At the same time, the international trend has been toward abolition of the death penalty (Hood, 2002; Trail, 2002) and cries for moratoria and investigations into the administration of the death penalty have become louder and more visible in the United States (Kirchmeier, 2002; Turow, 2003; Vollum, Longmire & Buffington-Vollum, 2004). In spite of these international and domestic trends, the use of the death penalty does not appear to be going away in the United States and has, in fact, flourished in recent years. Over the past three decades death row populations across the country have increased rapidly and in 1999 the largest number of executions were carried out since its reemergence in 1976 (Death Penalty Information Center [DPIC], 2007a). In Texas alone a record 40 executions took place in that year, the peak of a steady increase in executions in that state beginning in 1982 (DPIC, 2007a). In 2005, the United States followed only China, Iran and Saudi Arabia in number of executions and stood alone among Western countries in retaining the death penalty (DPIC, 2007a).

One factor that contributed to the apparent explosion of executions in the late 1990s was the passage of a piece of legislation referred to as the Anti-terrorism and Effective Death Penalty Act (AEDPA). This act, signed into law by President Bill Clinton in 1996, placed severe restrictions on successive federal habeas corpus petitions by death row inmates (del Carmen et al., 2005). It also limited the amount of time a defendant had to file an appeal based on new evidence (del Carmen et al., 2005). An even more extreme policy on this can be observed in Virginia's 21-day rule in which a defendant has only 21 days to appeal based on newly discovered evidence (ACLU of Virginia, 2003). It is no surprise that, on average, condemned inmates in Virginia spend the least amount of time on death row prior to execution at just over five years (DPIC, 2007a).

Another factor that potentially contributed to the increased use of the death penalty in the late 1990s is a public that seemingly embraced the death penalty. Support for the death penalty soared in the 1990s reaching a 65 year high in 1994 at 80% (Bohm, 2007). The "get tough on crime" policies that flourished in the 1990s included increasingly hard-line attitudes about the use of the death penalty (Tonry, 2004). Moral panics about predatorial murderers and monstrous individuals who prey on the innocent contributed to a public wishing to rid the world of such dangers. The death penalty satisfied this desire. And, the increasingly sanitized and de-humanized machinery of the death penalty allowed the public to disengage from the moral dilemma of state-sanctioned killing (Johnson, 1998; Lifton & Mitchell, 2000). The human voices at the center of this punishment were rarely heard.

This explosion in the use of the death penalty brought with it increasing attention from all directions. It has become one of the de jour controversial issues in the realm of criminal justice. The rapid increase in its use occurring in the late 1990's and early 21st century also brought on a greater degree of scrutiny and controversy at the state, national, and even international level. Issues surrounding wrongful convictions and the potential of innocent inmates being executed (Niven, 2004) and international disdain for the United States' use of the death penalty (Hood, 2002; Trail, 2002) have become particularly potent in the national psyche, often driven by substantial media coverage. Perhaps, in part related to these factors, the public has become more ambivalent about the death penalty with general support declining since 1995 (DPIC, 2007a). The public is increasingly interested in alternatives to the death penalty such as life in prison without parole. In fact, studies have shown that support for the death penalty declines significantly when true life sentences are available (Bohm, 2007). In one poll, support declined below 50% when the option of life without parole was offered (DPIC, 2007a). A true sign of changing attitudes comes from a study in which a majority of Texans, notoriously the staunchest supporters of the death penalty, were found to lack confidence in the death penalty (Vollum et al., 2004). Perhaps the greatest signifier that sensibilities about the death penalty are changing comes from the fact that its use has declined. The number of executions in 2005 (53) represents a 46% decrease from the record number in 1999 (98) (DPIC, 2007a). Nevertheless, we are still executing far more inmates annually than we had in the first two decades of the modern, post-*Furman*, death penalty era. Although it is not certain what to make of current trends, it cannot be denied that a dialogue surrounding the death penalty has heated to a boil.

Although many perspectives are expressed and acknowledged in the ever-increasing dialogue surrounding the death penalty, these voices have predominantly come from those on the periphery of the actual execution. The death penalty has provided fodder for political and academic debate for centuries. This is as true today as anytime in American history. The death penalty took center stage in the 2000 presidential campaign as the republican candidate (George W. Bush), the Texas governor who presided over the greatest number of executions in the modern (post-*Furman*) era, went head to head with the more "liberal" democratic vice president. In the end both presidential candidates supported the death penalty on the basis that it was a general deterrent (Turow, 2003), even though evidence doesn't support this argument (Cochran & Chamlin, 2000; Fagan, 2005). Other popular rationale for the death penalty include reducing prison populations and the costs associated with them, providing justice for victims and co-victims, incapacitation of irredeemable criminals, and "just deserts" retribution necessary for maintaining order in society (Turow, 2003). Conversely, some politicians are now taking stands against the death penalty, especially in regard to the contemporary attention being given to wrongful convictions in capital cases. In Illinois, for example, former Governor George Ryan called for a moratorium on executions and put together a commission to study the death penalty. The commission concluded that the death penalty was virtually beyond repair, recommending that it be abolished and calling for sweeping reforms if it were to be maintained (Turow, 2003). In the end, Governor Ryan commuted all death sentences to life sentences prior to leaving office. Other states have followed Illinois' lead in calling for moratoria and developing commissions to study the death penalty and its application (DPIC, 2007a).

The death penalty has also dominated much of the Supreme Court's time over the last several decades (del Carmen et al., 2005). In fact, some of the loudest voices regarding the death penalty come from those on the Supreme Court. Following years of chipping away at the "death is different" doctrine and the associated heightened scrutiny and safeguards initially intended for capital cases (Vollum, 2005), recent decisions have begun to diminish the use of the death penalty. Just in the last five years, the Court has declared the death penalty for mentally retarded offenders (*Atkins v. Virginia*, 2002) and for juvenile offenders (*Roper v. Simmons*, 2005) unconstitutional. It has also prohibited judges from making the final death sentence determination (*Ring v. Arizona*, 2002). These three cases alone effectively invalidated hundreds of death sentences (DPIC, 2007a), making a strong statement about the appropriate application of the death penalty. Most recently, the Supreme Court has reiterated and potentially expanded the notion that those suffering from severe mental illness to the point of delusion at the time of execution should not be executed (*Panetti v. Quartermain*, 2007). Additionally, the Supreme Courts of Kansas and New York in recent years have declared their states' death penalty statutes unconstitutional (DPIC, 2007a).

Academics also provide strong voices in regard to the death penalty. In fact, Radelet and Akers (1996) published an influential article in the debate about the deterrent value of the death penalty that was based solely on a survey of perspectives of criminal justice and criminology academicians in the United States. In it they reported that an overwhelming majority (92.6%) of criminology and criminal justice professors and researchers did not believe the death penalty to be an effective deterrent (Radelet & Akers, 1996). More recently, Robinson (2008) has published a book devoted to examining the views of death penalty "experts," most of whom are academics. Finally, the general public as well as protestors and activists have become increasingly vocal in regard to the death penalty (See, for example, Kirchmeier, 2002, Lynch, 2002, and Vandiver, Giacopassi & Gathje, 2002). Volumes of research and literature have accumulated regarding public opinion and public attitudes about the death penalty, and the views of activists on both sides of the issue have become more prevalent in the media.

Indeed, much has been written about the death penalty in America. Issues surrounding opinions about the death penalty (Bohm, 2007; Bohm, Clark & Aveni, 1991; Cochran, Boots & Heide, 2003; Durham, Elrod & Kinkaid, 1996; Vollum, Longmire & Buffington-Vollum, 2004), rationale and arguments for and against the death penalty (Bedau & Cassell, 2004, Bohm, 2007; Radelet & Borg, 2000a; Turow, 2003), and the social, psychological, and political ramifications of the death penalty (Bowers & Pierce, 1980; Cochran & Chamlin, 2000;

Hood, 2002; Radelet, 1989; Sarat, 2001) have been thoroughly covered and debated[1]. Many voices are heard loud and clear in regard to the death penalty. Opinion, perspectives and rhetoric are not lacking. Yet very little is known about the opinions and perspectives of those most closely tied to and impacted by the death penalty and executions: the condemned inmate and his or her victim's survivors (hereafter referred to as co-victims[2]). It is rare that one is exposed directly to the perspectives and opinions of the condemned offender or even the co-victims. These are voices that have become silenced—or at least muffled—in the midst of the "noise" of these other groups.

The present study breaks this silence by exploring the statements made by both parties immediately surrounding the execution of the offender: the final statements made by the condemned and the statements made by co-victims to the media at the time of the execution. In effect, the present study, in the words of Charles Ragin (1994), "gives voice" to these groups who otherwise tend to go unheard in the ever-increasing discourse on the death penalty. This is an important step toward a fuller understanding of the death penalty. The death penalty is a social reality from which humanity has been obscured by political, academic, and philosophical rhetoric and discourse. By giving voice to these groups most directly affected by the death penalty, the reality of human relationships, human emotions, human needs, and human suffering can be more fully considered in the context of the death penalty and the crimes that precede it.

In this book, the voices of these groups are examined via the unique communiqué that exists in the moments directly surrounding an execution: the last statement of condemned inmates and statements made by co-victims at the time of execution. But first the literature surrounding two key areas salient to the study are discussed: 1) the literature pertaining to the human context of the death penalty, the

---

[1] The works cited here represent only a sampling from the voluminous body of literature that exists in the context of each of these areas. A more thorough consideration of this literature is outside the scope of the present work.

[2] "Co-victims" is the preferred term for those who have lost a loved-one to murder. "Victim's family" is overly limiting to the exclusion of close friends and other non-family individuals who shared an emotional connection to the victim. "Survivor" is potentially confusing as it may confuse those who literally survived the murderer's attack with those who only experience the loss of their loved-one.

people who are most closely tied to the death penalty and its process and who are most directly impacted or affected by it, and 2) the literature on restorative justice and specifically it's practice in the context of the death penalty. As this study puts a human face and perspective on the death penalty process, particularly as regards the condemned and their co-victims, the literature on the human context of the death penalty more generally is important to consider. As will be clear, the impact of the death penalty and executions is broad and far-reaching. Chapter II addresses this impact and the various individuals most acutely affected by the death penalty process. From the original crime to the broad social ramifications of the death penalty, the examination extends beyond offenders and co-victims. Notably the impact of the death penalty on criminal justice personnel, offenders' family members, and society at large (both national and international) is addressed. In the end, a better understanding of the extensive casualties of the death penalty hopefully emerges. The chapter concludes with a discussion of the primary mode by which co-victims currently have a voice in the capital punishment process: victim impact statements.

Chapter III pertains to restorative justice and the death penalty. As a primary focus of this book is to account for the themes of both the condemned and co-victims' statements at the time of execution, it is only natural to consider the potential principles of restorative justice which are expressed. As restorative justice concentrates on the connection between offender, victims and the community and the healing and repair needed in the aftermath of crime, it is a logical step to assume that such a process plays a role for some individuals experiencing the lengthy and often troubling process of the death penalty and execution. Indeed, as Arrigo and Fowler (2001) point out, a default "death row community" is created each time an offender is sentenced to death. Connections are natural (although perhaps unwelcomed) in this context and this study explores further any such connection between offender and co-victims by examining their statements at the time of execution. Chapter III begins with a brief overview of the theory and principles underlying restorative justice followed by a more specific consideration of one of the predominant applications of restorative justice: victim-offender mediation (VOM). It concludes with an examination of restorative justice practices in the context of the death penalty.

Chapters IV and V provide the reader with the objectives of the present study and the methodology by which these objectives are met.

This is an exploratory study of the thematic content of both condemned offenders' and co-victims' statements made during the time of executions. In Chapter IV, the prior related research and literature—what little there is—is addressed. The specific objectives and guiding questions for this inductive study are also outlined in Chapter IV. I also address the limitations of the study, which are by no means insubstantial. Nor are they overwhelmingly detrimental or catastrophic. Chapter V presents the methods by which the present study was conducted, including data collection, coding, and analytical processes. Most importantly, the sources of statements of both condemned inmates and co-victims are indicated and discussed as are the methods for coding, interpreting and analyzing the themes therein. Finally, the reliability and validity of the present study are discussed.

Chapters VI and VII present the results of these analyses in regard to the last statements of the condemned and the statements of co-victims, respectively. Included among these analyses are in depth qualitative examinations of the major themes of statements. Here the reader is presented with the actual words of these two populations in the context of the major thematic messages found among them. The themes of these statements are also examined in the context of various factors, including general demographics as well as variables related to the crime, the trial and the execution event. Finally, the restorative and non-restorative nature of these statements are examined.

In the final chapter, I briefly consider some of the broader conclusions and implications that can be drawn from these findings. I also incorporate an examination of the condemned and co-victim statements in conjunction with one-another. This adds another dimension to the primary analyses of last statements of the condemned and statements of co-victims by drawing the two together in a form of pseudo-dialogue. Finally, I consider the lessons learned about both the death penalty and about research on these populations in the context of the death penalty. Included are implications for future research. It is my hope that, in the end, this study provides some insight into these neglected participants in the death penalty process, the impact of that process in the search for humanity, justice and healing, and the future hope of attaining these lofty goals with or without the death penalty.

CHAPTER II:

The Human Context of the Death Penalty

Goffman (1959, 1967, 1974) would characterize the death penalty and all the events and circumstances surrounding it as human dramas. Foucault (1975) referred to this drama as the "spectacle of the scaffold." Of course, Foucault (1975) was referring to the spectacle of public executions. Although modern executions are carried out in a much more inconspicuous and controlled (some say "bureaucratic") manner (Burnett, 2002), the dramatic elements remain. That is, the death penalty occurs in the context of the meaningful interaction of human actors. From the murder which sets its inevitable consideration in motion to the final rituals surrounding the execution, real human drama is at the center of the death penalty. Not only is it an expression of law and punishment in response to horrible criminal acts and unimaginable violent victimization, it is also a statement about or reflection of society as a whole. The death penalty and its use tell us something about cultural values and patterns of interaction in human societies. But, while it may be reflective of social culture, it also has an impact on society. Garland (1990) writes of criminal punishment generally: "Instead of thinking of punishment as a passive 'expression' or 'reflection' of cultural patterns established elsewhere, we must strive to think of it as an active generator of cultural relations and sensibilities" (p. 250). The death penalty, being the most extreme and severe of all current penal sanctions in the United States, is arguably the most potent "generator" of human consequences. In this chapter these human consequences and the broader human context of the death penalty and all events surrounding it are considered.

I begin with a consideration of that event which precedes all modern death penalty cases—homicide.[3] The first human casualty in the context of the modern death penalty begins here with the victims and co-victims of the crime whose victimization logically precedes any consideration of the death penalty. Specifically, the impact homicide has on co-victims and their resultant needs are examined. I then turn my attention to the human casualties of the death penalty and executions themselves. Three realms of the death penalty and its human casualties are considered. First, the capital punishment process which encompasses the time period commencing from sentencing through the long and often delayed residence on death row for the condemned is examined. The human drama surrounding this process occurs in the context of what Arrigo and Fowler (2001) call the "death row community." Members of this community include the condemned and his or her loved-ones as well as the co-victims of the condemned's offense. Also, this "death row community" includes what Reid (2001) calls the "functionaries" in the system including the correctional staff, members of the media, and members of the legal community who struggle with the often long and complicated legal appeals that are raised during this period. Each of these members is impacted in their own ways by the capital punishment process that brings them together. Second, the last days of a condemned inmate and the "rituals of death" which accompany them are discussed. From deathwatch to "deathwork" and ultimately to the death chamber, these rituals include human actors who are inevitably impacted and transformed by the execution. Third, the broader social context of the death penalty is considered. Specifically, questions regarding whether capital punishment in America has the desired effect of deterring and diminishing violent victimization in society, comports with international sensibilities, and/or serves to offer justice and maintain social order in a society in which violent crime has become endemic are addressed. Finally, I conclude by bringing the discussion back to the co-victims of the violent murder which catalyzed the capital punishment process in the first place. Here I examine the role of victim impact statements (a rare circumstance in which victims are "heard" in

---

[3] Although the death penalty historically has been used for crimes other than homicide and that it remains available for some non-homicide crimes in federal and military jurisdictions in the United States today, in the "modern" death penalty era, it is a sanction virtually exclusively reserved for particular acts of homicide.

criminal cases) in capital cases and the policies and practices surrounding them in Texas.

SURVIVORS OF HOMICIDE (CO-VICTIMS)

The Impact of Homicide on Co-Victims

It is a commonplace to assume that losing a loved one to an act of homicide is one of the most traumatic losses one can experience. To have someone's life suddenly ended at the hands of another person leaves most survivors or co-victims at a loss for how to make sense of what has happened and how to find peace and healing in the wake of such a tragedy (Dicks, 1991; Geberth, 1992; King, 2003; Rock, 1998). In addition to the responses and emotions common among those who are grieving the loss of a loved one, a homicide raises additional feelings of horror and fear as a result of the intentional and violent actions of another person which caused the death (Rock, 1998). Geberth (1992) states, "[t]he grieving process under these circumstances is more intense and is commonly accompanied by acute feelings of rage and anger as well as a sense of injustice and helplessness" (p. 92). It is safe to say that the experience of loss among homicide co-victims defies, to some degree, the typical characterization of the experience of loss.

However, in spite of the unique nature of loss experienced by homicide co-victims, research has shown that the grieving process follows the same general pattern as that resulting from death and loss in other circumstances (Brown, 1991; Geberth, 1992). Kubler-Ross (1969) identified the five primary stages of grief in her landmark book *On Death and Dying*: (1) denial and isolation, (2) anger, (3) bargaining, (4) depression, and (5) acceptance. Others have presented similar conceptualizations of the grieving process. Westberg (1962) employed ten stages to illustrate the grieving process: (1) shock, (2) emotion, (3) depression and loneliness, (4) physical symptoms of distress, (5) panic, (6) guilt, (7) hostility and resentment, (8) inability to return to usual activities, (9) hope, and (10) affirmation of reality. Doyle (1980) outlined grief in only three stages: (1) shock, protest, anger, and disbelief, (2) intense emotion, and (3) final adaptation. Although these conceptualizations of grief differ, they present very similar pictures of the grieving process and contain many common elements. The National Organization of Victim Assistance (NOVA, as cited in

Geberth, 1992) identifies similar stages specifically applied to survivors of homicide victims. These stages and their characteristics are:

1. DENIAL: shock, confusion, avoidance, refusal to participate in acknowledgments, crying, physical pain, weakness, nausea, sleep disturbances, loss of appetite.
2. PROTEST or ANGER: anger at self, loved one, God, the world, irritability, lack of concentration, frenzied activity, fatigue.
3. DESPAIR: urge to recover what was lost, slower thinking and actions, sorrow, agony, depression, hopelessness and powerlessness.
4. DETACHMENT: apathy, indifference, decreased socialization, disengagement from the world, absent spontaneity and effect.
5. RECONSTRUCTION OF LIFE: spasms of grief, a loss is forever (pp. 91-92).

It is important to note that the grieving process for homicide co-victims, although following similar patterns of grief as those experienced as a result of loss in more "normal" circumstances, is unique in many ways. Sprang, McNeil & Wright (1989) state that "[a]lthough grief is a common human experience, mourning for families of murder victims is more profound, more lingering, and more complex than normal grief (p. 159) and further note that "[t]he cruelty of this act adds to both the depth and extent of the grieving." (p. 162).

Researchers have cited numerous factors that set the loss of a loved one as a result of murder apart from other experiences of death and loss. Few events experienced in life can produce the level of terror as that of murder. As a result of this added level of terror, co-victims often experience heightened feelings of fear and vulnerability (Brown, 1991; Magee, 1983) in addition to the other more common responses such as anger and despair. Moreover, such fear and vulnerability may be accompanied by desires for revenge or retaliation (Lifton & Mitchell, 2000; Sarat, 1997). And, the perceived injustice of the act will often result in rage (Rock, 1998). Parkes (1993) cites the following factors as some that make the loss of a loved one at the hands of a murderer particularly difficult to deal with: "witnessing of horrific circumstances," "threat to the life of the survivor or other loss of personal security," and "death by human agency" (p. 49). These factors, generally unique to loss associated with murder, not only exacerbate the grieving process by presenting an element of terror and fear, but also, according to Parkes (1993), contribute to the likelihood that psychological problems will arise and persist in the wake of the traumatic event.

There are also other more mundane stressors which invade the normal grieving process for homicide co-victims. The first is the manner in which co-victims are notified or come to learn about the murder. Co-victims are likely to learn about the death of their loved one from law-enforcement officials, often only being provided with limited or inaccurate information and often in the process of an investigation—not the ideally sensitive manner in which to be informed of such a loss (Brown, 1991). Others may learn about the murder via the media (Brown, 1991), an extremely impersonal way in which to find out such news. Second, murder "produces unforeseen demands on the family such as identifying the body...and dealing with the media" (Brown, 1991, p. 193). Such tasks can add extreme stress on top of an already emotionally painful event and also force a public element into an otherwise private grieving process. Third, due to the nature of the death, co-victims may become preoccupied with the level of brutality and suffering associated with the murder and feel they "need to know the details of the death" (Sprang et al., 1989, p. 163). Finally, murder often is not seen as a socially acceptable manner of death in society (Brown, 1991). Brown (1991) explains: "Because it is a frightening way to die, others may try to blame, at least in part, the murder on the victim so they can sustain the illusion that murder couldn't happen to them" (p. 193). Indeed, one of the earliest scholarly studies on homicide invoked the concept of "victim precipitation" as a common factor in murders (Wolfgang, 1958). Such a de-legitimization of the death only serves to invalidate the feelings associated with the loss and stunt the grieving process for co-victims.

These unique factors, often interrupting the normal grieving process, may lead to difficulties in psychological adjustment and psychological disorders among homicide co-victims (Freedy et al., 1994; Freeman, Shaffer & Smith, 1996). Specifically, homicide co-victims are especially prone to Post Traumatic Stress Disorder (PTSD) (Freedy et al., 1994; Freeman et al., 1996). PTSD is an anxiety disorder which arises in individuals who have experienced extremely traumatic events and usually involves recurring re-experiencing of the traumatic event. This re-experiencing may come via dreams, vivid recollections, or virtual "reliving" of the event in the form of hallucinations, flashbacks, or other sensory illusions (American

Psychiatric Association, 1994). It also may be manifested in an opposite manner of avoidance and detachment. Such things as low levels of affect, avoidance of other people or places which may remind one of the traumatic event, and a general sense of apathy about the future are all associated with PTSD (American Psychiatric Association, 1994). Other symptoms include irritability, altered sleep patterns, difficulty concentrating, hypervigilance, and heightened states of arousal (American Psychiatric Association, 1994). The high level of PTSD in the case of homicide mixed with the unique stressors and factors which interrupt the normal grieving process make the loss of a loved one to a homicide a particularly difficult loss from which to recover. Homicide co-victims are faced with a trauma from which they will likely never fully recover.

On top of the inherently difficult grieving process is added the fact that the co-victim must now be subjected (whether directly or indirectly) to the criminal justice process regarding the apprehension, prosecution, and punishment of the offender responsible for the death of their loved one. Many consider this to be an additional traumatizing event for co-victims. In fact, research has found that "PTSD prevalence for victims involved in the criminal justice system may be substantially higher than that of crime victims in general" (Freedy et al., 1994, p. 463). Some refer to this as a form of double-victimization (Brown, 1991; Magee, 1983). For example, Sprang et al. (1989) contend that "[f]amily members of murder victims are victimized twice: first by the criminal and second by the system" (p. 162).

As previously mentioned, one of the first forms of contact a co-victim might have immediately surrounding their finding out about the death of their loved one is with law enforcement officials in the process of the investigation. The news of and circumstances surrounding the murder are often presented in a cold and detached manner. Brown (1991) gives us the following depiction:

> Survivors have described detectives and police who have been part of the crime scene as reporting the news of their loved one's murder as if they were reciting their rank and serial number. The officials focus on the formality of the occasion and the evidence that needs to be gathered. Often the traumatized survivors' questions and demands for answers are overlooked. Details are often withheld from the family because the investigation is still pending or ongoing. Prized

> possessions of the murder victim can be held as evidence for years. (p. 191).

As the case proceeds through the criminal justice system to trial and ultimately punishment, the co-victim continues to be pushed to the periphery. As Brown (1991) notes, "Murder is considered a crime against the state, not a private crime against a family. Because this is a 'depersonalized' crime, interaction between court and family can be limited, or information can be given without concern of its impact" (p. 189). Indeed, the very nature of the criminal justice system in the United States is to remove the victim as an agent in the process. Such removal inevitably increases the feelings of isolation and alienation already inherent in the trauma of losing a loved one to murder. Until recently, co-victims were offered very little opportunity to be involved in the criminal justice process surrounding the adjudication of the offender responsible for the death of their loved one. Although their role remains a marginal one, as we will see in later sections, some efforts have been made in recent times affording them both participation in and consideration from the criminal justice process.

The Needs of Homicide Co-Victims

The most common rhetoric surrounding homicide co-victims' needs centers on the notions of healing and closure (incidentally, these are words often invoked as rationale for the death penalty, as well). Indeed, healing and closure, notions comprising the broader array of psychological and emotional needs following loss or trauma, are key final elements in the grieving process as discussed above and are necessary factors in overcoming PTSD. But, what does it mean to attain healing and closure? And how, if at all, can these needs sufficiently be met? In regard to the first question, Brown (1991) offers the following:

> They need to resolve the murder enough psychologically to move it from present (active) memory and stimulus to past (still remembered but less activated) memory. Survivors need to feel complete again and to live a satisfying life despite the murder (p. 195).

Brown further suggests that these needs are not extraordinarily complex or complicated but are common needs of humans in many circumstances and situations. In fact, the natural progression of the grieving process is to come to a point of acceptance or to "move on" from the traumatic event thus obtaining some semblance of healing or closure. But the second question regarding how such needs can be met is much more elusive. Although much has been offered in the way of a nice, linear, stepwise process in which humans grieve, even Kubler-Ross (1969) suggested that reality was not so simple—that the process will vary from individual to individual and is contingent upon the particular circumstances of the grief. One may experience the stages of grief multiple times, looping back from one stage to a previous one or multiple stages of grief may even occur at the same time. The grieving process creates very personal needs and their nature and extent vary widely across individuals. The way one obtains any sense of healing or closure will largely depend on the individual and the circumstances which surround him or her. Put very simply:

> Survivors need most of all to be able to grieve—for all that entails for them, for whatever meaning it has for them, and in whatever manner it feels right. Short of hurting themselves or others, there are no right and wrong ways to grieve (Brown, 1991, p. 195).

Individual or group therapy are obvious suggestions to help an individual to deal with grief and loss (Brown, 1991; Cerney, 1999) but there are other forms of support that can be provided in the community and in the criminal justice system which can significantly contribute to the experience of closure and healing for co-victims (Magee, 1983). Sprang et al. (1989) consider social support systems to be integral to the healthy grief process for homicide co-victims. They assert that "[n]onjudgmental compassion and support of concerned others helps survivors cope with the difficulties of grief work" (Sprang et al., 1989, p. 163).

Considering the role of the community and the criminal justice system in potentially responding to the needs of homicide co-victims, there are other important needs which arise in the wake of murder. The most obvious is a sense of justice or retribution. As Magee (1983) puts it, "[i]n the aftermath of murder, which is perhaps the most profound injustice, families need some sense of counterbalancing justice." Associated with the natural anger and rage co-victims experience, this need for justice may be more accurately depicted as a need for revenge rather than retribution. Again, the form and extent of this need will vary across individuals (Magee, 1983). Related to this is the need for co-victims to come to terms with the manner in which the victim died—to understand or comprehend what has happened. This may include a desire to know the details of the crime and whether or not and to what degree the victim suffered prior to death (Sprang et al., 1989) and may even extend to the need to confront the killer in some way. Underlying all of this is a need for some form of reparation or reconciliation, a return to some level of normality. Healing, closure, justice, retribution, understanding all relate to this. All share the goals of reconciliation and repair.

Magee (1983) believes that all these needs must be met by not just the community at large but by the criminal justice system, as well. He cites a report from the Families of Homicide Victims Project of New York City's Victim Services Agency:

> We have learned...that families expect from the criminal justice system something more subtle and more complex than just punishment of the offender. These families have experienced the failure of what is perhaps the most fundamental task of society—to preserve their physical safety. They feel vulnerable, helpless, and set apart. They look to the police and courts to give them formal acknowledgement of the wrongs against them. They expect from the courts a ritualistic expression of regret and concern (Magee, 1983, p. xv).

The needs of homicide co-victims run deep and are far too often neglected by society and by the criminal justice system. Recent gains for victims' rights may be offering some advances in the willingness and ability of the criminal justice system to attend to the needs of victims and co-victims. The question that remains and which is pertinent to the present study is: Can the death penalty meet these needs? Before this question is addressed I turn now to the more direct human and societal impact of the death penalty and executions.

THE HUMAN CASUALTIES OF EXECUTIONS AND THE DEATH PENALTY

The death penalty has an impact on humans and society at three levels. First, the process of capital punishment creates what Arrigo and Fowler (2001) refer to as a "death row community" in which numerous individuals are connected (whether they want to be or not) in the often long drawn out process that extends from the crime to the years the condemned awaits death on death row to the final appeal and ultimately to the moment of execution (and perhaps beyond). This lengthy process involves many individuals and undoubtedly has a significant impact on their lives. Second, the rituals surrounding the actual execution (as distinct events independent of the more general capital punishment process) require the participation and contribution of many individuals, relying on the direct input of some and a more passive role of others. Regardless of the degree of involvement in these rituals, they play a significant role in the execution of the condemned and in the lives of those touched by it. From "deathwatch" and "deathwork" to the execution chamber, human lives are profoundly transformed (both literally and figuratively) by this macabre event. Third, the death penalty has an impact on the community and larger society in which it exists and in which executions occur. Indeed, the very foundation of the death penalty as a penal sanction rests upon the assumption that it has just such a social impact. Although, whether the nature of this impact comports with the objectives of the death penalty, as we shall see, is debatable.

I refer here to those impacted by executions and the death penalty as "casualties" because that is precisely what they are. The state sanctioned killing of a human being has irrefutable impacts on communities and many individuals in society. Smykla (1987) reiterates this point:

> Physical death is only one part of the death penalty. The consequences of capital punishment vibrate throughout the social structure and include persons in an ever widening circle of impact. The circle begins with the offender and victim and expands to include the families of the victim and offender, jurors, judges, prison guards, wardens, other inmates on death row, witnesses to an execution, governors, attending physicians, attorneys, society, and reformers, to name a few. (p. 331)

Smykla (1987) goes on to argue that "all persons included in the capital punishment circle can be seen as victims" (p. 332). Kane (1986) extends this beyond the capital punishment circle: "The consequences of capital punishment are not confined to the individual who has been sentenced to die, but tear at the entire social fabric of those who stand on the periphery of an act of violence" (p. 33). From the jurors who must make the difficult decision of whether or not to condemn a defendant to death, to the correctional staff who must take part in the execution, to the witnesses who must view this macabre event, to the larger community which must bear the responsibility for sanctions implemented on its behalf, the strains and dissonance surrounding this most ultimate penalty are palpable. The consequences are human casualties.

The Capital Punishment Process and the "Death Row Community"

The process of capital punishment is only beginning when a suspect has been apprehended, convicted, and sentenced to death. Although the sentencing of a defendant is often depicted as a "final" social event emanating from a criminal incident, this is far from the reality in capital cases. On average, a condemned inmate in Texas will spend 10.43 years on death row prior to actual execution (Texas Department of Criminal Justice, 2005a). According to the Bureau of Justice Statistics (BJS), nationally the average wait is 9.17 years (BJS, 2002). The reality is that a majority of those sentenced to death have not reached (and may never reach) the execution chamber. As of 2002, only 12% of all defendants sentenced to death in the United States since 1977 have been executed (BJS, 2002). Over one-third (37%) have received other dispositions[4] (BJS, 2002). The death penalty process is long, and the outcome is far from clear and certain. Thus commences a nebulous and ambiguous process which many individuals must endure over a lengthy period of time.

During this time, the capital punishment process will involve numerous and variant individuals, impacting their lives in many ways. The most obvious impact of this process is on the inmates who must await their own death and experience the ups and downs of the often false hopes surrounding appeals, clemency hearings, and pleas for executive mercy. This impact extends to death row inmates' family and friends as they vicariously experience the process along with their condemned loved one (Smykla, 1987). The other obvious but often less considered impact is on the co-victims of the crime who must also suffer the uncertainty about the conclusion to this traumatic event in their lives. With each new hearing, they are confronted with the

---

[4] "Included persons removed from a sentence of death because of statutes struck down on appeal, sentences or convictions vacated, commutations, or death by other than execution" (BJS, 2002).

possibility of a change in status of the person responsible for their loss and pain and in many cases must participate in the hearings and be faced with reliving their experiences again and again. There are other less obvious individuals who must also suffer this process. As Arrigo and Fowler (2001) point out:

> Arguably, the death row phenomenon consists not only of those offenders awaiting execution, but also of those correctional and support staff working the unit, as well as those family members of victims and prisoners who anticipate inmate execution (p. 44).

Arrigo and Fowler (2001) suggest that the extensive and intensive capital punishment process creates what they term a "death row community" in which these divergent individuals become intricately tied to one another in the context of the death penalty and the circumstances surrounding its implementation. Those impacted by the capital punishment process extend beyond the inmate and co-victims and the "death row community" to the original jurors who must decide whether or not to sentence the defendant to death (Fleury-Steiner, 2004; Sarat, 2001), clergy and other spiritual advisors who often visit and consult inmates as they await execution (Pickett & Stowers, 2002; Prejean, 1993; Ingle, 1989), the appellate courts and clemency boards who must re-consider death sentences, executive officers (usually the state's governor) who must decide whether or not to grant inmates mercy and spare their lives via stays, commutations, or pardons (Kobil, 1998), members of the media who sometimes cover both the trial and the actual execution (Gillespie, 2003; Johnson, 1998; Reid & Gurwell, 2001), and attorneys who represent them throughout this process (Mello, 1989; Wollan, 1989). Indeed, the capital punishment process is wide-reaching, involving a substantial variety of individuals (Smykla, 1987). The toll this process takes on all individuals involved cannot be denied; however, for the sake of this chapter, the focus here will be limited to those identified by Arrigo and Fowler (2001) as comprising the "death row community": the correctional staff[5], condemned inmates, condemned inmates' family and friends, and co-victims.

---

[5] Here, "correctional staff" refers to all employees or agents of the corrections department who are involved in any part of the care, treatment, monitoring, or interaction with a condemned inmate. This includes, in addition to prison administration and custodial staff, individuals who work under civilian contract, volunteer, or otherwise devote their time to serving the corrections

Correctional Staff

Robert Johnson (1998), in his landmark study of death rows, executions and those he terms "death workers," provides a rich examination of the death penalty process leading up to execution and the individuals who come face-to-face with it. Specifically, he addresses the social world of those working on death row—the keepers of the "living dead" (Johnson, 1981, 1998). The death row population Johnson (1981) refers to as the "living dead" present a particularly stark working environment for correctional staff:

> Living death is here intended to convey the zombie-like, mechanical existence of an isolated physical organism—a fragile twilight creature that emerges when men are systematically denied their humanity. The image...serves as a dramatic summary statement of the death row experience, encompassing its central psychological features of powerlessness, fear, and emotional emptiness (p. 17).

There is little debate that working in an environment with such a peculiar population takes a toll on individuals and the individuals most directly impacted are those who work most closely and persistently with the death row population—the correctional officers. Death row guards come face-to-face with the reality of the death penalty on a daily basis. They have a unique position among correctional officers. The population which is their charge is one at the end of the line—one that literally has no future. The hopelessness among this population creates a heightened sense of tension and fear among correctional officers (Johnson, 1998). With nothing to lose, death row inmates present a particular source of fear for those who work directly with them (Johnson, 1998). Although research indicates that death row inmates are no more dangerous than other inmates (Buffington-Vollum, 2004), the fear among death row officers is a reality. And, this fear has ramifications: "The main casualty of fear, then, is simple human compassion, the absence of which contributes to the distinctively cold interpersonal climate on death row" (Johnson, 1998, p. 113).

Working on death row also creates a sense of futility in the working lives of these correctional officers. As Johnson (1998) notes:

---

department in the death penalty process and/or execution. This would include, for example, cooks, psychologists, medical professionals, and spiritual/religious personnel.

> Death row guards are enjoined solely to preserve the bodies of the condemned—to feed them in their cells or in common areas, to conduct them to out-of-cell activities, to watch them at all times. In large measure, the officers are reduced to intrusive waiters and unwanted escorts (p. 109).

Death row officers usually receive special training which includes such things as "suicide prevention" and "medical emergency preparedness" (Flack, 1993, p. 75). They are also required to monitor the inmates more heavily than those in general population (e.g. counts are often every hour as opposed to only periodically throughout the day) (Flack, 1993).

Correctional officers who work on death row often come to have some form of connection to those inmates with whom they work and interact so intensively (Johnson, 1998; Flack, 1993). It is, in part, for this reason that death row officers generally are not allowed to participate in executions (Johnson, 1998). This policy can be seen as tacit acknowledgement on the part of correctional management that the fact that officers are overseeing the incarceration of inmates who will be killed is one likely to produce heightened levels of psychological dissonance, stress and anxiety. Indeed, as Johnson (1998) points out, these keepers of the "living dead" often experience a very real sense of loss when an inmate is finally executed.

"Correctional staff" can be extended to also include support staff or secondary workers in the correctional system. These are usually individuals who do not work exclusively for the correctional system but are hired for specific purposes or have functions in the "death row community." Some examples are clergy or spiritual advisors who come into the prison to counsel death row inmates (Ingle, 1989), doctors and other medical professionals who attend to inmates in the case of attempted suicide or other health problems (Physicians for Human Rights, 1994), and psychologists, psychiatrists and other mental health professionals who counsel and, if necessary, reform or restore inmates' mental health, sometimes through the use of medication (Ewing, 1998; West, 1975; Physicians for Human Rights, 1994). We may even extend this notion of support staff to attorneys who visit with their death row clients on a regular basis as they prepare for appeals and clemency hearings (Wollan, 1989). Although many of these individuals—especially the latter—are by no means employees of the correctional system, they are definitely a part of the "death row community" in that they spend significant amounts of time in the death row environment and interact with a variety of individuals in that setting. Each of these individuals also faces the reality that they are working with individuals whose lives will (most likely) be ended by the state. This is a reality that often conflicts very directly with the ethics and objectives of their particular professions.

The Condemned and Their Families and Friends

The impact of the capital punishment process is most acute for the individual sentenced to death. As stated previously, the condemned inmates have been characterized by Robert Johnson (1981) as "living dead," but more importantly they come to define themselves as such:

> Some death row inmates, attuned to the bitter irony of their predicament, characterize their existence as a living death and themselves as the living dead. They are speaking symbolically, of course, but their imagery is an appropriate description of the human experience in a world where life is so obviously ruled by death. It takes into account the condemned prisoners' massive deprivation of personal autonomy and command over resources critical to psychological survival; their suspicion in a stark, empty, tomblike setting, marked by indifference to basic human needs and desires; and their enforced isolation from the living, with the resulting emotional emptiness and death (Johnson, 1981, p. 110).

In later work, Johnson (1998) comes to define the outcome of this experience as a literal form of dehumanization, one in which an individual's very personhood is removed: "Condemned prisoners thus typically suffer a more extensive and insidious form of dehumanization…literally losing their human attributes" (p. 209).

Although much of the focus on the death penalty in the context of the Eighth Amendment's prohibition of cruel and unusual punishment has focused on the execution itself, an argument can be made that the confinement of the condemned awaiting execution represents the truly cruel and unusual aspect of the death penalty. Camus (1960), in his seminal essay "Reflections on the Guillotine," offers the classic statement of this point:

> Having to face an inevitable death, any man, whatever his convictions, is torn asunder from head to toe. The feeling of

> powerlessness and solitude of the condemned man, bound and up against the public coalition that demands his death, is in itself an unimaginable punishment. (p. 204).

More contemporarily, Johnson (1981) offers the following observations of men awaiting execution:

> The suffering of prisoners under sentence of death must be recognized as a major human cost of capital punishment as it is administered today...for all intents and purposes, a death sentence amounts to death with torture in a society that has explicitly renounced torture as a remnant of barbarism (p. 129).

Espy (1989) makes a similar point:

> Only one who has endured the experience can fully understand the thoughts and emotions of a person who has been condemned to die at the hands of the executioner. Such an individual is kept in close confinement, deprived of all the creature comforts of life, forced to contemplate a sudden and violent death by a means already ordained and known to him or her. It is a period during which the soul and spirit of any mortal is severely tested (p. 27).

Indeed, the inherent loss of humanity associated with death row confinement and the very notion of awaiting a state-imposed death is a harsh reality of the capital punishment system. The following words of a death row inmate express this well:

> Seven years ago I began the process of awaiting my man-made appointment with death. Since being condemned to death, my days have been spent dealing with the guilt of having been convicted of taking the lives of two human beings, confronting the very real possibility of my own violent death, and coping with the anger, resentment, frustration, helplessness, and grief of having five friends taken from my side to be ritualistically exterminated. These have been nine long years of fighting to maintain my sanity, of growing, and of holding onto a sense of humanity in an environment maintained specifically for the purpose of bombarding the

> senses with hopelessness. It is almost impossible to maintain a sense of humanity in a system that ignores the fact that you are a living, breathing human being—a system where you are recognized only as a number, a compilation of legal issues open for debate, a 20- to 50-page legal brief before tribunals that will determine your fate without ever knowing you, as something human--a piece of tainted meat to be disposed of (Giarratano, 1989, p. 193).

The message is simple: capital punishment, by definition, strips away individuals' humanity and in doing so creates a class of casualties unique within the criminal justice system and modern democratic societies. Johnson (1998) contends that this removal of the most fundamental right—the right to live and be human—is tantamount to torture. Specifically, Johnson (1998, pp. 200-201) highlights the five primary elements of psychological torture and illustrates how they apply to the circumstances of the condemned: 1) Total control, 2) Isolation, 3) Personal humiliation, 4) Uncertainty, and 5) Physical debilitation and exhaustion. Although these five elements might be just as easily applied to non-death row confinement, the added element of impending execution elevates the condemned's status to that of particularly torturous circumstances and adds a level of literal dehumanization.

As can be gleaned from the extensive quotes above and from the reality of death row confinement as analyzed and described by Johnson (1981, 1998), a death sentence has severe psychological and emotional ramifications for the condemned. Based on interviews with thirty-seven death row inmates in Alabama, Johnson (1981) identified three primary psychopathological characteristics of the death row environment and confinement: powerlessness, fear, and emotional emptiness. Although these factors are not unique to the death row setting, Johnson (1981) notes that "[f]ew manmade environments offer stress surpassing that produced by confinement under sentence of death" (pp. 4-5). He goes on to offer other analogous circumstances, suggesting that French penal colonies, Russian forced labor camps, and Japanese World War II POW camps may qualify.

It is not so much the actual conditions of the environment that offers a salient analogy to these settings, but the helplessness and hopelessness of the human situation in them. It is from this perspective that Johnson (1981) applies Kubler-Ross's five stages of grief to the process of adjusting to a death sentence noting that her proposed stages "have been observed in the research on death row inmates" (pp. 8-9). Certainly the adjustment to a death sentence can be viewed in similar terms as an adjustment to terminal illness, as was Kubler-Ross's original point of analysis in developing her stages of grief. But, we also know that elements such as helplessness and hopelessness, especially when coupled with extreme stress, are likely to result in depression and other psychological disorders (Abramson, Alloy & Matalsky, 1989; Abramson, Seligman & Teasdale, 1978). Indeed, Bluestone and McGahee (1962), based on psychological interviews and examinations, found that death row inmates displayed numerous psychopathological symptoms including delusions, obsessive characteristics, withdrawal, acute anxiety, and psychopathy.

The extreme emotional and psychological stress of knowing one will be killed mixed with the conditions of confinement inevitably lead many to become mentally ill or experience any of a range of psychological disorders (Bluestone & McGahee, 1962; Miller & Radelet, 1993). It is no surprise that the extensive number of years an inmate must spend in such a setting awaiting their inevitable death creates what can only be referred to as human casualties—the death that comes at the end is only the final destruction in a long process of decomposition.

Thigpen (1993) suggests one other troubling aspect of the extended period of time an inmate spends on death row—the changes they experience as individuals. In spite of the deterioration death row inmates experience as documented above, many also make positive changes in their lives. Thigpen (1993) notes that death row inmates often make deep personal changes attempting to salvage their lives and make themselves better people. The sad reality is that they are given the time to make such changes, in which they may attain some level of redemption, but the opportunity to fulfill such promise of redemption is denied when the death chamber is their final destination. Thigpen (1993), drawing on his years of experience as warden of a prison which houses death-row, states the following:

> I found that the person we were executing may not be the same type of person who committed the crime. I believe that individuals do have the ability to change and that over the course of time they spend on death row some rather dramatic changes occur. I always will wonder about the good this man might have accomplished if his sentence had been commuted to life without parole. (pp. 56-57).

Indeed, in the end, the condemned inmate who dies by execution is a true casualty of the death penalty process. We can argue over the relative value of a condemned murderer's life, but we can not deny that a human life is lost. And, we can never know the true potential such a life might have had when that life is ended by the hands of the state[6]. This is not to say that there aren't those individuals who will never aspire to lead more pro-social lives or attain any semblance of a pro-social potential with their lives. Certainly, there are plenty of examples of individuals who will never change for the better. But, to deny the possibility for such change and redemption is to deny something very fundamental to individuals and to human societies.

The condemned are not the only ones who suffer their fate and the process catalyzed by their actions. Their families often share in their suffering and also suffer in their own ways, often bearing the brunt of an outraged society bent on retribution in addition to mourning the loss of their loved-one and enduring the ups and downs of the long judicial process of capital punishment trials and appeals. We turn, again, to the timeless words of Albert Camus (1960):

> [T]he relatives of the condemned man then discover an excess of suffering that punishes them beyond all justice. A mother's or a father's long months of waiting, the visiting-room, the artificial conversations filling up the brief moments spent with the condemned man, the visions of the executions are all tortures (p. 205).

One of the earliest considerations of the impact of capital punishment on the condemned's family was by the renowned trial attorney Clarence Darrow. Darrow's (1957) argument against the death penalty was best presented in his eloquent summation as defense attorney in the famous Leopold and Loeb murder trial:

> Here are these two families, who have led honest lives, who will bear the name that they bear, and future generations must

---

[6] I draw your attention to one case as an example: Stanley "Tookie" Williams was recently executed in California for gang-related murders which he admits he committed. Williams used his time in prison awaiting execution to make personal, spiritual and social change. In 2000, Williams was nominated for a Nobel Peace Prize for his efforts, primarily through writing books for teens, to stop gang violence and to stop young kids from choosing a path of gang membership and crime. For more information go to www.tookie.com.

> carry it on. It is a hard thing for a father to see his life's hopes crumble into dust. Should he be considered? Should his brothers be considered? Will it do society any good or make your life safer, or any human being's life safer, if it should be handed down from generation to generation, that this boy, their kin, died upon the scaffold?
>
> Have they any rights? Is there any reason…why their proud names and all the future generations that bear them shall have this bar sinister written across them? How many boys and girls, how many unborn children, will feel it? It is bad enough, however it is. But it's not yet death on the scaffold. It's not that. (p. 85).

Darrow's words bring to light the destructive pall of stigma and long-term impact of this punishment for those related to the condemned. Recent research indicates that the consequences of the death penalty process for death row inmates' family members are severe. Beck Britto & Andrews (2007) found that symptoms of depression and PTSD were common results of the stress family members experience as their loved one proceeds through the criminal justice system toward execution. Norgard (in King, 2005) characterizes the psychological state of many family members as one of "chronic grief," a grief prolonged by the extensive waiting period preceding the inevitable and predetermined death of their loved-one. She lists some of the symptoms experienced: "repeated nightmares, sleepless nights, difficulty concentrating, impaired short-term memory, hyper-vigilance, a constant aching grief, and episodes of uncontrollable crying" (p. 3). She also notes that the grief results not only from the impending loss of their loved-one but also from the co-victims' loss of their loved-ones and the fact that their family member is responsible for that loss.

The response by the larger community also plays a role in the grief of the family members. Fear, helplessness, horror and guilt are all related to the "chronic grief" experienced by those with family members facing the death penalty (Beck et al., 2003; Beck et al., 2007; King, 2005). The (often negative and even caustic) response in the community and the stigma which accompanies these circumstances are major factors in the development and prolonged nature of these destructive symptoms and disorders. The words of a wife of a death row inmate indicate this reality: "I got a lot of death threats, a lot of people being nosy who wanted to strike out and hurt. And it did"

(Dicks, 1991, p. 95). As their family member is one of the "condemned" being punished for his or her horrible act, so are the families enduring their own condemnation and suffering a fate not warranted by their own actions.

The Co-Victims

The co-victims' experience of the capital punishment process is unique in that they have already suffered the most severe trauma in the loss of their loved one to murder. As previously mentioned, this trauma carries with it a heavy emotional and psychological burden which includes intense mourning and grieving, psychological deterioration, and the need for healing. The process that follows carries two possible ramifications: 1) an opportunity for co-victims to obtain the healing they desire. This may be manifested in terms of justice, revenge, closure, or resolution or offer an opportunity for co-victims to be heard and have their feelings or perspectives validated (DPIC, 2007b; Dicks, 1991; Lifton & Mitchell, 2000); 2) the death penalty process may exact a form of secondary victimization on co-victims only prolonging their period of grieving and interrupting their healing process (DPIC, 2007b; Dicks, 1991; King, 2003; Lifton & Mitchell, 2000; Murder Victims' Families for Reconciliation, 2005).

In line with the first possibility is the contention by many advocates of the death penalty that it serves to provide co-victims with justice, closure and healing. In fact, those opposing the death penalty are often painted as "anti-victim," "pro-criminal" or just plain insensitive to the suffering and needs of co-victims (Lynch, 2002; Vandiver et al., 2002). The implication is that the death penalty is the appropriate and most effective method by which to meet the needs of co-victims of murder. Certainly many victims desire and demand revenge, vengeance, and retribution (Lifton & Mitchell, 2000; Sarat, 1997). And, capital punishment may be perceived to meet these needs. But, as we've seen in the previous discussion of the needs of homicide co-victims, there are many more fundamental individual needs. Healing, closure, and psychological adjustment are but a few. Are these needs met with the sentencing of an offender to death? The answer is unclear. Some co-victims express relief and satisfaction that the offender has been sentenced to death, but often this is followed by extreme dissatisfaction as the process takes years and sometimes decades before the finality of the execution (Gross & Matheson, 2003). The continual process of hearings, judicial decisions, and potential changes in status for the offender may be an added source of strain on co-victims and often simply serve as catalysts of painful memories and further trauma (Gross & Matheson, 2003). This is only exacerbated by the media attention that such cases often attract—usually focusing on the offender and not the victims (Gross & Matheson, 2003). It is also questionable whether the protracted capital punishment process can adequately meet the justice or retribution elements often cited as central concerns of co-victims. The finite moments of conviction and death sentence and, later, execution may provide victims with opportunities to experience justice, be heard, or find some semblance of healing and closure. But, the nature and length of the death penalty process seems to counter-balance what might otherwise be constructive forces for co-victims.

Some co-victims are more direct about the impact of the capital punishment process on them. The group Murder Victims' Families for Reconciliation (MVFR) is composed of individuals who have lost loved-ones to murder and who oppose the death penalty. They vehemently assert that not only does the death penalty violate their sensibilities as crime victims, it actually serves to impede their healing and ability to find closure (Murder Victims' Families for Reconciliation, 2005; King, 2003). A form of secondary victimization is often cited by those in this group and others who share their experiences and views. In a recent statement to Connecticut's state legislature in support of a bill which would abolish the death penalty in that state, one co-victim referred to the capital punishment process as "heinous, incredibly cruel and traumatizing" for co-victims (Death Penalty Information Center, 2005b). Others go further, stating that capital punishment denies co-victims the right and opportunity to truly find healing and reconciliation by removing the one person with whom they must find reckoning (King, 2003). In restorative justice terms, it further ruptures the relationship (whether a desired relationship or not) that is at the center of any real chance of finding healing and closure (King, 2003; Umbreit et al., 2003).

For some co-victims the execution represents that final moment in which the trauma of the capital punishment process will finally end and in which they will finally find justice and closure. For these individuals, the hope is that they will walk away from the execution feeling relief and peace. And, undoubtedly, some will. For others it is one more act of violence and harm in the lives of people who have had more than their share of both—it is an act that denies these co-victims the exact things that others hope to find in it: reconciliation, healing, and peace. But, one thing is certain for all co-victims: the execution signifies some form of finality in their lives. And, whether willing and active participants or not, they are a part of this finality—a ritualistic and macabre finality unlike anything else conducted in human societies. It is to these "rituals of death" that our attention now turns.

Rituals of Death

The Deathwatch

The actual execution "event" begins with a period known as "deathwatch" (Johnson, 1981, 1998; Purdum & Parades, 1989)[7]. The procedures surrounding deathwatch vary from state to state, sometimes beginning weeks prior to execution when the death warrant is read to the condemned inmate (Purdum & Paredes, 1989) and other times beginning only shortly before the execution. At this time, the offender is moved from death row to the "death house" where he will await execution (Purdum & Paredes, 1989). The "death house" is usually located in a facility separated from death row (Johnson, 1998).

In Texas, the inmate is transported to the death house shortly before the scheduled date of execution, often on the day of the execution itself (Sunriver Cartel, 2000). Thus begins a meticulous monitoring process. According to one correctional officer (cited in Johnson, 1998, p. 144): "We record everything, missing nothing. If he turns over in his bed, we note it. How much he eats, how much coffee he drinks, how many cigarettes he smokes—we record it all." Below is a typical record of the hours an inmate spends on deathwatch in Texas[8]:

12 midnight – 12:45 a.m.	Standing at cell door talking with inmate in adjacent cell.
1:00 a.m.	Sitting on bunk drinking coffee and reading a letter.

[7] For the sake of the present discussion, and in line with Texas' general procedure, Johnson's (1998) definition of deathwatch will be employed: "the last hours before an execution" (p. 142).

[8] Although TDCJ no longer makes such records available on their website, they are still provided to media in regard to particular executions and are available in the open records of each execution maintained by TDCJ's public information office.

1:30 a.m. – 1:45 a.m.	Sitting on bunk writing a letter.
2:45 a.m.	Writing a letter.
3:05 a.m.	Refused breakfast meal. Drank only a carton of milk.
3:15 a.m. – 4:00 a.m.	Sitting on bunk reading a paper.
4:45 a.m.	Kneeling on floor writing a letter.
5:30 a.m. – 6:45 a.m.	Sleeping.
6:55 a.m.	Talking with Assistant Warden Robert Parker.
7:30 a.m.	Showering.
8:19 a.m.	Escorted to visitation room to meet with his mother, Bessie Barefield; sister, Mary Barefield; and brother, Louis Stokley.

Last Meal Request: Double-meat cheeseburger, french fries.

Clothing to be worn: Blue shirt, blue pants, personal shoes.

10:05 a.m.	Refused afternoon meal. Continued visit.
10:30 a.m.	Barefield's sisters, Linda Barefield and Georgia Walker, join visit.
12:36 p.m.	Visit ended. Returned to cell and prepared for transport to Huntsville Unit.
1:00 p.m.	Departed Ellis enroute to Huntsville Unit.
1:20 p.m.	Arrived at Huntsville Unit. Placed in holding cell.

The detached temporal record-keeping of the "death-log" is striking. The presentation of a process of great gravity and idiosyncrasy is done with such normalcy that one may as well be reading the shipping manifest of a product being delivered to a warehouse to await sale. But, underlying that apparent normalcy is a process involving great human drama and real pain, suffering, and emotion.

It is during this time that the condemned must say his last goodbyes to his family and friends. They are often allowed an extended period of time for interaction. Lifton and Mitchell (2000) summarize: "the boxing up of his possessions, his last meal, a final visit with loved ones and his spiritual advisor, a change of clothes, a picture taken, the reading of the death warrant, and then the 'last walk'." (p. 82).

It goes without saying that this is a time of great stress and emotion for the inmate awaiting death. Fyodor Dostoyevsky, who himself once awaited his own death at the hands of the executioner, offers the following analysis:

> But the chief and worst pain may not be in the bodily suffering but in one's knowing for certain that in an hour, and then in ten minutes, and then in half a minute, and then now, at the very moment, the soul will leave the body and that one will cease to be a man and that's bound to happen; the worst part of it is that it's certain! (1958, pp. 20-21).

As indicated in the death watch log above, inmates rarely have an appetite and rarely sleep more than short periods. They are often offered certain medications to keep them calm or counteract anxiety. Indeed, many inmates suffer extreme anxiety and sometimes attempt to commit suicide (Gillespie, 2003).[9]

The condemned inmate is not the only one who suffers during the rituals of death surrounding the deathwatch. It is at this time that family and friends must say their last goodbyes to their loved-one. Joseph Ingle (1989), a spiritual advisor for death row inmates, offers the following observation of the last visits with condemned inmate David:

> On the evening of 11 July, the volunteer attorney, the paralegal, and I joined 11 members of David's family for a visit with him. There were 36 more hours to live. For three

[9] This is one primary reason for the intensive monitoring during "deathwatch" and one of the great ironies of the death penalty—we work very hard to not allow them to "cheat the executioner."

> hours we crowded into the noncontact visiting area and talked with him through the glass barrier. Three small children, aged three through five, enlivened the occasion by talking with their uncle through the glass. David teased them, put happy smiles on their faces, and sought to uplift all of our spirits. His stepfather, a quiet and large man, radiated strength for all of us. David's mother relived some of the memories she shared with her son. David spoke intently to his younger brother, who was clearly having an especially difficult time. At one point David asked me to take special care in helping his brother make it through the ordeal. Although all the family members suffered, the pain of David's 12-year-old daughter was perhaps the most visible. She had not seen her dad in years, and she had difficulty expressing her love amid the horror of this occasion. She broke down in tears several times, and it was only David's constant support and encouragement that kept her intact (pp. 118-119).

Referring to the next day's final visit just hours before David would be executed, Ingle (1989) writes:

> As David was led away, I gazed about me. His daughter was sobbing in Susan's firm embrace, watching her father leave for the last time, shouting, "Please don't kill my daddy." The small children were near hysterics, his mother's shoulders were heaving with sorrow, and his stepfather tried to comfort us all.
>
> We remained transfixed. None of us moved. It was as if by holding the moment, by not moving, we could retain David with us. We stood planted in the middle of the prison corridor like fixtures. Then a prison colonel, the head of the execution team, entered the hall and walked through our midst. The spell was broken, and we stumbled to the parking lot, wailing, grief-stricken, and inconsolable. Society's retribution had produced a family bereaved, a wounded child, and another mourning mother (p. 121).

This can only be compared to similar situations when family and friends say goodbye to a loved-one with a terminal illness (Vandiver, 1989). The difference here being that the soon-to-die individual is healthy and that the potentially calming thought that the death will bring a relief from physical suffering is not present. In fact, as illustrated in Joseph Ingle's description above, the condemned inmate may be the one trying to comfort his family and friends rather than the other way around. Vandiver (1989) adds that "[f]amilies of condemned prisoners must also cope with the knowledge that their relatives' deaths are actively desired" (p. 128). Contrary to situations in which a terminal illness is culpable, their loved-one's life will be brought to an intentional, calculated and premature end by agents of the state—an end they will likely witness just hours after saying their goodbyes.

Aside from correctional officers and administrative staff, the last people to spend time with the condemned inmate are usually their attorneys and spiritual advisors. These are the people who have probably come to know the inmate as well as anyone over the many years since the capital punishment process began and, as Johnson (1998) points out, often "serve the useful end of buffering the emotional impact of the execution on the prisoner" (p. 149). The unwitting connection or even friendship that has often developed can make these last hours powerfully difficult for these professionals. Attorneys may have to face what represents the ultimate failure of their efforts to save their defendant's life (Johnson, 1998; Wollan, 1989)[10] and members of the clergy or other spiritual advisors must often offer consolation and comfort while preparing the condemned inmate emotionally and spiritually for an event that may violate their own religious sensibilities (Ingle, 1989; Lifton & Mitchell, 2000; Pickett & Stowers, 2002). For these people, their connection to a condemned inmate has potentially serious personal consequences, often deteriorating their emotional and even physical well-being.

"Deathwork": Correctional Staff and Executions

The work of correctional staff surrounding the deathwatch and execution is a highly ritualized process. It is critical to correctional administration and staff that the last hours and actual execution go smoothly and exactly according to plan. The routines and rituals

[10] The case of Texas defense attorney Keith Jagmin illustrates this well. Following his one and only capital case, Jagmin, a respected and successful lawyer, descended into a state of depression and drug addiction which led to professional suspension and ultimately to the loss of his license. Jagmin cites his deep feelings of failure and responsibility for the death of a client he had become close to as the genesis of these problems.

provide important functions in reducing anxiety for those involved and ensuring uniformity and predictability. These routines and rituals are often "practiced" several times prior to each execution, much like actors on a stage rehearse before a show (Thigpen, 1993).

As previously mentioned, the correctional staff that oversees this process is different from those who supervised the offenders on death row: "death row officers normally are not involved in executions; the execution team is assembled from officers who have had little or no contact with the prisoner prior to the deathwatch" (Johnson, 1998). The separation of those officers who work on death row from the actual deathwatch and execution is perceived as necessary and functional in that it reduces the stress which would inevitably arise from participating in the death of an offender one has come to "know." The lack of prior contact between those on the deathwatch team and the condemned offender serves to mitigate the stress and trauma of the execution on those who must carry it out (Johnson, 1998). Johnson describes the role and function of the deathwatch team:

> The tasks of the deathwatch team are service, surveillance, and control. Their ultimate objective is to keep the prisoner alive and 'on schedule'—that is, to move him through a series of critical and cumulatively demoralizing junctures beginning with his last meal and ending with his last walk. When the time comes, they must deliver the prisoner up for execution as quickly and unobtrusively as possible (Johnson, 1998, p. 142).

When the actual execution is finally carried out, the impact ripples throughout the prison and correctional community in which it occurs. There is virtually no level of correctional staff which is left untouched by an execution. From the cooks who must prepare the final meal to correctional officers who must tie the inmate down, to the medical professional who must pronounce the executed person dead, the breadth of participation among correctional staff and contracted employees in executions is unlike any other activity occurring in prisons. A one-time warden from South Carolina emphasizes this reality:

> It is important to understand that the execution team we assembled and trained included many of the staff's disciplines. In addition to uniformed and other operational staff, our chaplain and maintenance, medical and human service

> personnel were directly involved. All took part in the practices and were included as team members (Martin, 1993, p. 61).

All play integral roles in the ritual that makes up the execution process and none are left untouched by the process. Johnson (1998) characterizes these employees as being involved in "deathwork."

Such "deathwork" has consequences for those who perform it. Although the correctional officers which take part in the death "team" or "squad" generally have not had contact with the inmate prior to transport to the unit containing the death house, they nevertheless feel the weight of their role in the execution of this individual. Many employ what Bandura (1990, 1999) would call mechanisms of moral disengagement to reduce any dissonance they feel as a result of their role in executions (Lifton & Mitchell, 2000). The ritualized process as described above, the sanitized nature in which the condemned are executed, the division of labor into highly specialized roles as one small part of a larger "death squad" and the authority of law and justice all offer deathworkers to morally disengage from the true nature of their actions (Johnson, 1998; Lifton & Mitchell, 2000; Osofsky, Bandura & Zimbardo, 2005). Bandura (1990, 1999) would argue that mechanisms such as diffusion of responsibility, displacement of responsibility, moral justification, dehumanization and euphemistic labeling all play a significant role in this process. Lifton and Mitchell (2000), referencing retired army lieutenant colonel Dave Grossman's analysis of killing in the course of war, give an apt description of this process:

> The various enabling mechanisms Grossman describes apply to those who carry out executions: the desensitizing and conditioning effects of the repeated rehearsals; various forms of emotional and technological distancing; a high level of anonymity and the defusing of responsibility; and moral distancing from the prisoner, who is seen in some way as nonhuman (p. 92).

In spite of such mechanisms, it is not uncommon for those involved to suffer forms post-traumatic stress disorders (PTSD) and other symptoms of anxiety and depression in the wake of executions. As a result death row and execution-team correctional staff are often required to submit to ongoing psychological testing and counseling. In

California, for example, correctional staff involved in executions are required to go through extensive pre- and post-trauma assessment and counseling to reduce stress and anxiety resulting from the execution (Vasquez, 1993). Lifton and Mitchell (2000, p. 83) make this point more broadly: "Whatever the dissolving of responsibility, there is evidence...that members of an execution team share a sense of collective taint...their relationship not only to death but to killing creates in them some sense of being psychologically or morally defiled."

Witnesses to the Execution

The execution itself draws these individuals together as they each witness the execution. Some participate in the execution as we have seen (correctional administration and staff) and others only observe the execution. But each bears witness to the state's deliberate killing of one of its citizens.

The macabre act of witnessing executions accompanies the history of capital punishment in human societies (Burnett, 2002; Domino & Boccaccini, 2000). The spectacle of public executions was once the crux of capital punishment and its intentions to deter others and uphold the rule of law (Bessler, 1997; Burnett, 2002). Foucault (1975) wrote of the "spectacle of the scaffold":

> In the ceremonies of the public execution, the main character was the people, whose real and immediate presence was required for the performance. An execution that was known to be taking place, but which did in secret, would scarcely have had any meaning. The aim was to make an example, not only by making people aware that the slightest offense was likely to be punished, but by arousing feelings of terror by the spectacle of power letting its anger fall upon the guilty person (pp. 57-58).

It was 17th and 18th century Europe to which Foucault referred when he wrote of the spectacle of the scaffold, but the issue of public executions persists today in the United States. Advocates of the death penalty often proclaim that it would be more effective if executions were televised (Gillespie, 2003) and in 2001, Timothy McVeigh's execution was broadcast on closed-circuit television so the thousands of co-victims of the Oklahoma City bombing could witness his death (Gillespie, 2003).

Although the idea of public executions is scarcely considered a viable reality today, the more intimate witnessing of executions by a select few, usually composed of family and friends of the victims and the condemned, attorneys and spiritual advisors for the condemned, as well as members of the media, is an integral part of the execution process and ritual. In Texas, "[p]olicy allows for up to five pre-approved witnesses requested by the condemned and up to five immediate family members or close friends of the victim to attend" (Sunriver Cartel, 2000). Additionally, specified members of the media are allowed to witness with representatives of the Associated Press, United Press International, the *Huntsville Item*, and reporters from the community where the crime was committed having first priority as media witnesses. As discussed in the previous section, correctional staff members are among others who "witness" directly the executions, some by participating directly in it and others by experiencing or participating in the rituals leading up to and surrounding it. These people are rarely left untouched or unaffected by the experience.

Morris Thigpen, former commissioner of the Alabama Department of Corrections, recalls the impact executions he presided over had on him: "After each execution, I felt as though I left another part of my own humanity and my spiritual being in that viewing room." (1993, p. 57). Lifton and Mitchell (2000) cite psychiatric research showing that "witnesses suffered from posttraumatic stress and 'experienced a high prevalence of dissociative symptoms...similar to that of people who endured a natural disaster'" (p. 168). The emotional and psychological impact of witnessing an execution is obviously most acute for those close to the condemned, but the experience is no less powerful for all who witness executions. Lifton and Mitchell (2000) indicate the pervasive psychological infiltration of executions for witnesses: "[B]y being there, if one really takes in the experience, one can readily feel implicated in the state killing, in the new 'murder.' The question, then, is what one does with that sense of self-condemnation, of guilt and shame, and of the taint of death" (pp. 168-169).

Of course, we might expect a very different experience among co-victims. The previously discussed needs of co-victims for closure, healing and finality are often cited as reasons for victims to witness the execution of the killer of their loved-one (Domino & Boccaccini, 2000). But, others suggest that it more often than not fails to meet these needs or desires and even may simply cause more trauma for co-victims (Domino & Boccaccini, 2000). Although Domino and Boccaccini (2000) examine public attitudes about the utility and appropriateness of co-victims witnessing executions, no research has been conducted examining the actual impact of witnessing on the co-victims. They conclude: "It is not enough to presume that victims' family members will attain satisfaction from viewing the execution. Even if satisfaction was guaranteed, it would most certainly be an inadequate satisfaction, shrouded with death and gloom" (Domino & Boccaccini, 2000, p. 74). More research is definitely needed to better understand the real impacts witnessing executions has for co-victims.

We must not forget that there is one more "witness" to the execution—the condemned him or herself. This is the last person heard from prior to the actual execution when he or she is allowed to make his or her last statements. These last statements represent one of the most unique communiqués in human societies. It is exceedingly uncommon for humans to be asked to make a statement before they are killed. When they have finished uttering the last words which will ever leave their mouths, they are put to death and their voice is forever silenced.

The Broader Social Context of the Death Penalty

A thorough consideration of the human casualties of the death penalty would be incomplete without acknowledging the social context in which it exists and the impact it has on the broader social world. The very foundation of capital punishment is predicated on this impact. Whether it is to set an example or warn others that extreme crimes will be met with extreme punishment and thus deter potential offenders or to mete out justice and retribution on behalf of a society wronged by such criminal acts, the purpose and function of the death penalty rests on the idea that it has a social impact. The fact that the death penalty is intended to exact just such impacts in society is manifest in its practice throughout the United States. Whether or not these intentions are borne out in reality and the degree to which there may be other latent social effects of the death penalty is less clear. In this section, this broader social impact of the death penalty will be discussed. Specifically, the impact on violence in society will be considered, asking the crucial question of whether the death penalty deters others from committing similar crimes. Capital punishment in the United States will further be considered in the international context, a social context that is becoming increasingly important. Finally, the issue of justice and retribution will be briefly examined.

Deterrence or Brutalization?

The impact of the death penalty on society, and particularly on homicide and violence in society, is widely debated in academic circles. On the one hand, proponents of the death penalty argue that the death penalty deters others from committing murder and thus is a positive policy for the reduction of violence. On the other hand, opponents argue that the death penalty brutalizes society, ultimately inspiring or catalyzing further violence in society. Research examining the relationship between executions and murder have proliferated but have rarely offered conclusive answers to the deterrence/brutalization question nor, when considered together, provided overwhelming evidence one way or the other. However, each side has research it can cite to back up its argument.

Historically, deterrence has been a fundamental basis for the death penalty. As Espy (1980) states, "the belief that capital punishment deters others from committing capital offenses has long been advanced as one of the most cogent arguments for the states doing the very thing it denies as a right of individual citizens—deliberately putting an end to human life" (p. 536). The idea that executing offenders will send a message to other potential criminals and thus deter them from committing such acts of violence is at the heart of capital punishment. Although the explicit use of such rationale has waned in recent decades (Bohm, 2007), it has not disappeared. In fact, in the 2000 presidential campaign both candidates invoked deterrence as the primary reason they supported the use of the death penalty (Turow, 2003). The logic underlying this position is appealing. It seems obvious that if one is threatened with death, they will be less likely to engage in behavior that would invoke such a penalty. Based on the notions that human behavior is rational and calculated, deterrence has dominated modern thinking about punishment in our criminal justice system (Bowers & Pierce, 1980). As philosopher Ernest Van den Haag (1982) points out: "[O]ur penal system rests on the proposition that more severe penalties are more deterrent than less severe penalties" (p. 326). He adds that "the most severe penalty—the death penalty—would have the greatest deterrent effect" (p. 327). But, empirical evidence regarding Van den Haag's logical proposition has been largely inconclusive.

Research on the deterrent effect of the death penalty has always brought controversy. In the mid-1970's economist Isaac Ehrlich (1975, 1977) presented evidence that the death penalty did, in fact, have a deterrent effect. Based on econometric analyses of the impact of several variables (including "execution risk" or the number of executions divided by the number of convictions for murder) on homicide rates for the time period 1933 to 1969, Ehrlich (1975) concluded that each execution prevented, on average, seven or eight murders. Ehrlich's research inspired a wave of studies on the deterrent impact of the death penalty. Although, some later econometric research has supported Ehrlich's original conclusions (Clonenger & Marchesini, 2001; Shepherd, 2004), the majority of the studies have failed to find that the death penalty deters murder (Cochran & Chamlin, 2000) and Ehrlich's research has been criticized as methodologically and statistically flawed (Fagan, 2005; Sorensen, Wrinkle, Brewer & Marquart, 1999). In fact, several studies have yielded findings suggesting just the opposite of deterrence, that the death penalty has a brutalization effect, serving to increase murder and violence in society.

Albert Camus (1960), in his eloquent critical essay *Reflections on the Guillotine*, wrote: "It is a penalty, to be sure, a frightful torture, both physical and moral, but it provides no sure example except a demoralizing one. It punishes, but it forestalls nothing; indeed, it may even arouse the impulse to murder" (p. 197). Although many such as Camus had suggested it previously, the notion of a brutalization effect of the death penalty was first formalized by Bowers and Pierce (1980). Bowers and Pierce (1980) explain that rather than having the intended effect of preventing murder and violence, the death penalty actually stimulates violence in society. They suggested that exposure to legitimized killing or "violent vengeance" would lead to internalization of such values and even imitation. From this perspective, the symbolic message of the death penalty is one that encourages rather than discourages violence in society. Clarence Darrow (1957), for example, posed the following question in arguing against the death penalty: "Do you think that children of our schools and our Sunday schools could be taught killing and be as kindly and as tender after it as before?" (p. 102-103). Espy (1980) characterizes the death penalty's overall social impact as one of "demoralization."

Bowers and Pierce's (1980) research provided compelling evidence of a brutalization effect and other research has supported this (Bailey, 1998; Cochran, Chamlin, & Seth, 1994; Thompson, 1997; Godfrey and Schiraldi, 1995). Another body of work, however, has found the death penalty to have no impact on murder rates (Sorensen, Wrinkle, Brewer & Marquart, 1999; Stolzenberg & D'Alessio, 2004). Most recently, researchers have begun to find evidence that the death penalty has *both* a deterrent and brutalization effect, potentially offering one explanation for findings of no effect. Cochran and Chamlin (2000, p. 689) make this argument:

> [E]xecutions can lead to both deterrent and brutalization effects. That is, executions deter some forms of criminal homicides while encouraging others through brutalization. The net effect, consistent with the extant research, is that these two opposing effects tend to cancel each other out, leading to an overall null effect.

It may also hold that the death penalty deters murder in some geographic areas and in some time periods but stimulates it in other areas and time periods (Shepherd, 2004). Much more research is needed to understand fully the circumstantial and contextual factors that play a role in the impact of the death penalty in society. In any case, the over-simplified view of the death penalty as a logical tool in deterring murderers, United States Presidential candidates aside, has all but disappeared from discourse on capital punishment. In fact, a 1996 poll of criminologists and other criminal justice academics (former presidents of ACJS, ASC and LSA) revealed that only 11.9% felt the death penalty was a deterrent to murder (Radelet & Akers, 1996) and none of them believed that the statement "[t]he death penalty significantly reduces the number of homicides" was accurate (Radelet & Akers, 1996, p. 13). More recently, Robinson (2008, p. 147) in a national study of the views of death penalty experts, found that only 9% believed the death penalty achieved deterrence in the United States.

The International Context

While other Western nations are either abolishing capital punishment or at least severely curbing its use, the United States remains among the countries that use the death penalty the most.[11] In fact, in the past decade, the United States has increased its use of the death penalty to record levels in the modern era (Hood, 2002). Moreover, until the

---

[11] In 2005, the United States trailed only China, Iran and Saudi Arabia in number of executions (DPIC, 2007a)

recent Supreme Court decision declaring the execution of juvenile offenders unconstitutional (*Roper v. Simmons*, 2005), the United States led all nations in the execution of juvenile offenders and was the only Western nation allowing the execution of juvenile offenders at all (DPIC, 2007a). Since 1990, Texas alone executed more juvenile offenders than any other nation[12] (DPIC, 2007a).

In a world climate leaning toward abolition of the death penalty, these facts place the United States in a precarious international position. Numerous international treaties have called for the abolition of the death penalty and in 2004 a United Nations resolution called for a world-wide moratorium on executions. To the degree that the United States does not succumb to pressure to fall in line with global sensibilities about capital punishment, potential international ramifications are a reality. International human rights organizations have cited the United States' use of the death penalty as one of the primary human rights concerns in the world today (Trail, 2002). Recently, the United States has even been held in violation of the Vienna Convention for refusing to allow foreign nationals charged with capital crimes to speak to their consulate (DPIC, 2007a). In the last decade, The United States' use of the death penalty on juveniles and foreign nationals increasingly threatened its status in international treaties, in some cases preventing its inclusion and involvement in such treaties altogether (ACLU, 2004; Trail, 2002). Only recently did the United States' Supreme Court finally put an end to the execution of juvenile offenders, a potential signifier of increasing alignment with international sensibilities.

In spite of the recent judicial ban on the death penalty for juvenile offenders, the United States remains divergent from the international community in regards to capital punishment. Although executions have declined over the last several years, they still remain higher than nearly all other nations (DPIC, 2007a). What's more, the number of crimes for which the death penalty can be used in the United States has increased (Bohm, 2007). This has potentially serious ramifications for the international interests of the United States. Whether we like it or not, the death penalty is a benchmark of a society's civility and morality in the global community. In spite of the United States' stance for human rights and of moral leadership, its use of capital punishment tarnishes its international image. It may have more serious and direct

---

[12] Since 1990, Texas has executed 13 men who were juveniles at the time of the crime; This is followed by Iran (8) and Pakistan (3) (DPIC, 2007a).

consequences as well. According to a report put out by the ACLU (2004), "[t]he most significant consequence of the United States' stance on the death penalty is its potential impact on national security" (p. 3). The report goes on to point out that "[i]nternational opposition to the death penalty also may be hindering U.S. efforts against international terrorism" (ACLU, 2004, p. 15). In this regard, the United States' refusal to abolish the death penalty has potentially serious and harmful implications for both American citizens and citizens of the world who look to the United States for social, political, and moral guidance.

No matter how one looks at it, the continued use of the death penalty presents significant contradictions for the United States' in the international community. Dicks (2000) summarizes this bluntly:

> Much of the rest of the world opposes this barbaric American rite. No country in the Western alliance, except the United States, kills its own citizens. We are always talking about what champions we are of human rights and then we have this murder by the state. Europeans think we're hypocritical. (p. 1).

The ramifications of this growing perception of the United States in response to its use of the death penalty are not yet fully clear. But, as the global community continues to become more congealed, it is clear that the United States' stance and policy on the death penalty will come under greater scrutiny and that international pressure will increase. Whether or not this will impact death penalty practices in the United States is another question.

Social Order and Justice?

Today, one of the dominating arguments for the death penalty is that it offers retributive justice. As Bohm (2007) points out, retribution has varying meanings. It is often equated with revenge or the popular notion of *lex talionis* or "an eye for an eye." (Bohm, 2007, p. 342). Another primary expression of retribution is associated with the notion of "just deserts," that the offender gets what he or she deserves. Bohm (2007) clarifies the distinction between these two perspectives: "[T]he principal difference between just deserts and revenge has to do with who repays whom, that is, whether the offender repays society (just deserts) or society repays the offender (revenge)" (p. 343). In a recent survey of attitudes among college students in Texas, 73.3% of those who supported the death penalty cited retribution as the primary reason for their support. 52.9% cited revenge-oriented retribution and 20.5% indicated a more just deserts- or proportionality-oriented perspective (Vollum, Kubena & Buffington-Vollum, 2004).

A sense that offenders must "get what they deserve" or receive just deserts as a result of their behavior and that one who commits particularly atrocious murders must be killed if justice is to be had is an increasingly common assertion. Some argue further that the death penalty is necessary to maintain social order via the credibility of law and criminal justice (Berns, 1982; Van den Haag, 1998). Berns (1982) proclaims:

> Capital punishment...serves to remind us of the majesty of moral order that is embodied in our law, and of the terrible consequences of its breach. The criminal law must possess a dignity far beyond that possessed by mere statutory enactment or utilitarian and self-interested calculations. The most powerful means we have to give it that dignity is to authorize it to impose the ultimate penalty (p. 339).

From this argument it follows that there is a moral necessity to apply the death penalty when someone commits murder, that to fail to exact such retribution is to fail in our moral duties as part of a society or community (Berns, 1982; See also, Steffen, 1998). Berns (1982) argues "[w]e punish criminals principally in order to pay them back, and we execute the worst of them out of moral necessity." (p. 333). From this point of view, retributive justice (and, by extension, the death penalty) is essential to a well-ordered and safe society and to argue otherwise (to argue against the death penalty) is to be selfish and to violate moral duties of community citizenship. Berns (1982), writing about righteous anger and retribution via capital punishment, states "[i]f men are not angry when a neighbor suffers at the hands of a criminal, the implication is that their moral faculties have been corrupted, that they are not good citizens" (p. 335).

Berns (1982) goes on to address the moral failure of the offender: "[T]hey have violated the foundations of trust and friendship, the necessary elements of a moral community, the only community worth living in" (p. 335). He also claims that in such a "moral community," its members are trusted to respect and obey the laws of that community and that "[t]he criminal has violated this trust, and in so doing has injured not merely his immediate victim but the community as such"

(p. 335).[13] Berns (1982) concludes that such a violation and injury not only warrants, but demands, that the death penalty be carried out.

Although Berns (1982) focuses on the harm or injury to the larger community in his philosophical argument for the death penalty, the more often heard sentiments favoring the death penalty as a form of retribution or justice center around the harm against the victim and the needs of co-victims. Often, cries for vengeance and retribution are on behalf of the co-victims and sometimes (although, less often) are voiced by the co-victims themselves (Lifton & Mitchell, 2000; Robertson, 2002). The claim that we have a duty to deliver justice and retribution for the victims and co-victims is one of the most dominant and emotionally powerful arguments for the death penalty. But, beyond this rhetoric, often used by prosecutors to secure death sentences or by politicians to appeal to citizens and policy-makers alike, is the reality that co-victims and their needs are largely ignored or forgotten in the aftermath of a tragic murder and the subsequent capital trial and appeals process (Freeman, Shaffer, & Smith, 1996; Magee, 1983). Many argue, however, that important gains have been made in responding to the needs and desires of co-victims of capital homicide. The most obvious example of this is the increased role granted to co-victims in capital trials. Specifically, co-victims are now allowed to present victim impact statements during capital sentencing hearings and are thus given some voice in a process that has traditionally relegated them to silent observers.

VICTIM IMPACT STATEMENTS

In the death penalty system, some gains have been made when it comes to the victims. Over the last decade, victims' (or more appropriately, co-victims') needs have been increasingly acknowledged and incorporated into the capital punishment process. Specifically, co-victims are now allowed to present statements at trial (*Payne v. Tennessee*, 1991; Belknap, 1992; Meek, 1992) and, in Texas at least, are allowed to view the execution (TDCJ, 2005c). Much of the "participation" co-victims are now afforded in capital cases can be

---

[13] It is worth noting here that Berns' language regarding an offender's violation of community trust and the injury caused to both victim and community mirrors that often professed by advocates of restorative justice. Interestingly, Berns' conclusion about the appropriate response to such injury (i.e. the death penalty) is diametrically opposite of what those advocating restorative justice would suggest.

traced to the proliferation of victim advocacy and victims' rights movements and organizations which have gained increasing strength in the legislative and criminal justice policy arena over the last few decades.

The modern advent of victim impact statements can be traced to the Victim & Witness Protection Act of 1982 in which it was mandated that written statements regarding the crime, defendant, and impact of the crime on the victims be allowed to be included with pre-sentence reports presented to judges to help them determine the appropriate sentence and/or restitution in a given case (Posner, 1984).

Victim Impact Statements and Capital Cases[14]

Although the Victim & Witness Protection Act of 1982 gave victims some voice in the adjudication process, it was not until a decade later that victims would begin being heard in capital cases (Belknap, 1992; Meek, 1992; *Payne v. Tennessee*, 1991; Schneider, 1992). In a series of cases at the end of the 1980s, the United States Supreme Court deemed VISs in capital cases to be in violation of the Eighth Amendment and thus unconstitutional (*Booth v. Maryland*, 1987; *South Carolina v. Gathers*, 1989). The focus of a capital trial, the Supreme Court opined, should be on the facts and circumstances of the *crime*, and not the impact of the crime on the victim's family and loved-ones (*Booth v. Maryland*, 1987). As Justice Powell stated, writing for the majority in *Booth v. Maryland* (1987), "[t]hese factors may be wholly unrelated to the blameworthiness of a particular defendant." Moreover, the Majority contended that any characterizations of the crime or defendant made by co-victims would likely be prejudicial and inflammatory, potentially leading to a sentence based more on caprice and emotion than on reason (*Booth v. Maryland*, 1987; For a more thorough discussion and deeper analysis of *Booth v. Maryland*, see Boudreaux, 1989).

In 1991, the Supreme Court had a change of opinion in regard to the admissibility of VISs in capital cases. In *Payne v. Tennessee* (1991), the Court effectively overturned *Booth v. Maryland*, asserting that the admission of victim impact statements in the sentencing phase

[14] For a thorough review of the relevant literature on, and issues surrounding, victim impact statements in capital cases, see the special issue of the Cornell Law Review on Victims and the Death Penalty: Inside and Outside the Courtroom, V. 88, N. 2, January, 2003. For a comprehensive bibliography on the topic, see Callihan (2003) in that issue.

of capital trials does not constitute an 8th Amendment violation as long as the information presented does not violate principles of fundamental fairness for the defendant. The ruling limited the statements, however, to only characteristics of the victim and the emotional impact of the crime on the victim's family. Statements characterizing the crime or the defendant would continue to be prohibited (*Payne v. Tennessee*, 1991). In spite of these limitations, victims now had a voice in the sentencing process of capital cases.

In recent years, most states have taken further steps toward providing victims a voice in criminal cases by adopting "victim participation" laws which "ensure that crime victims have an opportunity to be active participants in a criminal case and have a voice in the way in which the defendant is sentenced or treated" (Erez, 1994, p. 17; See also, Beloof, 2003). These laws have provided for two forms of victim impact statements afforded to victims in criminal cases: written and allocuted (Erez, 1994). The written form is the most common and constitutes the typical written statement attached to pre-sentence reports given to judges in which the impact of the crime on the victims is communicated. The allocuted, or spoken, form consists of an oral statement voiced by the victim during the sentencing phase of a trial. This form of VIS is most common in capital cases, where a jury decides whether or not the defendant will be sentenced to death or life in prison and is asked to consider both aggravating and mitigating circumstances in doing so. As of 2003, 33 of the 38 states with the death penalty allowed victim impact statements to be admitted in capital cases (Blume, 2003).

This increasing participation of victims in the sentencing phase of capital trials has not come without controversy. Some researchers and critics have suggested that victim impact statements unduly prejudice capital jurors toward death by playing on their emotions, attitudes, prejudices, and predispositions (Eisenberg, Garvey & Wells, 2003; Myers & Greene, 2004; Sarat, 2001). Further, it has been suggested that the admission of VIS lends to arbitrariness and capriciousness in death penalty decisions in that when jurors relate to victims or perceive them as respectable, they will be more likely to sentence the defendant to death (Eisenberg et al., 2003; Luginbuhl & Burkhead, 1995; Myers & Arbuthnot, 1999; Phillips, 1997). Research has supported these claims[15]. Studies of mock jurors have indicated that the mere presence

[15] For a very thorough review (which is beyond the scope of this book) of the research and issues surrounding the prejudicial nature of VIS in capital cases see Myers and Greene (2004).

of victim impact evidence in capital trials increases the likelihood that jurors will sentence the defendant to death (Luginbuhl & Burkhead, 1995; Myers & Arbuthnot, 1999). In these studies, some mock jurors were presented with victim impact evidence while others were not. Those exposed to the VIE were significantly more likely to suggest the punishment of death (Luginbuhl & Burkhead, 1995; Myers & Arbuthnot, 1999). Other studies of mock jurors have found that subjects who are exposed to VISs from victims perceived as "respectable" are more likely to sympathize with the victims and perceive them as more socially "valuable" (Myers & Greene, 2004) or express outrage for their suffering (Greene, 1999; Greene et al., 1998). Further, those exposed to VISs from "respectable" victims attached less weight to the mitigating evidence presented on the defendant's behalf in comparison to subjects who viewed VISs from less respectable victims (Greene et al., 1998). Others have added that such effects open the door for racial bias in capital sentencing decisions (Blume, 2003). Given what is already known about the racial bias inherent in capital cases in regard to the victims' race,[16] Blume (2003) concludes that "expansive VIE will inevitably make way for racial discrimination to operate in the capital sentencing jury's life or death decisions" (p. 280). Aguirre, Davin, Baker, and Lee (1999) conducted a study of pre- and post-*Payne* capital cases and found that "cases in which victim impact evidence is presented are much more likely to result in a sentence of death" (p. 305) and that Latino defendants are particularly vulnerable when victim impact evidence is presented.

Although such evidence, largely based on mock juror studies, pointed to biasing effects of VIE, other studies have not supported these findings. Davis and Smith (1994a), in an examination of the presence of victim impact statements and actual sentence outcomes in criminal cases, found that victim impact statements had no effect on the harshness of the sentence. Rather, factors such as the seriousness and nature of the crime were the most determinative. A recent study of capital jurors in South Carolina tells us something different. Eisenberg et al. (2003), in their study based on the Capital Jury Project being conducted out of Northeastern University, failed to find significant relationships between VIE and sentencing outcomes in capital cases. In

[16] The landmark Baldus (Baldus, Pulaski, & Woodworth 1983, 1986, 1998) study as well as other subsequent studies (Ekland-Olson, 1988; Keil & Vito, 1995) have concluded that cases in which the victim is a racial minority are much less likely to garner a sentence of death than cases in which the victim is White.

their study, they examined factors related to victim admirability, crime seriousness, aggravating and mitigating circumstances, and other case characteristics. Using Probit regression models, the researchers found little or no relationship between VIE and jurors' sentencing decisions. The authors concluded that it is "salient facts" which drive capital juries' sentencing decisions, not emotional responses to victim characteristics or victim impact statements (Eisenberg et al., 2003).

Although most attention has been on the potential negative impact of victim impact evidence in capital trials, some have argued the opposite, claiming that there are positive impacts which need to be considered (Alexander & Lord, 1994; Erez & Roeger, 1995). Erez and Roeger (1995) suggest several potential positive outcomes of the use of VIE and VIS in all forms of criminal trials: 1) an increase in victim satisfaction with justice, 2) a decrease in victims' feelings of helplessness and lack of control, 3) an increase in victim cooperation which aids the criminal justice process and enhances the efficiency of adjudication, and 4) an increase in awareness about the harms and loss which result from crime. Several studies have examined victim satisfaction with the VIS process and the findings are inconclusive. Researchers working with Mothers Against Drunk Driving (MADD) provide evidence of victim satisfaction, showing that 56% of victims of drunk drivers who had the opportunity to present victim impact statements were satisfied with the criminal justice system while only 14% of those not given the opportunity were satisfied (Alexander & Lord, 1994). Other studies have failed to replicate this finding. Davis and Smith (1994b) and Erez, Roeger and Morgan (1997) found little or no relationship between victim impact statements and satisfaction with the justice system. In fact, Erez (1994) even suggests that "filing a VIS may, by heightening their expectations that it will influence the outcome, decrease their level of satisfaction with the sentence should they then feel that their input has had no effect on the sentence" (p. 24). More research is needed to adequately understand the impacts of victim impact statements on victims and the criminal justice process. To date, no similar research has been conducted looking specifically at co-victims in capital cases nor have studies adequately addressed the latter three potential positive outcomes of VIS as indicated above.

Victim Impact Statements in Texas

In Texas, VISs are commonly introduced during the sentencing phase of capital trials. Until recently a victim's right to participate in criminal procedure was not formally acknowledged by statute. However, following the *Payne* decision, Texas prosecutors began introducing victim impact testimony at the sentencing stage of capital trials. Consequently, the issue made its way to the Texas Court of Criminal Appeals where the court, citing the Texas Code of Criminal Procedure (Article 37.071, sec. 2a) which permits admission of evidence "as to any matter the court deems relevant to sentence" as well as the *Payne* decision, held that victim impact testimony is admissible (*Ford v. State*, 1996). In Texas, jurors are required to answer yes to two factors to consider the option of a sentence of death: 1) Is the defendant likely to present a threat or future danger to society in the future, and 2) Is the defendant directly responsible for the death of the victim? Upon answering in the affirmative to both questions, the jury is then asked to consider any mitigating factors which would warrant mercy and a sentence of life in prison instead of death:

> Whether, taking into consideration all of the evidence, including the circumstances of the offense, the defendant's character and background, and the personal moral culpability of the defendant, there is sufficient mitigating circumstance or circumstances to warrant that a sentence of life imprisonment rather than a death sentence be imposed (Texas Code of Criminal Procedure, Art. 37.071, Sec. 2(e)).

It was the mitigating circumstances requirement that opened the door for the presentation of victim impact statements at the sentencing stage of capital trials in Texas. The latitude established for admissibility of evidence regarding mitigating factors regarding the defendant was effectively extended to evidence about the victim and the impact of the crime on the victim's family (*Ford v. State*, 1996). In *Smith v. State* (1996) and *Mosley v. State* (1998), the Texas Court of Criminal Appeals qualified the admissibility of victim impact statements. In *Smith,* holding that "[b]oth victim impact and victim character evidence are admissible…to show the uniqueness of the victim, the harm caused by the defendant, and as a rebuttal to the defendant's mitigating evidence" (*Mosley v. State,* 1998, p. xx).

In 2001, the Texas Legislature amended its Rights of Crime Victims provision of the Texas Code of Criminal Procedure to include the right to "complete the victim impact statement, and to have the victim impact statement considered by the attorney representing the state and the judge before sentencing" (Texas Code of Criminal

Procedure, Article 56, sec. 13(a)). Although not directly applying to their role in capital sentencing, the legislation was a big step in the legitimacy of the use of victim impact statements in capital cases in Texas, a use that has subsequently become relatively routine.

CHAPTER III:

Restorative Justice and the Death Penalty

Restorative justice is a theoretical paradigm which views crime as a violation or rupture of relationships in society and argues that repair of this rupture should be the primary goal of a society's response to crime. Healing, reconciliation, and transformation among victims, offenders, and communities are primary objectives under this paradigm. The idea of restorative justice in the context of the death penalty may, at first glance, seem something of a paradox. Indeed, killing an offender is antithetical to many of the restorative ideals. However, many have begun to incorporate principles of restorative justice into the death penalty process. As the previous chapter indicated, there is an especially strong need for healing and transformation among those who are impacted by capital murder and by the death penalty process; foremost among them are the co-victims. Although less often considered, offenders' families, community members, correctional staff, and others exhibit similar needs for healing and transformation in the aftermath of capital murder and the death penalty process. Restorative justice appears to provide some paths toward this healing and transformation.

In this chapter, I begin by giving a brief overview of restorative justice, what it is, what it is not, and how it applies to the three groups most directly involved in it: victims, offenders, and communities. This is followed by a discussion of restorative justice in practice. Restorative justice has come to be applied in a wide variety of settings and has taken many differing forms. Encounters between victims and offenders will be the primary focus here as it is most directly relevant to the present study. Specifically, programs known as victim-offender mediation (VOM) or victim-offender mediation/dialogue (VOM/D), the most common form of victim-offender encounters in the United States, will be considered in depth. Finally, restorative justice will be considered in the context of the death penalty. In this last section, the apparently paradoxical notion of restorative justice in the context of the death penalty will be addressed as will the actual use of VOM between capital murder co-victims and death row inmates. The potential for restorative justice to provide healing and transformation for not only the co-victims but for offenders' families and others impacted by capital murder and the death penalty will be considered.

RESTORATIVE JUSTICE: A BRIEF OVERVIEW

The practice of what has come to be known as restorative justice has existed in human societies as far back as history is recorded (Bianchi, 1994; Braswell, Fuller & Lozoff, 2001; Daly & Immarigeon, 1998; Llewellyn & Howse, 1999; Van Ness & Strong, 1997). Although rooted in ancient and diverse traditions and practices, the contemporary restorative justice movement (particularly in Western societies) is only in its infancy. The genesis of this modern movement toward restorative justice can be traced to Howard Zehr's paradigmatic book "Changing Lenses" (1990).

Zehr (1990) presented restorative justice as a counter paradigm to the dominant retributive model of justice in Western societies. Noting that retributive justice has failed, not only to reduce crime but also to provide victims and communities justice and to repair the harm caused by crime for victims, offenders and communities, Zehr (1990) suggests that it is time for a paradigm shift, a change of "lenses." A retributive lens, according to Zehr (1990), views crime as a violation against the state, relegates the needs and rights of victims to secondary status by making the state the victim, focuses on determination of guilt and punishment for the offender, and offers little or no consideration of the community in the justice process. It also myopically focuses on the anger- and revenge-oriented victim and community responses to crime, neglecting other important emotional responses and needs. A restorative lens, on the other hand, views crime as "a violation of people and relationships" in which there is a tear or rupture in these relationships that needs repair and restoration (Zehr, 1990, p. 181). Although it acknowledges that anger and revenge are natural responses to crime, it also views other important needs and responses as important and argues that for meaningful repair and transformation in the aftermath of crime, we must look beyond anger and vengeance. A restorative lens also views the involvement and participation of all who are impacted or harmed by crime as essential to the justice process: victims, offenders, and community members alike. For restoration to occur, according to Zehr (1990), the needs of each must be considered and attended to. The following table (Table 1) illustrates these oppositional aspects of the retributive and restorative models of crime and justice.

Table 1
Zehr's (1990, pp. 184-185) Retributive Lens/restorative Lens Comparison

Retributive Lens	*Restorative Lens*
Crime defined by violation of rules (i.e., broken rules)	Crime defined by harm to people and relationships (i.e., broken relationships)
Harms defined abstractly	Harms defined concretely
Crime seen as categorically different from other harms	Crime recognized as related to other harms and conflicts
State as victim	People and relationships as victims
State and offender seen as primary parties	Victim and offender seen as primary parties
Victims' needs and rights ignored	Victims' needs and rights central
Interpersonal dimensions irrelevant	Interpersonal dimensions central
Conflictual nature of crime obscured	Conflictual nature of crime recognized
Wounds of offender peripheral	Wounds of offender important
Offense defined in technical, legal terms	Offense understood in full context: moral, social, economic, political

But, what, more specifically, is restorative justice? In a later article, Zehr & Mika (1998, p. 54) continue their comparative approach to defining restorative justice:

> Where conventional justice is law and punishment oriented, we conceive of restorative justice as a harm-centered approach: the centrality of victims, the obligations of offenders (and the meaning of accountability), the role of the community, and the active engagement of all parties in the justice equation are distinctive elements, we believe, of such an approach.

A more concise definition is offered by Marshall (Cited in Zehr & Mika, 1998, p. 54): "[A] process whereby all the parties with a stake in a particular offence come together to resolve collectively how to deal with the aftermath of the offence and its implications for the future." Van Ness and Strong (1997, p. 42) offer a more multi-layered definition of restorative justice:

- It is a *different way of thinking* about crime and our response to it.
- It focuses on the *harm caused by crime*: repairing the harm done to victims and reducing future harm by preventing crime.
- It requires offenders to take *responsibility* for their actions and for the harm they have caused.
- It seeks *redress* for victims, *recompense* by offenders and *reintegration* of both within the community.
- It is achieved through a *cooperative effort* by communities and the government.

Clearly, there are numerous and variant definitions of restorative justice, but the underlying ideas and objectives are the same. In the end, the goal of restorative justice is transformation (as opposed to retribution) (Cose, 2004; Llewellyn & Howse, 1999; Van Ness & Strong, 1997; Zehr & Mika, 1998). This transformation comes from reparation of the harm that crime causes and this reparation includes attending to the needs of each of the parties impacted by the crime (Zehr, 1990). Central to this transformation is the objective of restoring relationships which have been ruptured by crime. In a more specific sense, restorative justice sets out to restore victims, offenders, communities, and the interrelationships therein in the aftermath of crime.

Victims

Restoring victims incorporates a variety of concepts and principles related to the needs of victims of crime. As Zehr (1990) states it, "[v]ictims have a variety of needs which must be met if one is to experience even approximate justice. In many cases, the first and most pressing needs are for support and a sense of safety" (p. 191). Contrary to these needs, the retributive process generally focuses on apprehending and convicting the offender with little attention given to the victims (aside from asking them questions which may lead to the apprehension and conviction of the offender, of course). Thus, the most fundamental initial aspect of restorative justice in meeting the needs of victims is the encouragement and facilitation of victim involvement and participation in the justice process. Christie (1977) observes that the criminal justice process essentially steals conflicts from crime victims by removing victim status from the individuals harmed by the crime and replacing them with the state as primary victim. Umbreit (1989a, p. 52) points out that "[t]he old paradigm of 'retributive justice' focuses upon the state being the victim and places the individual victim in a passive position with little, if any, participation in the justice process." Restorative justice aims to reverse this, placing the status of victim back into the hands of those who actually experience the victimization, thereby empowering victims and making them active participants in the justice process.

By allowing the victim an active role in the justice process, the restorative process is better equipped to redress the harm that has been done to victims. Such redress may include restitution in which the offender compensates the victim for the harms he or she caused. Although this seems feasible in cases of property crimes or crimes in which property is damaged, it is much more difficult to imagine the role of restitution in cases of violence. Nevertheless, restitution is often an important (if not primary) aspect of the restorative justice process, even in cases of violent crime (Immarigeon, 1996; Van Ness & Strong, 1997). As Zehr (1990) points out however, "[r]estitution represents recovery of losses, but its real importance is symbolic" (p. 192). The real importance comes from the vindication that it represents, the acknowledgment of a wrong and acceptance of responsibility. Ultimately, the goal (whether accompanied by restitution or not) is for things to be "made right" (Zehr, 1990). These less instrumental and tangible forms of redress may include finding answers such as why the offender violated the rights of the victim or simply understanding the situation and circumstances that brought the offender to their actions. Often such answers serve to calm anxiety and fears that otherwise accompany the ambiguity and seeming arbitrariness surrounding crime (Immarigeon, 1996). Zehr (1990) claims that "[v]ictims need reassurance, reparation, vindication, empowerment, but they especially need to find meaning" (p. 194). This meaning is often an avenue toward healing or closure and often comes from a process of reconciliation with the offender.

Reconciliation between victim and offender has come to be a cornerstone of restorative justice (Van Ness & Strong, 1997). Although use of the term reconciliation has drawn some controversy due to the fact that "reconciliation" implies a prior relationship with the offender and a desire to maintain it (See, for example, Umbreit, Vos, Coates & Brown, 2003 who prefer to use the term "mediation"), it's use here refers to the more general process of righting a wrong and settling a dispute—or, as Webster's New World Dictionary puts it, "to bring into harmony" (p. 1187). In the case of reconciliation with the offender, there may be a prior relationship which needs repair for the victim to move forward with the healing process. If there is no prior relationship, one has been created (regardless of intent or desires) by the crime and must be reconciled for meaningful justice to take place. Moreover, reconciliation offers the victim an opportunity to obtain answers from the one person who might be able to provide them and to glean meaning in the context of a negative and traumatic experience. Immarigeon (1996) gives the following account of a process of reconciliation practiced in Canada:

> [V]ictims discovered that offenders were also human beings; victims' emotions were released and fears subsided while they obtained peace of mind; victims' stereotypes of offenders were challenged in some ways; forgiveness and reconciliation were evident where victims, through dialogue, developed compassion toward offenders and empathy for their social conditions (p. 474).

Perhaps the most powerful aspect of a victim's reconciliation with the offender is the potential for forgiveness. Gehm (1992) offers the following regarding the importance of forgiveness:

> Forgiveness (a) helps individuals forget the painful experiences of their past and frees the subtle control of individuals and events of the past; (b) facilitates the reconciliation of relationships more than the expression of anger; (c) decreases the likelihood that anger will be misdirected in later loving relationships; and (d) lessens the subconscious fear of being punished because of unconscious violent impulses (p. 544).

Others have reiterated the importance of forgiveness in the healing process and for obtaining peace and closure in the face of being wronged or traumatized (Cose, 2004; Dickey, 1998; Dzur & Wertheimer, 2002; Enright, 2001; Estrada-Hollenbeck, 1996; Fitzgibbons, 1998; Ransley & Spy, 2004). Estrada-Hollenbeck (1996), reporting on an analysis of victim and offender narratives regarding forgiveness, concludes the following:

> The results of this study suggest that forgiveness does contribute to improved relationships between the victim and the perpetrator, compared to when forgiveness does not occur. In this way, forgiveness is a contributor to the restoration of justice to the extent that it restores a neutral or positive relationship between the victim and perpetrator (pp. 311-312).

Although forgiveness is often conceived in the context of an interrelationship between victim and offender accompanied by contrition or apology on the part of the offender, such two-way interaction is not essential (although, from a restorative justice perspective, it is ideal) to the process of forgiveness and the power it holds for the victim. Reciprocation and two-way interaction is not always possible, but for the victim, forgiveness remains an important element in healing and restoration.

It should be noted that the notion of "victim" in the context of restorative justice extends beyond the primary victim of a crime to "secondary victims" who include the family and other loved-ones of the primary victim and even others who are impacted by the crime such as the offender's family and friends (Van Ness & Strong, 1997). From a restorative justice perspective, these other individuals suffer harm as a result of the crime and are thus victims. The restoration of relationships for these "secondary victims" is just as important in the context of restorative justice as that for primary victims, and all the components mentioned above must be considered for all of these victims. In cases of homicide as well as cases in which the victim is a young child, secondary victims (or, co-victims) play an even more central role in the restorative justice process, as the actual victim is unable to actively participate. In any case, the restoration of relationships and repairing of harm caused by crime should incorporate all who have been impacted by the crime. If restorative justice is about restoring relationships in the wake of crime, all impacted individuals and relationships must be taken into account.

Offender

The restoration of the offender is seen as no less important to the restorative justice approach to crime. And, contrary to the currently predominant retributive paradigm of criminal justice, offenders are required to play an active role in the justice process in the wake of their criminal action. The primary focus of restorative justice in regard to offenders is on accountability and responsibility (Zehr, 1990; Van Ness, 1997; Zehr & Mika, 1998). For the restorative process to be successful, the offender must own up to their actions and the harms that they have caused. This may occur through direct interaction between the offender and the harmed parties including the victim or victims, co-victims, and community in general. Being confronted with the harm that has resulted from his or her actions is a particularly powerful aspect of this, but the offender is also often required to take specific actions to redress the harm or compensate the victims and/or community who have been violated and harmed. As Zehr and Mika (1998) put it, "[o]ffenders' obligations are to make things right as much as possible" (p. 51). Van Ness and Strong (1997) characterize the obligation and role of the offender in restorative justice as one of "recompense." They define recompense in comparison to the more currently dominant goal of retribution:

> Retribution is defined as deserved punishment for evil done…the offender is merely a passive recipient of punishment, [a] punishment that does not help repair the injuries caused by crime [but] simply creates new injuries; now both the victim and the offender are injured. "Recompense," on the other hand, is something given or done to make up for an injury. This underscores that the offender who caused the injury should be the active party, and that the

> purpose of punishment should be to repair as much as possible the injury caused by the crime (p. 38).

Such recompense may include specific compensation such as restitution or a more broad engagement in a process of reconciliation with those harmed. In both cases the objective is to work toward repair of the harm that one has caused.

In conjunction with the needs of victims, reconciliation offers offenders an avenue to right the wrong they have created by helping in the healing of their victims but also an avenue toward their own healing. Contrition and apology on behalf of the offender and expressed to the victim have particular power in aiding in the healing and closure and experience of justice for victims (Estrada-Hollenbeck, 1996). But it is also often cited as transformative for the offenders as well, especially if an apology is reciprocated with forgiveness by the victim (Umbreit et al., 2003). Moreover, Haley (1989) notes that opportunities for expression of contrition and remorse on the part of the offender not only are restorative for the offender but also contributes to a decline in criminality. In the end, the reconciliation process is conducted in the hope that resolution and healing for both victim and offender will be generated and that the likelihood for continuing criminality and crime in the community will be diminished.

This approach to "dealing with" offenders may be perceived by many to be "soft" or otherwise lenient (Llewellyn & Howse, 1998). From the perspective of the retributive paradigm, which focuses on punishment and "just deserts," restorative justice approaches to crime and criminals is depicted as letting offenders off easy and not holding individuals responsible for their actions. In reality, advocates of restorative justice argue, the restorative model offers greater avenues toward holding offenders responsible for their actions by requiring direct accountability and ownership of actions. Dickey (1998) offers an eloquent summary of this reality:

> It is not forgetting; it is not condoning or pardoning; it is not indifference or a diminishing of anger; it is not inconsistent with punishment; it does not wipe out the wrong or deny it. Indeed, it relies on recognition of the wrong so that repair can occur. It also relies on the taking of responsibility for the wrong in a personal and social way (p. 108).

The retributive model, on the other hand, in effect discourages actual accountability by pitting the offender against the state in an adversarial process in which it is in the interest of the offender to deny guilt or remain silent (Wright, 1996).

Ultimately, the final goal of restorative justice as it concerns offenders is reintegration (Van Ness & Strong, 1997). Van Ness and Strong (1997) offer the following description of reintegration in the context of restorative justice:

> When we speak of reintegration we mean re-entry into community life as a whole, contributing, productive person. This means more than simply tolerating the person's presence in the community. Reintegration requires relationships characterized by respect, commitment and intolerance for—but understanding of—deviant or irrational behavior.

Braithwaite (1989), although at the time not writing specifically about restorative justice, noted the fundamental importance of reintegrating offenders into communities in the reduction of crime, recidivism and associated harms. Specifically, he argued that offenders who fail to be reintegrated following crime will be less integrated and connected with the community (rather, they will be stigmatized) and will thus be more likely to continue violating the norms of that community. Restorative justice emphasizes the importance of relationships and connections in society and of maintaining these relationships. Reintegration of offenders (and all others impacted by crime) into their communities is critical to this.

Communities

The broader community must not be ignored in the restorative justice process. As crime is viewed as violation of relationships, the community in which such relationships exist and flourish becomes central to any meaningful justice process. A broad goal of restorative justice is to repair or restore ruptures in the community and these interrelationships therein. Many of the aforementioned principles and practices serve this goal in that they attempt to mend these ruptures between members of the community and to ultimately restore community peace and order. Van Ness and Strong (1997) point out that "[t]he victim's and the offender's need for resolution, and the…community's need for public safety, must be addressed in the same process" (p. 38). Thus, as with victims and offenders, the community and its members must be allowed to directly participate in the justice process. As previously mentioned, there are secondary victims who must be considered. But, there are also general community members who experience crime even more indirectly through the impact it has on their sense of security and safety and the integrity of the geographical space in which they reside and which they share with others. Moreover, cohesion, interdependency, and connection in communities are critical elements in minimizing crime (Braithwaite, 1989; Bursik, 1988; Sampson & Groves, 1989; Savage & Kanazawa, 2002). Restorative justice sets out to foster, maintain and repair this cohesion, interdependency and connection.

VICTIM-OFFENDER ENCOUNTERS: RESTORATIVE JUSTICE IN PRACTICE

Although true restorative justice is intended to redress the harm to each the victim, offender, and the community, some of the most predominant and effective restorative efforts have focused primarily on the victim and offender. Indeed, the practice of restorative justice in contemporary North American societies is cited as first being observed in 1974 with a victim-offender reconciliation program (VORP) in Ontario, Canada (Daly & Immarigeon, 1998). Programs in which the victim and offender are brought face-to-face to engage in dialogue and work toward reparation and restoration are many and diverse. Collectively referred to as "encounter" programs, such approaches have become "pillars of a restorative approach to crime" (Van Ness & Strong, 1997, p. 68). Some specific forms of encounters include family group conferencing (FGC), victim-offender panels (VOP), and victim-offender mediation and dialogue (VOM/D). FGC is an approach popular in Australia and New Zealand in which family conferences (involving the victim, offender, and each of their families) are held to determine what should be done to best resolve the harm caused by the (in most cases, juvenile) offender (Moore & O'Connell, 1994; Morris & Maxwell, 1998; Van Stokkom, 2002). VOPs, in which victims meet and engage in dialogue with offenders other than those who directly victimized them, have become popular in cases in which the specific offender is unknown or refuses to participate or in which victims are too frightened or traumatized to confront their actual offender (Van Ness & Strong, 1997). Research on VOPs have shown beneficial impacts for both victims and offenders. Van Ness and Strong (1997) report "a dramatic change in attitudes of offenders and in the likelihood of recidivism" and that "82 percent [of victims] reported that it had helped in their healing" (p. 76).

Although there is a wide range of varying approaches to victim-offender encounters in the pursuit of restorative justice, Victim Offender Mediation (VOM)[17] is one of the most common manifestations (and the manifestation most salient to the present study) (Umbreit et al., 2003). Based on the original conceptualization of VORP[18], VOM is a process in which victim and offender are brought together to engage in a dialogue with the aid of a trained mediator or facilitator (Gehm, 1998; Umbreit et al., 2003). Participation in VOM is always voluntary on the part of the victim and is usually voluntary on the part of the offender. The encounters only occur after each has gone through at least one preparation meeting with the mediator "in which they explore the participant's experience of the event, the nature of the harm caused, and potential avenues for repairing the harm" (Umbreit et al., 2003, pp. 11-12). Umbreit (1998) gives an overview of the process highlighting four phases:

1. case referral and intake;
2. preparation for mediation, at which time the mediator meets with the parties separately prior to the mediation session in order to listen to their stories, explain the program, invite their participation, and prepare them for the face-to-face meeting;
3. mediation, at which a trained third party mediator (most often a community volunteer) facilitates a dialogue that allows the victim and offender to talk about the impact of the crime upon their lives, provide information about the event to each other, and work out a mutually agreeable written restitution agreement; and

---

[17] Although many programs are referred to as Victim Offender Mediation and Dialogue (VOM/D) programs, the shortened version of simply Victim Offender Mediation (VOM) has become the more common name. This latter name will be the primary term used throughout this book.

[18] As noted by Umbreit et al, 2003, the use of the name VORP has fallen out of favor due to the assumption implicit in the term reconciliation that victims have, or desire to have, a relationship with their offender and thus to "reconcile" that relationship. Many, such as Umbreit, argue that the use of the word "mediation" is more appropriate.

4. follow-up, which monitors restitution agreements (online journal).

The actual mediated encounter begins with each sharing their experiences of the crime (sometimes including previously written or prepared statements) and the aftermath of the crime (Umbreit et al., 2003). Sometimes family members or other community members are also present and participate (Van Ness & Strong, 1997). Finally, in addition to follow-up on restitution agreements, follow-ups or continued monitoring may be used to ensure compliance with other obligations such as specified actions which may serve restorative purposes (e.g. particular forms of community service or specialized treatment or therapy) or even that punishment (although this is a controversial aspect in the context of restorative justice) is adequately carried out (Daly, 1999; Garvey, 1999).

In line with the general principles of restorative justice, VOM is intended to repair the harm caused by crime and restore those impacted by cooperatively and peacefully determining the best resolutions for everyone. Although the focus of VOM is primarily on the victim and offender, the goals of such a response to crime is much broader. Gehm (1998) cites the following broad objectives of VOM:

> [T]o reduce victim trauma, to humanize the criminal justice process, to increase offender accountability, to provide meaningful roles for victims, to provide restitution, to create opportunities for reconciliation between victim and offender, to enhance community understanding of crime and criminal justice, to break down stereotypes, and, in combination with other sanctions, to reduce reliance on conventional punishment (online journal).

Umbreit et al. (2003) add that it "holds offenders directly accountable to the people they victimized, allows for more active involvement of...community members (as participants or as volunteer mediators) in the justice process, and can potentially suppress further criminal behaviors in offenders" (p. 12). Research has shown that these objectives are shared by both victims and offenders who have engaged in VOM. Umbreit et al. (2003) report that victims chose to engage in VOM out of "a desire to receive restitution, to hold the offender accountable, to learn more about the 'why' of the crime and to share their pain with the offender, to avoid court processing, to help the offender change behavior, or to see that the offender was adequately punished" (p. 24). They go on to report that offenders "wanted to take direct responsibility for their own actions, to pay back the victim, to apologize for the harm they caused, and to get the whole experience behind them" (pp. 24-25).

Research on VOM suggests that these goals are generally met with overwhelming satisfaction on the part of both victims and offenders (Coates & Gehm, 1989; Latimer, Dowden, & Muise, 2001; Nugent, Umbreit, Wiinamaki & Paddock, 2001; Umbreit, 1996; Umbreit, 1998; Umbreit et al., 2003). Umbreit (1996), in a comprehensive study of four VOM programs in Canada, found that 89% of victims and 91% of offenders were satisfied with the outcome of mediation and that 91% and 93%, respectively would participate in mediation again (p. 381). Moreover, Umbreit (1996) reports that satisfaction with the criminal justice system overall is higher for both victims and offenders when they participated in mediation. Among victims, 78% of those who participated in mediation reported general satisfaction with the criminal justice system in comparison to only 48% of victims who did not participate in mediation. For offenders, 74% of mediation participants and 53% of non-participants reported satisfaction with the criminal justice system. Umbreit (1996) also found both victims and offenders were significantly and substantially more likely to perceive the justice system as fair if they had participated in VOM. A recent meta-analysis of 35 prior analyses of VOM programs supports these findings (Latimer et al., 2001). As Umbreit et al. (2003) conclude, based on a thorough review of prior studies, "[e]xpression of satisfaction with VOM is consistently high for both victims and offenders across sites, cultures, and seriousness of offenses." It is typical that eight or nine out of every ten participants express satisfaction with the process and outcomes (Umbreit et al., 2003).

Beyond the high levels of satisfaction, research has also indicated overwhelming success in securing agreements and the meeting of obligations and commitments resulting from VOM (Coates & Gehm, 1989; Umbreit et al., 2003). Coates and Gehm (1989), in an analysis of 37 victims and 23 offenders, found that written agreements and contracts resulted in 98% of cases in which victim and offender engaged in mediation. Umbreit et al. (2003), in reviewing a broad array of prior studies, report that restitution (whether manifested in monetary terms, community service, or direct service to the victim) is successfully completed in 80 to 90% of VOM cases. Umbreit et al. (2003) further report that the use of VOM as a diversion produces resource and cost savings. They conclude that "[t]he potential cost savings of VOM programs when they are truly employed as alternatives rather than as showcase add-ons is significant" (Umbreit et al., 2003, p. 34). A final focus of research is on the impact of VOM on re-offense. A meta-analysis conducted by Nugent et al. (2001) suggests a significant difference between re-offense in cases in which mediation occurred and cases in which it did not. Nugent et al. (2001) found that "VOM participants were only about 60% as likely to reoffend over a 1-year period as were non-VOM participants" (p. 16). Similarly, Umbreit, Coates and Vos (2001a), having conducted research on juveniles offenders, reported that "18 percent of the program youth re-offended, compared to 27 percent for the comparison youth...[and] also tended to reappear in court for less serious charges than did their comparison counterparts" (p. 32).

Umbreit et al. (2001a) assert that "victim offender mediation is one of the more empirically grounded justice interventions to emerge" (p. 29). Based on the research as indicated above, it is hard to disagree. And, as a result, modest gains in the utilization of VOM over the last decade can be seen. In 1998 there were more than 290 VOM programs operating in the United States (Umbreit, 1998), and over 1300 programs worldwide (Umbreit et al., 2001a). Recently, VOM has even enjoyed increased media attention and interest, being profiled and discussed on numerous popular news and talk shows (Szmania, 2005). As the use of VOM has gained momentum in recent years, its application has broadened in scope. Although initially expected to be exceedingly difficult to implement in cases of violent crimes such as rape, aggravated assault, and murder, VOM has been found to be successful even in cases of extreme violence (Flaten, 1996; Umbreit, 1989b; Umbreit, Coates and Vos, 2001b; Umbreit et al., 2003), in addition to its more traditional application in cases of less severe crime. Moreover, VOM has been implemented and operated by a range of groups, agencies, and organizations in a variety of settings. Although often operated by groups independent of the traditional criminal justice system (e.g. religious groups, non-profit organizations), VOM is also practiced in the context of probation, correctional facilities, prosecutors' offices, victims' services, and law enforcement (Umbreit et al., 2003, p. 22). VOM is increasingly being used in prison settings (Immarigeon, 1996) and in cases of violent crime. As will be discussed in the next section, VOM has even begun to be used on death row.

Texas is one state which has made increasingly wide use of VOM and enjoyed great success employing it in the context of their correctional system, particularly in cases of violent crime. In Texas, which employs victim-offender mediation and dialogue (VOM/D), sessions are arranged by the Victim Services Division of the Texas Department of Criminal Justice (TDCJ). In response to pressure from crime victims and victims of violent crime in particular, Texas created the Office of Victims Services (later to become the Victim Services Division) in 1989. In 1991 the first mediated session between a homicide co-victim and the killer of her daughter was held. The first full-blown VOM/D program session was conducted in 1995. Texas' program, as it deals with particularly difficult cases of violence, is especially rigorous in its preparation of both victim and offender (sometimes spending up to a year in preparation for a mediation session) and in the management of actual sessions. The following is a detailed checklist for VOM/D sessions in Texas:

- Mediator reviews ground rules/establishes purpose.
- Victim makes opening statement (brief preview of expectations).
- Offender makes opening statement (brief preview of expectations).
- Victim begins dialogue.
- Victim and offender continue interaction.
- Lunch break.
- Mediation resumes.
- Mediation (sic) clarifies/summarizes.
- Victim and offender continue interaction.
- Mediator reviews Affirmation Agreement process, if applicable.
- Mediator facilitates brainstorming/consensus/signing of Affirmation Agreement.
- Victim and offender make closing statements.
- Mediator concludes mediation.
- Mediator interviews and debriefs offender/victim separately (Umbreit et al., 2003, p. 83).

Upon consent by both parties, sessions are routinely videotaped and used in subsequent debriefing sessions with both victims and offenders. These debriefings, aided by video of the session, are used in the context of both short-term and long-term follow-ups, both of which are deemed very important (Umbreit et al., 2003, pp. 83-84).

By 1996 there were more than 200 requests by victims for mediation (Umbreit et al., 2003). Since then, Texas' VOM/D program has enjoyed great success. In an in depth analysis of 22 VOM/D sessions and 39 participants (20 victims and 19 offenders), Umbreit et al. (2003, p. 127) found that all victims reported being either "very satisfied" (95%) or "somewhat satisfied" (5%). All 19 offenders reported being "very satisfied" (p. 173). VOM/D in Texas also was found to have positive long-term effects. For example, 60% of victims reported that the process enriched their religious or spiritual life and 73% felt that VOM/D gave them a more positive and peaceful outlook on life. Offenders likewise reported gaining a lot of long-term benefits from VOM/D. All but one (94%) reported that it gave them a newfound understanding of how their criminal actions impacted others; 72% reported that it gave them a more positive outlook on life and increased ability to cope with life events (Umbreit et al., 2003). The specific qualitative statements made by both victims and offenders only add to the strength of these findings.[19] Their overwhelmingly positive and transformative theme can be well expressed in the words of one mother of a homicide victim: "If everybody in the country would do it we'd have a better world because I know it makes you a better person and it makes them a better person" (Umbreit et al., 2003, pp. 129-130).

RESTORATIVE JUSTICE PRINCIPLES IN CAPITAL CASES

The idea of restorative justice occurring in the context of the death penalty is seemingly paradoxical. In fact, many have questioned the viability of restorative justice in the context of any punishment (Braithwaite, 1999; Zehr, 1990). Braithwaite (1999) claims that punishment is a sign of weakness which fails to reduce crime and only serves to perpetuate and increase harm in society. Like Zehr (1990), who was the first to formalize much of the contemporary principles, Braithwaite (1999) argues that restorative justice should *replace* punitive responses to crime, not simply supplement them. As

---

[19] To read the statements of VOM/D participants and a more thorough review of the findings presented here, see Chs. 4-6 in Umbreit et al. (2003).

previously discussed, Zehr's (1990) conceptualization portrayed restorative justice as the diametrical opposite of retributive (i.e. punitive) justice. The notion that restorative justice can possibly be incorporated into the death penalty process, then, brings us right up against the most punitive of sanctions and presents a great challenge in application. The death penalty is the antithesis of offender restoration and reintegration. Note the following selected "signposts" of restorative justice provided by Zehr & Mika (1998, pp. 54-55):

- Show equal concern and commitment to victims and offenders, involving both in the process of justice;
- recognize that while obligations may be difficult for offenders, they should not be intended as harms and they must be achievable;
- encourage collaboration and reintegration rather than coercion and isolation.

These are only a select few of the "signposts" of restorative justice but it becomes immediately clear that the very nature of the death penalty violates some of the most fundamental principles of restorative justice. Nevertheless, the notion of restorative justice in the context of the death penalty has begun to be discussed by scholars and practitioners (Arrigo & Williams, 2003; Eschholz, Reed, Beck, & Leonard, 2003; King, 2003; Radelet & Borg, 2000b; Umbreit et al., 2003; Umbreit & Vos, 2000) and restorative justice principles have even begun to be incorporated into the death penalty process in some states (King, 2003; Umbreit et al., 2003; Umbreit & Vos, 2000).

In December, 2003 a conference on restorative justice and the death penalty was held in Durham, NC and was sponsored by the Duke Death Penalty Clinic, the Eno River Unitarian Universalist Fellowship, and People of Faith Against the Death Penalty. (DPIC, 2007c). The conference was entitled "Restorative Justice and the Death Penalty, Exploring the Human Costs" and was organized with the goal of exploring the ability of restorative justice to offer peace and healing to those who have been impacted by the death penalty (including co-victims, offenders' family and friends, and community members). According to conference organizers, "[t]he hope for those attending the conference is that they will find community with one another and that they will leave with information helpful to themselves and/or to others" (DPIC, 2007c).

One of the primary focal points of the conference was exploring and attending to the needs of co-victims of capital murder as well as to those of offenders' families and others impacted by the murder and the aftermath of the murder. As previously addressed in Chapter II, there are numerous casualties of both murder and the death penalty process and the needs of these casualties are complex and diverse. It's fair to suggest that restorative justice practices potentially offer the best avenue for supplying the needed healing, closure, and transformation among co-victims, offenders, offenders' families and the community in the wake of capital murder. But, the death penalty and capital trial processes present some significant barriers to such ideals and practices.

The death penalty process often only contributes to or exacerbates the grief and harm of the crime by failing to attend to these needs, and inherently inhibits the potential for meaningful restorative justice processes. Although some might argue that restorative elements exist in the context of victim impact statements offered by co-victims at trial, such allocutions often have little restorative value (Arrigo & Williams, 2003; See also, Obold-Eshleman, 2004). In fact, according to Arrigo & Williams (2003), "VIS, as presently employed, not only instill a desire for vengeance in decision makers but, correspondingly, inhibit the possibility of empathy, compassion, and forgiveness directed toward the offender" (p. 604). And, they note, instead of producing healing and catharsis, "resentment, anger, and vengeance...often accompany (or follow) the experience of such intensely charged and deeply felt victim allocutions" (Arrigo & Williams, 2003, p. 604). Indeed, the adversarial nature of VIS and the capital trial process inherently pits co-victims and offenders' families against one-another. Research has found that these are two groups who share a similar grief and who often desire and benefit from dialogue or interaction with one-another (Eschholz et al., 2003; King, 2004). However, the current capital trial process only serves to split them further apart and impede meaningful restorative interaction and healing on the part of co-victims and offenders' families (Eschholz et al., 2003).

Arguments for restorative justice reforms in the context of capital trials and the death penalty process have begun to be heard in academic, legal, and community circles (Arrigo & Williams, 2003; Beck et al., 2007; DPIC, 2007b; Eschholz et al., 2003). Advocates of restorative justice point to the supreme need for justice and transformation in cases of capital murder and argue that bringing individuals impacted by such crimes together offers the best opportunities for meaningful healing for all—co-victims, offenders,

offenders' families, and the community (Arrigo & Williams, 2003; Eschholz et al., 2003; King, 2003, 2005). It is with this intent that the practice of restorative justice has started to be incorporated into the death penalty process. Indeed, Texas has begun implementing victim-offender mediation/dialogue between death row inmates and their co-victims.

Texas is one of the rare states which offer VOM in the context of cases of extremely violent crimes and which has extended availability to capital cases. Moreover, Texas has a very rigorous training process for mediators and preparation process for participants. Umbreit and Vos (2000) point out that "[m]ediation staff in the Texas program are trained in humanistic dialogue-driven style of mediation that frequently involves little, if any, preparation of the parties prior to the mediation session" (p. 67). In the death row cases, preparation is extensive taking as long as up to a year (although, the time of preparation may be shortened due to impending execution dates). In 2000, Umbreit and Vos (2000) presented preliminary analyses of Texas' use of VOM/D between death row inmates and their co-victims. Their study included two cases of VOM/D in which three co-victims participated. In one case, the granddaughter of one of the victims and sister of another participated. In the other, the mother of a victim participated. All three co-victims and both of the offenders participated voluntarily. Umbreit and Vos (2000) reported extremely positive results from the VOM/D sessions. Based on extensive interviews with each of the participants, they concluded the following:

> All were moved beyond their expectations, all were relieved, all reported significant progress on their healing journeys, and all were grateful. The extent of the actual healing and transformation that took place for the offenders can never be documented beyond their self-reports in these interviews held a matter of weeks before their executions. All 5 persons point to the same set of components to account for their response; these included careful, compassionate preparation, gentle and unobtrusive guidance during the session, and above all, the opportunity for genuine, human face-to-face encounter, which increases, rather than decreases, offender accountability and responsibility. The 5 participants were unanimous in their hope that this potentially healing process can be made more available for both victims and offenders (Umbreit & Vos, 2000, pp. 84-85).

A follow-up study by Umbreit et al. (2003) included one more case which included one more co-victim (the mother of the victim). Again, the outcomes were all reported as extremely positive. Each participant reported that "the experience was powerful and healing, and they were relieved and renewed" (Umbreit et al., 2003, p. 261).[20] Of course, the researchers note that much more qualitative and quantitative research is needed for a fuller understanding of the effectiveness of VOM/D for meeting co-victims' and offenders' needs in capital cases.

But what of others who are impacted by the death penalty—those Arrigo and Fowler (2001) refer to as "the death row community?" In accordance with restorative justice, the healing of all who are a part of this community should be considered. Although VOM/D offers restorative opportunities for co-victims and offenders, the broader community and, more specifically, the offenders' family remain neglected. As Eschholz et al. (2003) report from extensive, in-depth interviews with capital offenders' family members, there is a strong need for restorative justice initiatives in capital cases on behalf of offenders' families. These families often suffer as much as co-victims, have the same needs for healing, and experience alienation and stigmatization in their communities. According to Eschholz et al. (2003), restorative justice offers the greatest opportunity to provide healing for this neglected group in capital cases. In fact, they note "many instances in which families were trying to do restorative justice on their own" (Eschholz et al., 2003, p. 173) but also that "[u]nfortunately, many of these families found that the traditional system of justice impeded their efforts at restorative justice" (p. 174). On the other hand, they found that "[o]ther family members desired restoration but needed help in their journeys" (p. 174). Unfortunately, little help in the death penalty process is currently forthcoming; in fact, the criminal justice system currently appears to only exacerbate the suffering and harm experienced by capital offenders' families (Eschholz et al., 2003).

As noted in Chapter II, the death penalty leaves many ruptures and casualties in its path. Restorative justice offers opportunities to repair these ruptures and reduce casualties. Eschholz et al. (2003) concluded their study of offenders' family members by noting that "[t]hese families are in need of healing. To that end, many desired to reach out

---

[20] For actual statements made by participants and testimonials to the positive outcomes of VOM/D in capital cases, see the actual Umbreit & Vos (2000) article and Umbreit et al. (2003) book.

and connect with victims' family members, their own communities, and to form new communities based on the shared experience of a homicide and trial" (p. 175). This sentiment can extend to all involved in the "death row community;" and, in the true spirit of restorative justice, the broader community and its role in the justice process must be considered. This is especially true in capital cases in which particularly horrible crimes are at center, emotions run high, and stigmatization is likely for all involved with the death penalty process. There is a need for healing and transformation for not just the co-victims, offender and offender's family, but for those other individuals touched by the death penalty such as correctional staff, attorneys, clergy, media, and many others. For healing and transformation to occur in the wake of such horrific and traumatizing crimes as well as the process of the death penalty, community support is critical, and a factor that is currently missing. It is the hope of many that the application of restorative justice principles in capital cases will provide these and other missing pieces and, ultimately, the healing and transformation so needed.

In spite of the apparent promise and potential of restorative justice in the context of the death penalty, some scholars seriously question the wisdom and viability of implementing it alongside a form of punishment which so blatantly violates its essential principles (Arrigo & Williams, 2003; Radelet & Borg, 2000b). Radelet and Borg (2000b), in a response to Umbreit and Vos's (2000) article on VOM/D and the death penalty, argue that restorative justice has no place in the capital punishment process. They argue: "By its very nature, the death penalty is not about forgiveness (however conceptualized), finding common ground, or reconciliation. Instead, it embraces the polar opposites: retribution, hatred, and denial of the offender's humanity" (Radelet & Borg, 2000b, p. 90). It is hard to disagree with them. And, there is good reason for restorative justice advocates to be skeptical about such applications. The very thought of restorative justice being practiced in the context of the death penalty may perhaps devalue the real goals of restorative justice. As Van Ness and Strong (1997) point out "[a] society cannot select certain features of the [restorative justice] model and omit others; all are essential" (p. 41). The death penalty, from a restorative justice perspective, is among the most grievous violations of certain features of restorative justice (particularly those related to restoration, respect, and reintegration of offenders). Similarly, death penalty abolitionists may find the incorporation of restorative justice into the death penalty process a bit unsettling as such practices have the potential to obscure the violent and non-restorative end product of executions. Radelet and Borg (2000b) offer the most cogent summary of these points:

> If the state is truly interested in promoting restorative justice between killers and the families of their victims—as we think it should be—the first step it needs to take is to abolish the death penalty and stop promoting the false belief that capital punishment is an effective way to foster the healing of families of homicide victims (p. 88).

Indeed, the abolition of the death penalty would be a positive reform from a restorative justice perspective; but, assuming that the death penalty persists, should potentially useful and positive restorative justice practices—practices that might best address the needs of co-victims, offenders' families, and communities—be forbidden because of philosophical semantics? Perhaps, as a colleague recently suggested, we should resist using the label "restorative justice" in regard to VOM/D and other such initiatives in the context of the death penalty. Nevertheless, the question must be asked whether we can use principles of restorative justice (whatever we choose to call them) to reduce harm and increase peace in the context of inherently non-restorative justice practices and punishments. There is no easy answer to this question. But, it is hard to deny that there can be meaningful dialogue and reconciliation for many individuals in spite of the death penalty. In cases in which the most severe harm and suffering (both from the crime and from the response to the crime) are inherent, the paths to healing offered by restorative justice are alluring.

CHAPTER IV:

Giving Voice to the Condemned and their Victims

This study endeavors to, in the words of Charles Ragin (1994), "give voice" to the two groups most directly impacted in capital cases: the co-victims of capital murder and the offenders condemned to death sentences for committing capital murder. Specifically, statements of co-victims made in the local newspaper in Huntsville, TX (where executions are conducted) at the time of an execution and the last statement given by offenders immediately prior to their execution are explored. This study is an attempt to observe and understand the sentiments and attitudes as expressed in the words of those with the greatest stake in the rituals of the death penalty and executions. In this chapter, the primary objectives of this exploratory study are discussed. But, first, the previous relevant research—what little there is—is addressed.

PREVIOUS RESEARCH ON OFFENDERS' AND CO-VICTIMS' STATEMENTS

Very little research on the statements of offenders and co-victims has been conducted. In spite of the centrality of offenders and co-victims to the death penalty process and to popular rationale about the use of the death penalty, little attention has actually been given to the thoughts and perspectives of these groups. Some of the most common expressions advocating the death penalty and executions refer to the particularly evil and irredeemable nature of offenders and to the need for justice for victims and co-victims (Lynch, 2002). But, little is actually known about these groups and less is known of their thoughts and expressions directly surrounding the implementation of the death penalty.

Although numerous journalistic accounts have reported statements made by death row inmates, actual analyses of statements made by condemned inmates are scarce in the literature. The accounts that have been published have predominantly been based on interviews (Dicks, 2000) or on letters (Arriens, 1997) or other personal accounts relayed by the condemned inmates (Pickett & Stowers, 2002; Prejean, 1993; Robertson, 2002). Others have been auto-biographical publications by death row inmates (Abu-Jamal, 1995; Rossi, 2004). Although these accounts are valuable in relaying the stories of (and, in a limited way, giving voice to) particular condemned inmates, they lack a systematic exploration into the broad array of thoughts and perspectives of condemned inmates. Further, they do not offer any opportunity to compare statements across a large sample of condemned inmates or to collectively characterize their perspectives.

One particularly salient opportunity to obtain the perspective of a large number of condemned inmates is to examine their last statements made at the time of execution. This is information that is generally available to the public (in Texas, it is freely accessible through TDCJ's website). Nevertheless, little research on these statements has been conducted. The lone known published analysis was conducted by Heflick (2005) who examined 237 last statements of executed inmates in Texas from January 1997 to April 2005. The researcher identifies six primary themes of last statements: "afterlife belief, silence, claims of innocence, activism, love/appreciation, and forgiveness" (Heflick, 2005, p. 329). Although Heflick (2005) briefly discusses and offers some examples of these six themes, he limits his study to a purely qualitative analysis and offers no indication of the prevalence of these themes or any factors that might relate to them. In one other known study, Slone et al. (2002), in a paper presented at the 2002 American Society of Criminology Meetings in Chicago, IL, analyzed the last statements of 285 executed offenders in Texas developing a simple typology consisting of four identified types of executed offenders: contrite, externalizer, philosopher, and defiant. They reported that 33% of the statements fit into the contrite category; 10% in the externalizer, 16% in the philosopher, and 12% in the defiant. They also examined the four different last statement types in respect to various offender and execution characteristics. Most interesting among their findings were that statements were more likely to exhibit "contrite" characteristics and less likely to be "defiant" when co-victims witnessed the execution.

A similar pattern was identified when the offender and victim were related. However, no significance testing was conducted, so any inferences or conclusions from these findings must be made with caution. Indeed, no solid consideration of findings or conclusions are offered by the authors and the results they do present seem to suggest a need for deeper analytical exploration of the statements and their proposed constructs. Overall, both the Heflick (2005) and Slone et al. (2002) studies are severely limited but offer some good descriptive elements in regard to the last statements of condemned inmates.

The situation is similar for statements by co-victims. Much of what has been written of co-victims and their perspectives has been either journalistic or anecdotal in nature, often incorporating short testimonials (King, 2003; Robertson, 2002). King (2003), for example, presents a collection of statements made co-victims against the death penalty (see also Murder Victims Families for Reconciliation, 2005). In her book, King tells the stories of several capital murder cases, incorporating extensive statements by family members of victims grouped under the headings of forgiveness, executing the vulnerable, grave injustices, and restorative justice. Although her book is not intended as solid research (and, in fact, intentionally only includes those co-victims who are opposed to the death penalty), it does offer a glimpse of the attitudes and perspectives of at least some co-victims. Other work has focused on interviews with murder victims' family members, occurring either while the offender is still alive on death row or years after the execution (Dicks, 1991). Little scholarly attention has been given to perspectives of co-victims in capital cases but even less has been offered in the way of statements at the time of execution.

Gross and Matheson (2003) rectified this problem by examining newspaper accounts of co-victims' statements at the time of execution. They note that "the great majority of newspaper accounts of executions include at least some description of the reactions of the victims' families and of any surviving victims." They then proceeded to systematically collect and analyze such accounts for executions conducted in the United States from 1999 to 2002. Using Lexis and Westlaw, the researchers compiled a total of 138 stories in which statements of victims' family were reported. Based on content analysis of these statements, Gross and Matheson (2003) found that "the statements made by family members of victims vary widely" (p. 489) and identify several predominant themes. Closure was the most predominant theme of co-victim statements with about 35% of statements expressing "relief that it finally happened" (p. 514). Within the category of closure, the authors note that sentiments vary with some expressing the symbolic meaning of the event for their path to healing and others expressing relief that the person is gone and no longer a potential threat. Others noted relief that the long drawn out process of hearings and appeals and waiting for execution had come to an end. Justice and vengeance comprise the second most prevalent theme found with about 25% of statements expressing some belief that justice has been done. Gross and Matheson (2003) found that abstract references to justice were often accompanied by more personal expressions of vengeance, sometimes expressed as happiness or joy found in the execution and other times in a desire for the offender to have suffered more. Other themes found were compassion (10%), a wish for clemency (7%) and forgiveness (6%). Interestingly, the authors note reference to an apology being made by the condemned toward the victim's family in 40 (29%) of the cases. In only eight of those cases did the co-victims accept the apology. More often they expressed skepticism about the genuineness of the apology or said nothing at all. Finally, in thirteen cases, co-victims reported anger that no apology was offered.

The overriding theme in many of the statements was dissatisfaction with the long process between the murder and the execution. But, it was not necessarily the duration of that period as much as the quality of it that was important. Gross and Matheson (2003) note that "what matters most to families is not the length of time leading up to the execution, but instead what happens during that time" (p. 493). In regard to closure, co-victims often expressed relief that their ordeal is finally over and that they can finally move on, something they were unable to do as long as they were required to relive the traumatizing events of the murder through the many appeals and hearings as well as the media reports. The lengthy process also appeared to add to desires for revenge among co-victims. Gross and Matheson (2003) conclude the following:

> The long and complex route from trial to execution seems to contribute to the desire for justice and vengeance. Some relatives are offended or hurt by the attention that is repeatedly focused on the defendant throughout this process and view the execution as an opportunity to redress the balance—to do something for the victim (p. 515).

In the end, it is hard to determine whether the co-victim statements are driven more by the original crime and loss of their loved one or by the death penalty process itself. What seems clear from Gross and Matheson's (2003) study, however, is that co-victims desire a more meaningful process of justice than what they are offered with the current death penalty system.

The studies discussed here as well as the numerous journalistic and anecdotal accounts of condemned offenders' and co-victims' statements offer some insight into the thoughts and perspectives of these two important groups regarding the death penalty and executions. But, this insight is limited. The journalistic accounts give some depth but offer little in the way of understanding either the immediacy or the diversity of perspectives directly surrounding the execution. The two cited studies offer good starting points, however, toward a meaningful examination of these two groups and their statements at the time of execution. The present research builds from these studies, incorporating their objectives into a broader study in which the statements of both groups are examined and in which statements are examined in the context of principles of restorative justice.

PRESENT STUDY

In an attempt to fill a void in death penalty research the present study examines the neglected perspectives of the two groups most directly impacted by capital murder and capital punishment: the co-victims and the condemned. The objective is to examine the perspectives and reactions of co-victims and condemned inmates at the time of execution through an exploration of their own statements. For the condemned, their last statements given moments prior to execution are examined. For co-victims, statements made to local newspaper reporters at the time of execution are examined. These two sources of statements made by the condemned and co-victims offer a unique opportunity to construct a form of pseudo-dialogue between these two most central groups in the context of executions and to consider that dialogue in relation to other factors surrounding the condemned, his or her actions, co-victims, and the death penalty process. By inductively examining the themes of the respective statements, the present study sheds light on these groups, their attitudes, emotions, thoughts and sensibilities surrounding the culminating event of execution.

Much has been written about the death penalty. There are volumes devoted to explicating the philosophical underpinnings of the death penalty from both a pro-death penalty and anti-death penalty stance (Acker, Bohm & Lanier, 1998; Bedau & Cassell, 2004; Bohm, 2007; Hood, 2002; Lifton & Mitchell, 2000; Sarat, 2001; Steffen, 1998; Turow, 2003; Zimring, 2003). Questions of deterrence, discrimination, retribution, justice, execution of the innocent and many other factors have been examined thoroughly in the legal and social science literature. Moreover, research on the attitudes and opinion of the public regarding the death penalty abounds. In all of this, certain voices are seriously neglected—the voices of those with the most direct stake in the death penalty and executions. Although the voices of philosophers, researchers, and other scholars have been heard loud and clear, the voices of the condemned and their co-victims have been virtually silenced. Smykla (1987) speculated why this might be:

> It may be that researchers are more interested in the political, legal, and sometimes moral issues of capital punishment. Another possible reason is that the relevant persons are shielded from the public and want to protect their privacy. Further, methodologies of some researchers may be too much guided by the philosophy of the physical sciences to allow them to enter these private worlds as humanists (p. 331).

It seems that in the nearly twenty years that have passed since Smykla (1987) wrote those words, not much has changed. During that time, however, the death penalty has increasingly been held out as requisite justice for victims, necessary for the deserved healing and closure for co-victims, and righteous retribution for particularly evil offenders. Also, during that time, victims' rights and victim empowerment movements have flourished. In spite of all of this, little has systematically been gathered in regard to co-victims' reactions to the severe crime of capital murder and the death penalty process and execution that follows; even less attention has been given to the reactions and perspectives of the condemned offender. In the scholarly discourse on the death penalty, the term "justice" is bandied about quite a bit, but it is rarely considered in the context of those on whose behalf justice is being exacted when an execution is conducted. Anecdotal accounts and the few relevant studies aside, we have neglected to examine the experiences and perspectives of those who are directly experiencing this "justice:" the co-victims and the condemned offenders.

Research Objectives

Ragin (1994), in outlining the primary goals of social research, presents the notion of "giving voice" as one important goal. Specifically, Ragin (1994) points to the importance of bringing to light the voice or perspective of marginalized or neglected groups[21]. The present study endeavors to do just that—to give voice to condemned inmates and their co-victims in the context of executions. Through an examination of the actual discourse of these groups at the time of executions, this study gives voice to these key stakeholders in the death penalty, attempting to produce systematically an understanding of these groups, their experiences of the death penalty and executions, and the meaning that the death penalty has for each.

The specific objective of the present study is to examine and explore the last statements of condemned offenders and the statements of co-victims made at the time of execution as reported in the local newspaper. These statements are examined in an exploratory and inductive fashion, with the ultimate goal of constructing meaningful categories or types of statements which represent the general themes of expressed attitudes, perspectives and emotions at the time of execution. In line with the "grounded theory" approach to social research, the statements are examined with the goal of inductively determining their meaning and developing theoretical categories based on the themes of the statements (Strauss & Corbin, 1990). In other words, typologies are developed in regard to each set of statements—one for the last statements of the condemned and one for the co-victims' statements reported in the newspaper. Content analysis (to be discussed further in the next chapter) is used to construct these categories and typologies.

Another primary (and less inductive) objective of the present study is to examine the content of these statements for signs of the principles of restorative justice. As previously discussed, concepts such as closure, healing, apology, forgiveness and peace are all central to the theory and principles of restorative justice. These are concepts expected to be found among the statements of the condemned and their co-victims in the context of execution. However, inductive processes comprise the primary approach to observing and reporting these and the other concepts found among the statements.

---

[21] For an interesting artistic form of this in regard to the death penalty, see the play *The Exonerated* (Blank & Jensen, 2004) in which the words of exonerated death row inmates are recreated in a one-act play.

Finally, the statements of condemned offenders and co-victims are examined in the context of other key factors surrounding the crime, the trial, the death penalty process, and the execution. Specifically, demographic information on the offender is examined as are factors relevant to his or her criminal acts. Also, the allowance of victim impact statements in capital trials and the presence of witnesses at executions (two factors which changed significantly over the time-period being studied) are considered in regard to the statements made by these groups.

General Research Questions

Although primarily an exploratory and inductive study, some general research questions are considered. In addition to a broad examination of the themes of both the last statements of the condemned and the news media statements of the co-victims and subsequent typology construction, the following research questions are considered in general guidance of the analyses. Each question is applied to both analyses of the last statements of the condemned and the statements of the co-victims in the local newspaper.

1. Do the themes vary across inmate and offense characteristics?
2. Have these themes changed over time?
3. Have they changed over time in regard to policy changes allowing victim impact statements to be presented during capital trials?
4. Have they changed over time in regard to policy changes allowing co-victims to witness executions?
5. Do the themes vary based on who witnesses the execution?
6. Are there signs of restoration or principles of restorative justice in the statements surrounding executions?

a. Perhaps as important here: Do statements indicate the death penalty as serving any restorative purpose or impeding it?

7. Do signs of restoration vary in respect to inmate and offense characteristics?

8. Do signs of restoration vary based on the level of participation of co-victims (i.e. giving victim impact statements at trial, witnessing the execution)?

LIMITATIONS OF THE PRESENT STUDY

This study is restricted to an examination of particular recorded statements of condemned inmates and their co-victims. Specifically, last statements of condemned offenders recorded and reported by TDCJ are the sole focus on the words of this population. Moreover, only statements of condemned inmates in Texas are included. Statements of co-victims are even more severely restricted with only statements made at the time of execution to the local newspaper in Huntsville, TX—*The Huntsville Item*—being included in the study. Although in both cases these sources offer a broad and generally thorough sampling of statements made by these populations, some important limitations must be noted.

First, it is important to acknowledge the somewhat "formal" nature of last statements made by the condemned. These are statements offered immediately prior to execution after the inmate has been secured in the lethal injection apparatus and as witnesses look on. The potentially artificial nature of statements made under these conditions cannot be denied. Moreover, some of the statements have been prepared beforehand, in several cases being submitted only in writing and not spoken at the time of execution. The degree to which statements were pre-prepared or extemporaneous may not be easily determined.

A more serious limitation occurs with the selected statements of co-victims. Only articles from Huntsville's local newspaper are examined in this study. Although *The Huntsville Item* is known for doing a thorough job of reporting on Texas executions, it must be acknowledged that stories as reported in a single newspaper are not necessarily representative of all such stories and media coverage. Likewise, statements given to reporters at *The Huntsville Item* may vary from statements given to other sources.

Most significantly, however, is the fact that only a particular portion of the population of co-victims are likely to be represented by the statements made to *The Huntsville Item* (or any media source for that matter). Statements of those co-victims who are unwilling to speak to the media and those who choose to avoid the execution of their offender are unlikely to be accounted for. Gross and Matheson (2003) give the following speculation regarding the biased nature of this sample:

> [T]hey are probably more likely to favor execution than those who do not show up or do not speak, and less likely to have come to terms with the murder. They may also be more articulate and vocal, higher status, and more likely to live in the vicinity of the execution (p. 487).

This problem is coupled with the fact that the accounts of co-victim statements that are reported are mediated through the reporters and editors of *The Huntsville Item*. In spite of these problems, and given the limited availability of information on these populations, the present study provides an opportunity to examine their thoughts and perspectives even if those thoughts and perspectives are to some extent mediated. Furthermore, the present study provides a platform from which other researchers can further give voice to these populations through other forms of systematic examinations.

CHAPTER V:

Data and Methodology

DATA COLLECTION

Data for the present study were limited to executions in Texas during the post-Furman era. Specifically, executions occurring between December 7, 1982 (the date of the first post-Furman execution in Texas) to March 3, 2004 (the last date of data collection), a total of 321 executions, were included in the analyses. Data were restricted to Texas for two reasons. First, Texas has executed by far the greatest number of inmates since *Furman* and offers an opportunity to examine statements in the most death penalty-prone state in the country (and one of the most death penalty-prone regions of the world). Second, condemned offenders' last statements are available and easily accessed through TDCJ's website along with other information about the offender and his or her crimes. Also, the local newspaper in Hunstville, TX (home of the "Walls Unit" where executions are held), *The Huntsville Item*, does a particularly good job reporting on executions and specifically reporting co-victim statements if such statements are offered.

The last statements of condemned inmates are recorded in inmate "facesheets" available on TDCJ's website (TDCJ, 2005b). The verbatim full-text of statements made by condemned inmates at the time of execution are transcribed by a TDCJ staff member who listens to the last statement through a PA system in a remote site. Periodically, written statements are given in addition to or in lieu of verbal statements. The facesheets indicate whether the statement was verbal or written. Facesheets were obtained for all 321 executions being analyzed in the present study. To enhance the validity of these statements (which are potentially subject to omissions or errors in transcription), the researcher used a triangulation of sources to check the accuracy and completeness of statements. Statements as reported by TDCJ were checked against two other sources: A book compiling executed Texas inmates' last statements from 1982 to June 22, 2000 (222 of the 321 statements in the present study) published by The Sunriver Cartel (2000) and *The Huntsville Item* (which often includes portions of the last statements in articles on the particular executions). The TDCJ facesheets were the primary source and in the case of discrepancies between two or more sources, the researcher deferred to the versions therein. However, in several cases, data were missing or incomplete in the facesheets. In these cases, the researcher attempted to use the other sources to record or fill in the missing data.

In spite of attempts to locate last statements for all 321 cases, 29 (9.0%) remained missing (See Table 2). For some of these 29 cases, statements were indicated as "not available;" others were simply not present in any of the sources. In analyses of the last statements of condemned inmates, these missing cases were excluded leaving 292 valid cases. Forty one (12.8%) of the condemned inmates declined to make a statement leaving 251 (78.2%) total statements. Of these, 235 of the inmates gave the typical last statement verbally directly prior to execution. Two only gave last statements in the form of a written document prepared in the days prior to the execution and 14 (4.4%) gave both spoken and written last statements. Although only 251 inmates gave last statements, all 292 non-missing cases were included in analyses. Those who declined to make a statement were not excluded as missing as their chosen silence equates to null responses on the identified themes and categories in the analyses.

Table 2
Proportion of Condemned Inmate Last Statements by Mode of Delivery

Total Cases = 321

Statement Form	**#**	**%**
Last Statements Given	251	78.2%
Spoken Only	*235*	*73.2%*
Written Only	*2*	*0.6%*
Both Spoken and Written	*14*	*4.4%*
Declined to Give Last Statement	41	12.8%
Missing	29	9.0%

Offender and offense information, as well as some limited information about victims was also obtained from TDCJ inmate facesheets. Additional information about the nature of each case was obtained from the Death Penalty Information Center's Execution Database (DPIC, 2007a).

Data regarding execution witnesses were obtained directly from TDCJ's executed offender files. TDCJ maintains detailed and complete files for each executed inmate which are available to the public, but not allowed to leave the TDCJ public relations offices. Several weeks were spent going through each file, locating and recording the official execution witness lists. These lists contain the name of the witnesses, their relation to the inmate (if witnessing on behalf of the condemned) and their relation to the victim (if witnessing on behalf of the victim or victims). Out of 321 cases, data regarding witnesses for the condemned were obtained for 313 (98%) and data regarding witnesses for the victim(s) were obtained for 314 (98%). In the other cases, adequate information was missing from the files.

Finally, co-victim statements were obtained through articles reporting on executions in *The Huntsville Item*. It should be noted that newspaper reports of executions exhibit inherent biases and reflect perceived interest and thus marketability of particular stories and angles. Based on an analysis of newspaper coverage of executions throughout the United States, Hochstetler (2001) states "[m]edia coverage of the death penalty plays to multiple audiences but ultimately is biased by sensationalism" (p. 8). Indeed, executions involving "celebrated" cases, offenders, or victims are going to be covered more heavily and in more depth, creating great variation in the material presented from case to case. Furthermore, Hochstetler (2001) found that newspaper coverage of executions predominantly reflected general support for the death penalty. Although *The Huntsville Item* is by no means immune to these biases (see, for example, Halmari, 1998), it does report on virtually all executions, creating a relatively consistent record of executions in Texas and the factors and issues surrounding them (Halmari, 1998).

For the present study, *The Huntsville Item* was chosen for several reasons. First, *The Huntsville Item*, being the local newspaper in the city in which TDCJ is centered and in which Texas' executions are carried out, coverage of executions is extensive. *The Huntsville Item*'s proximity to the death house is literally several city blocks, offering easy access to TDCJ's facilities and media events (which are common surrounding each execution). Moreover, the public relations office of TDCJ generally has a close relationship with *The Huntsville Item.*[22] Second, *The Huntsville Item* specifically assigns a reporter to attend and report on each execution (Reid & Gurwell, 2001). TDCJ reserves a witness position for *The Huntsville Item* reporter for every execution. Finally, as *The Huntsville Item* serves a relatively small community, death penalty and execution stories often receive considerable attention, often appearing on the front page (Halmari, 1998). This coverage includes statements made by co-victims.

Articles were obtained via microfilm at Sam Houston State University's (a university located in Huntsville, TX) Newton Gresham Library. Articles appearing within two days of each execution were obtained in an attempt to restrict statements to those directly surrounding the execution. For example, if an execution was held on January 9th, articles appearing during the five day period from January 7th to January 11th were collected. Direct quotes of co-victims are the primary focus of analysis in the present study. However, reporter or third party characterizations of co-victim statements or sentiments were indirectly included in some cases. The inclusion of such characterizations was minimal and only used when they were simple and direct references to statements made by co-victims and as support for direct quotes made by co-victims. More interpretive third-party statements were not included.

Co-victim statements were obtained for 159 execution cases. There was only one instance in which copies of the newspaper were missing for necessary dates, leaving 320 valid cases for analysis in regard to co-victim statements. However, analyses of co-victim statements were conducted with regard to a base of cases in which a statement was found (N = 159). Unlike the statements of condemned inmates, it can not be concluded that no reported statement equates to a null response in regard to the statement themes. In such cases it is unknown whether the co-victim(s) gave statements that were not reported or gave statements to other sources. Therefore, analyses of co-victim statements proceeded with an N of 159.

---

[22] Currently, in fact, TDCJ's primary public information officer in Huntsville is a past *Huntsville Item* reporter who covered TDCJ and Executions.

CODING AND OPERATIONALIZATION OF KEY CONCEPTS

Coding of key concepts began inductively in a process referred to as "open coding" (Berg, 2004, p. 278; Strauss & Corbin, 1990). Strauss and Corbin (1990) define open coding as "[t]he process of breaking down, examining, comparing, conceptualizing, and categorizing data" (p. 61). The open coding process is primarily qualitative and intended to "open inquiry widely" (Berg, 2004, p. 278) withholding interpretations and conclusions until all material is coded. Open coding is an initial and tentative coding process in which the researcher begins formulating categories which can characterize the different properties and dimensions of the data. The objective at this point is to "analyze the data minutely" (Berg, 2004, p. 279; Strauss & Corbin, 1990), paying particular attention to commonalities and distinctions among the data. This collective process can be referred to as grounded categorization in which key concepts are inductively identified and conceptualized. Once these concepts are determined and clearly defined, more specific coding of the statements is conducted.

In the present study, from the initial open coding process was developed content coding protocols (one for last statements of the condemned and one for co-victim statements) which were then used in the coding of the statements into the grounded categories and subsequently used for reliability checks. These protocols are exhibited in Appendixes A and B, respectively. These protocols may also be used for replication in the future or with other populations or samples. These protocols include clear descriptions of each category indicating the criteria for inclusion under each respective category. In the present study, coding was done with a series of binary (yes/no) variables with a "1" indicating that the category theme was present in the statement and a "0" indicating that it was not. Statements could be coded under multiple categories and often were. Specific themes were determined via the open coding and grounded categorization process. From these were determined broader thematic categories through grouping these specific themes together. It is these broader theme categories that are the major focus of analyses.

ANALYTICAL TECHNIQUES

As indicated above, analyses in the present study are primarily qualitative and inductive in nature. The first step was to openly examine statements, identifying themes and messages. Common themes were identified in an attempt to develop a typology of statements. Furthermore, distinctions between themes were examined. The different types were then described in regard to their substance and content as outlined in the coding protocols. Finally, the specific thematic "types" were aggregated into meaningful broader thematic categories or "types" of statements.

The primary mode of analysis flowing from the general qualitative examination is content analysis. Weber (1985) gives the following definition of content analysis:

> Content analysis is a research methodology that utilizes a set of procedures to make valid inferences from text. These inferences are about the sender(s) of the message, the message itself, or the audience of the message. The rules of this inferential process vary with the theoretical and substantive interests of the investigator (p. 9).

Content analysis is generally used to reduce verbal or written messages to discrete and meaningful categories that capture some element of the particular messages. It may be used to characterize and organize messages at numerous levels. Weber (1985) identifies the following units as potential data elements in content analysis: word, word sense, sentence, theme, paragraph, and whole text (pp. 22-23). Content analysis allows the researcher to quantify qualitative data by being able to compute the frequency with which each category of message content is present in the data. Moreover, such quantification allows for analysis in respect to other quantitative variables.

There are two primary forms of content analysis: Manifest and latent. Manifest content analysis is defined as analysis of "those elements that are physically present and countable" (Berg, 2004, p. 269). Such elements might be specified words or phrases that represent particular concepts or categories. Latent content analysis, on the other hand, requires a more interpretive approach to the data. Berg (2004) describes this as "an interpretive reading of the symbolism underlying the physical data" (p. 269). An analysis of the general themes of messages, without specific regard to particular words or phrases, would best be described as latent content analysis. Latent content analysis is generally considered a more qualitative approach although it may include quantitative coding of latent messages (Berg, 2004).

As the present study is primarily an exploratory and qualitative one, analyses of condemned inmate and co-victim statements are limited to traditional latent content analysis in which the general themes of messages are the units of analysis (Berg, 2004; Riffe et al., 1998)[23]. Specific words (although important in determining the theme) are not the primary focus of analysis. Also, the source of the messages is not of central concern to the analyses. Although such sources and their potential relation to the statements and their themes are important, it is not within the scope of this study to systematically incorporate them into the analyses.

An extensive typology of both the last statements of the condemned and the statements of co-victims in the press were constructed. Each statement was coded into conceptual categories in accordance with the message portrayed in the statement and was coded into multiple categories when multiple conceptual themes were expressed. Binary codes were used for each category, with a "1" recorded if the theme was present and a "0" recorded if it was not. Following the coding of statements into specific thematic categories, broader thematic categories composed of two or more of related specific themes were constructed. It is these "major" themes that are the focus of analyses in the following chapters.

Each set of statements (of the condemned and of the co-victims) were then analyzed by looking at frequencies of each major thematic category and examining them in respect to numerous offender, offense, and victim characteristics. Included among these characteristics were temporal indicators examined to ascertain whether a change in thematic content had occurred over time. Further, the major themes of statements were examined in respect to factors surrounding the capital case and the execution such as admissibility of victim impact statements and witness presence at executions. In regard to these

---

[23] Although latent content analysis is the primary mode of analysis in this study, it should be noted that manifest content is often denotative of particular themes and thus plays a role in classification of content. Moreover, specific words and phrases are identified as indicators of particular content in the coding protocol. As others have noted, the difference between manifest and latent content is often subtle and a wise approach to content analysis is to rely on a "middle-ground" or blend of the two forms (Berg, 2004; Riffe et al., 1998). This is the case with the present study.

descriptive analyses, nonparametric statistical tests were conducted to assess statistical significance.

SOME NOTES ON RELIABILITY AND VALIDITY

Reliability and validity are particular concerns with latent content analysis (Weber, 1985). Indeed, because of the qualitative nature of this analytical technique, it is inherently more difficult to establish reliability and validity when coding and analyses are more interpretive and less objective than typical quantitative research. Moreover, consistency and replicability (i.e. reliability) often suffer due to ambiguous or unclear category definitions coupled with rich and complex textual data (Weber, 1985). For the present study, I attempted to diminish such concerns by first clearly and thoroughly defining concepts and categories based on the initial open coding process. These definitions and descriptions were incorporated into coding protocols, one for the themes of the last statements of the condemned and one for the themes of statements of co-victims. These protocols are presented in Appendix A and Appendix B, respectively. Two coders were given a sample of 26 last statements of condemned inmates (10.4% of statements obtained) and 26 co-victim statements (17.2% of statements obtained) to code in accordance with that protocol and intercoder agreement and reliability was examined. Intercoder reliability was assessed first using a basic percentage agreement measure then by using Chronbach's alpha which statistically assesses reliability among multiple items (in this case, multiple coders' scoring of items). Chronbach's alpha was chosen because of the nature of the data. The low variability in responses on most of the thematic categories (with a null, or 0, code being much more likely in most cases as there were so many binary code options and only a handful usually present in each given case) made the use of more conventional measures of interrater reliability such as Scott's Pi or Cohen's Kappa untenable (see Wimmer & Dominick, 2000 for a discussion of these and other conventional methods). Instead, each code was treated as a dummy variable and inter-item (each coder representing a different item for each theme) reliability computed via Chronbach's Alpha (Trochim, 2001). Both the percentage agreement and Chronbach's Alpha for each thematic category, as well as overall agreement on all categories are reported for last statements of the condemned in Table 3 and co-victim statements in Table 4.

Table 3
Interrater Reliability for Condemned's Last Statement Themes-Three Raters (Researcher and Two Interraters): Percentage Agreement and Chronbach's Alpha

Last Statement Theme	% Agreement	Alpha
Apology to Co-Victim(s)	100.0%	1.00
Apology to Own Family/Friends	96.2%	0.92
Apology to God or Other Deity	100.0%	N/A
Asks for Forgiveness from Co-Victim(s)	96.2%	1.00
Asks for Forgiveness from Own Family/Friends	94.2%	0.82
Asks for Forgiveness from God or Other Deity	92.3%	0.88
Wish to Turn Back Time	96.2%	N/A
Apology/Asks Forgiveness-Unspecified	90.4%	0.90
Prayer for Self	92.3%	0.86
Prayer for Others	94.2%	0.91
Prayer-Unspecified	88.5%	0.85
Preaching	92.3%	0.90
Proclamation of Faith/Giving Self over to God	92.3%	0.85
Afterlife	94.2%	0.94
Gratitude/Thanks to Family & Friends	94.2%	0.94
Gratitude/Thanks to Criminal Justice Staff	92.3%	0.63
Gratitude/Thanks to Lawyers	96.2%	1.00
Gratitude/Thanks to Chaplain/Spiritual Advisor	94.2%	0.87
Gratitude/Thanks to Media	100.0%	N/A
Gratitude/Thanks to God or other Deity	96.2%	0.90
Acceptance of Responsibility for Specific Capital Murder	92.3%	0.81

Table 3 (continued)

Last Statement Theme	% Agreement	Alpha
Taking Responsibility for Other Bad Acts or Crimes	96.2%	0.87
Minimize/Rationalize Actions or Agency	96.2%	0.92
Claim of Innocence	100.0%	1.00
Death Penalty or Execution is Hypocritical/Killing is Wrong	96.2%	0.83
Death Penalty or Execution Does Not Bring Peace or Closure	96.2%	0.92
Death Penalty or Execution is Not Justice	94.2%	0.82
Death Penalty or Execution is Inhumane	100.0%	N/A
Death Penalty or Execution is Not a Deterrent	100.0%	N/A
Death Penalty or Execution Only Creates More Victims	100.0%	N/A
Death Penalty or Execution is Wrong	96.2%	0.95
Condemns Police/CJ Officials	98.1%	N/A
Condemns CJ System or Government in General	94.2%	0.70
Condemns Co-Victim(s)/Victim(s)	100.0%	1.00
Anger or Resentment Toward Own Lawyers	100.0%	N/A
Anger or Resentment Toward Witnesses at Trial	100.0%	1.00
Anger or Resentment Toward CJ Officials/CJ System	100.0%	1.00
Anger or Resentment Toward Co-Victims	100.0%	N/A
Forgives Others	92.3%	0.91
At Peace (Non-Religious)	92.3%	0.85
Personal Transformation	92.3%	0.77
Humanizes Self	100.0%	1.00
Wish Co-Victims Peace or Closure	92.3%	0.93

Table 3 (continued)

Last Statement Theme	% Agreement	Alpha
Wish that Execution Brings Justice	100.0%	N/A
Well-Wishes and/or Love to Family/Friends	90.4%	0.90
General Expression of Love	86.5%	0.90
Words of Encouragement to Family/Friends	90.4%	0.93
Words of Encouragement to Others on Death Row	94.2%	0.83
Fate	90.4%	0.89
Helplessness	100.0%	N/A
Release	84.6%	0.73
Filibuster	100.0%	N/A
Recital of Song or Poem	100.0%	N/A
Cheer for Sport's Team	100.0%	1.00
Statement or Act of Defiance	100.0%	N/A

OVERALL PERCENTAGE AGREEMENT:

W/Rater #1: 95.3%

W/Rater #2: 95.7%

Table 4
Interrater Reliability for Co-Victim Statement Themes-Three Raters (Researcher and Two Interraters): Percentage Agreement and Chronbach's Alpha

Co-Victim Statement Theme	% Agreement	Alpha
Looking Forward to Execution	94.2%	0.82
Satisfaction with Death	86.5%	0.73
Happy to be Present at Execution	90.4%	0.85
Gratitude to State of Texas/CJ System	96.2%	N/A
Grateful for Apology	98.1%	N/A
General Satisfaction with Last Statement of Condemned	100.0%	N/A
Dissatisfaction/Frustration with Lack of Remorse or Apology	100.0%	1.00
Dissatisfaction/Frustration with Lack of Acknowledgement	100.0%	1.00
Dissatisfaction/Frustration because of Claim of Innocence	96.2%	1.00
Dissatisfaction/Frustration with No Claim of Responsibility	98.1%	1.00
Dissatisfaction/Frustration with Condemned's Statement or Demeanor	100.0%	1.00
Dissatisfaction/Frustration with CJ System/Delay	86.5%	0.90
Dissatisfaction/Frustration with Media	100.0%	N/A
Questions the Truthfulness of Statement	100.0%	N/A
Dismisses Condemned's Words or Sentiments	92.3%	0.77
No Happiness/Joy/Satisfaction from Execution	94.2%	0.77
Personalized Death Penalty Support	98.1%	N/A
Abstract Death Penalty Support	98.1%	0.95
Criticism of Protestors	100.0%	N/A
Death Penalty or Execution Opposition	100.0%	1.00

Table 4 (continued)

Co-Victim Statement Theme	% Agreement	Alpha
Death Penalty Doesn't Solve Anything	98.1%	0.92
Dehumanization of the Condemned	98.1%	1.00
Denial of Personal Malevolence	90.4%	0.89
Demeans the Character of the Condemned	92.3%	0.63
Prayer for Victim/Co-Victims	100.0%	N/A
Prayer for Condemned	98.1%	1.00
Prayer for Family of Condemned	100.0%	N/A
God's Judgment	98.1%	N/A
Proclamation of Faith	100.0%	N/A
Death Penalty in the Bible	100.0%	N/A
Execution Brings Healing and/or Closure	98.1%	N/A
Execution Brings Peace or Relief	94.2%	0.86
Conclusion	94.2%	0.92
No More Appeals, Trials, or Hearings	96.2%	N/A
Beginning	98.1%	0.92
Won't Bring Them Back	96.2%	0.87
No Healing or Closure	88.5%	0.86
Prior Reconciliation	94.2%	0.82
Execution was Traumatizing	96.2%	1.00
Justice for Victim	96.2%	N/A
Justice for Society	88.5%	0.80
Desire to See or Inflict Harm or Suffering	100.0%	1.00
Death Penalty/Execution Not Harsh Enough	100.0%	1.00
Just Deserts	90.4%	0.87
Comparison of Suffering of Victim & Condemned	100.0%	1.00

Table 4 (continued)

Co-Victim Statement Theme	% Agreement	Alpha
Forgive	98.1%	0.95
Don't Forgive	100.0%	1.00
Rejects Apology	100.0%	1.00
Sympathy for Condemned	98.1%	0.92
Sympathy for Condemned's Family	96.2%	0.96
Condemned No Longer Presents a Threat to Co-Victim(s)	100.0%	N/A
Condemned No Longer Presents a Threat to Others/Society	100.0%	1.00
Extermination	94.2%	0.83
Speaks to Qualities of Victim	100.0%	1.00
Memorializes or Honors Victim	98.1%	0.92
Wishes for Peace/Release for Victim	98.1%	1.00
Reference to Victim's Murder	98.1%	N/A
Wished to Witness Execution	100.0%	1.00

OVERALL PERCENTAGE AGREEMENT:

W/Rater #1: 96.7%

W/Rater #2: 96.8%

Percentage agreement is the most basic way to assess reliability in content analyses. Although commonly used as a measure of reliability, it is often criticized for not taking into account intercoder agreement that occurs simply by chance (Wimmer & Dominick, 2000). Nevertheless, it does tell us something about the reliability of the thematic categories and the clarity of definitions of those categories and the criteria by which messages are interpreted into these categories (Trochim, 2001). In the present study, agreement is generally very high, in most cases above 90%. Although, in many cases, agreement is at 100%, this may simply occur due to the fact that a theme was not present in any of the coded statements. To overcome the possible exaggeration of reliability offered by percentage agreement, Chronbach's Alpha reliability scores are also computed. Generally, Alpha values were relatively high for the different thematic categories indicating strong reliability in their measurement across the three raters. Unfortunately, there were several categories for which Chronbach's Alpha could not be computed due to the fact that no coders coded that category as being present in any of the sample of statements being coded. Nevertheless, the fact that all coders agreed to the absence of these themes in these cases is indicative of a high rate of agreement among coders. Finally, the overall percentage agreement (indicated at the bottom of Tables 3 and 4) indicates a very high rate of agreement across all items. Overall, reliability appears to be strong in regard to the definitions, descriptions, and measurement of these qualitatively determined thematic categories of both the condemned and co-victim statements.

Validity refers to the extent to which a variable measures what it is purported to measure. Establishing validity is particularly difficult in latent content analysis in which concepts and categories are determined to a great degree based on the interpretation and subjective judgment of the researcher (Weber, 1985). Nevertheless, steps can be taken to minimize problems with validity. Assessment of validity in the current study is limited to face validity. Face validity is a form of validity that exists when items used to measure a concept appear valid on their face or logically align with the concept being measured (Schutt, 2004). Face validity is examined in the present study in two ways: First, the coding protocols in Appendix A and Appendix B give clear descriptions of the concepts identified and analyzed in the present study and second, by assessing agreement among coders on the definitions and descriptions of categories and concepts as developed in the process of initial, open coding. This latter indicator of face validity is illustrated well by the high levels of intercoder agreement exhibited in Tables 3 and 4 regarding the content that aligns with particular defined categories. Overall, evidence is relatively strong that the thematic categories of statements of both the condemned inmates and the co-victims are, at the least, face valid.

A final (and unavoidable) issue of validity concerns the ontological nature of verbal statements. We must ask the question whether, and to what degree, verbal statements accurately reflect, represent or indicate the actual reality of feelings, thoughts or emotions. In conducting latent content analysis, the researcher is inherently drawing inferences about these realities from such statements. But, the degree to which this reality can adequately be inferred from these sources is impossible to measure. Of course, this is a problem inherent in virtually all research in the social sciences. Manifest indicators of reality such as responses to survey items or interviewer questions, physical actions, and verbal or written statements are commonly used to gauge human and social realities. Indeed, these are the observable options available to us as social scientists. Although we can learn a lot about thoughts, emotions, feelings, attitudes and perspectives from such observable data, we must acknowledge the limitations of verbal statements for providing an accurate portrayal of such underlying realities (Riffe et al., 1998; Potter, 2004). This is particularly true in the present study as it attempts to get at particularly sensitive and painful thoughts and emotions.

REFLEXIVE NOTE

There is a common concern and criticism of qualitative research, that it violates the value-neutrality and objectivity required to qualify as "scientific" inquiry. Although this view has been challenged by many (Berg, 2004; Ferrell, 1998) and such hard-line positivistic perspectives have waned somewhat in social sciences (Ragin, 1994), it remains necessary to allay some of these concerns that accompany studies such as the present one.

Reflexivity is a tool by which a researcher owns his or her biases and acknowledges personal subjectivity in respect to his or her research. It means to reflect, to look into oneself to gain an understanding of one's psyche and the lens through which one observes the social reality he or she examined. Through reflexivity, the researcher admits that value-neutrality is a façade in regard to the selection, development, analysis, and interpretation of research topics. Berg (2004) puts it this way:

> The fact is, research is seldom undertaken for a neutral reason. Furthermore, all humans residing in and among social groups are the product of those social groups. This means that various values, moral attitudes, and beliefs orient people in a particular manner (p. 155).

Tunnell (1998) argues further that reflexivity is not only necessary but also desirable and preferable to positivistic methodologies proclaiming to be objective and neutral: "Reflexivity is a fundamental component of the sociological tradition. Little progress toward developing full understandings of the textures of crime and its seductions is possible without a critical, reflexive methodology" (p. 214). In this brief section I will reflexively shed light on my own biases and subjectivity in approaching this study and will discuss attempts made to fairly check these biases as I progressed through the project and examined and interpreted the data.

As someone who is unequivocally opposed to the death penalty, there is no doubt that I brought my own biases to this project. The very fact that I have an interest in the topic stems, in part, from my subjective perspective in regard to the death penalty. The fact is that my opposition to the death penalty was cultivated in a culture not conducive to such opposition. Specifically, it was only during my time spent in graduate school in Huntsville, TX, where the largest concentration of executions in the Western world are carried out, and where the predominant belief is that the death penalty is a moral imperative, that I began to think about the death penalty and my own feelings about it. Prior to that, I had never lived in a state which had the death penalty and it had been a relative non-issue. Confronted with it as I was in these later years, I came to find it to be an illogical policy and repugnant practice. I also became fascinated with the culture and perspectives that surrounded it and determined to attempt to understand the various attitudes that existed in this context. As much as I may disagree with many of the attitudes and perspectives supporting the death penalty, I have a much greater interest in understanding them and the underlying feelings and emotions that drive them than I do in condemning those who hold them or express them. It was in the interest of further developing this understanding that I chose to examine the words of the condemned inmates and the words of their co-victims for the present study.

Originally, the intention of this project was to only study the last statements of the condemned. One of the great by-products of the decision to examine both of these populations' statements in the present study has been that it has had a sort of counter-balancing effect on my biases. Being confronted with not only the words of the condemned but also the words of the co-victims—those who have been so harmed and damaged by the acts of the condemned—influenced me to be more neutral, to see both sides of the death penalty. Although I could sympathize with the condemned inmates who were being put to death by the state, I sympathized greatly with the horror, pain, loss, and suffering experienced by the co-victims at the hands of the condemned. Furthermore, searching newspaper articles for the co-victim statements, as well as examining official facesheets for last statements of the condemned, I was often confronted with the horrible details of the murderous acts of these individuals and the violent deaths of the victims. As someone already opposed to the death penalty, I was surprised at the feelings that arose when reading accounts of the crime and the co-victims' responses and clear pain and suffering. I naturally felt sad and disturbed, but also often felt angry at and repulsed by the individuals who could commit such atrocious acts. I was able to empathize with those who support the death penalty based on these reactions and feelings. But I also found a profound sense of transformation among those who had committed the acts that so abhorred me and could empathize with them, as well, as they lived their last minutes before they too would be the victims of killing.

As I worked my way through all the data, I found that I was in a much more neutral place as I reflected on both sides of these transactions of violence and killing. In knowing the details of the crimes, I was able to avert any over-identification or over-empathizing with the condemned inmates; and by having a general sense of the transformations many of the condemned had made in their lives, I was able to avoid over-empathizing with the pain and anger of the co-victims. These subjective realities put me in a good place to openly examine the words of these groups.

I also took some more pragmatic steps to avert overly-biasing subjective analyses as much as possible. First, I went into the study with very little in the way of formalized expectations or hypotheses. Instead, the objective was to first engage with the statements with an open mind as to what these statements would say, represent, mean, or indicate. Through the previously mentioned iterative process of open coding, I was able to go through all statements before drawing any conclusions or noting any patterns, commonalities, or distinctions. This was done several times before specific conceptualizations were constructed. Also, through feedback from external coders (with differing subjective perspectives from my own), I was able to check my conceptualizations and interpretations.

Some researcher subjectivity is inherent to the very nature of any study. This study is no exception. It is my belief that my personal subjectivity could be both a help and a hindrance to the value of this study but that, in the end, it was mitigated by the factors discussed above. We are left, then, with the words of the condemned and the words of the co-victims to tell us what it is we want to know. I have done my best to faithfully represent these words in the pages that follow.

CHAPTER VI:

Last Statements of the Condemned

In the last statements of condemned inmates we are offered an extremely unique form of human expression, not only because the individual will be killed in a matter of moments, but also because the individual has often had many years or even decades to contemplate his or her final moments. We turn, again, to Camus (1960) for perspective on this reality:

> As the weeks pass, hope and despair increase and become equally unbearable. According to all accounts, the color of the skin changes, fear acting like an acid. 'Knowing that you are going to die is nothing,' said a condemned man in Fresnes. 'But not knowing whether or not you are going to live, that's terror and anguish.' Cartouche said of the supreme punishment: 'Why, it's just a few minutes that have to be lived through.' But it is a matter of months, not minutes. Long in advance the condemned man knows that he is going to be killed and that the only thing that can save him is a reprieve, rather similar, for him, to the decrees of heaven. In any case, he cannot intervene, make a plea for himself, or convince. Everything goes on outside of him. He is no longer a man but a thing waiting to be handled by the executioners. He is kept as if he were inert matter, but he still has a consciousness which is his chief enemy (pp. 200-201).

It is in his last statements that the condemned can reassert his agency, become more than a "thing" and finally "intervene, make a plea for himself, or convince." The last statement is an opportunity to take back some semblance of control that has been stripped from the condemned in the death penalty process—if unable to have control over his life, he can at least have some control in his death. In effect, the condemned is able to shed the "thinghood" of Camus' assessment and re-establish his humanity at the very point at which it is being extinguished forever.

In this chapter[24] these last statements of executed offenders in Texas are examined. Major themes found across these statements are first identified and discussed and examples of statements representing each major theme are provided. Following this qualitative exposition of the major thematic elements of the last statements of the condemned, statement themes are examined in regard to the characteristics of the condemned, their offense, and the context of their time on death row. Tables presenting descriptive statistics representing the relationship between statement themes and the multitude of factors in each of these areas are displayed and discussed. Finally, the last statements are analyzed in the context of restorative justice and restorative principles. The objective here is predominantly descriptive. Little is known about the final thoughts and perspectives of this population and rigorous attempts to shed light on their thoughts and words are lacking. Therefore, the focus of this chapter is to "give voice" to this population by describing and shedding light on the things they say in the moments which are their last.

MAJOR THEMES

The most striking initial impression one has when observing the last statements of condemned inmates is the diversity of sentiments expressed by the inmates. This is indeed a heterogeneous group of individuals with a variety of thoughts and perspectives as expressed in their final words. Nevertheless, one is also struck by commonalities among the last statements. There are definitely identifiable, common themes in the words of these men and women as they face death.

Through the inductive process of open coding, ten primary themes expressed in last statements of the condemned were identified. As indicated in Table 5, each of these primary themes comprise of more specific statement themes (secondary themes). In total, 56 specific secondary themes were identified and coded. 52 of these were used to make up the more general primary themes which are the focus of the

[24] Portions of this chapter are included in a forthcoming article in the journal *Contemporary Justice Review* entitled "Giving voice to the dead: The last statements of condemned inmates" (Vollum & Longmire, Forthcoming).

analyses in this chapter[25]. Table 5 indicates each of these themes (both primary and secondary) and the percentages of cases in which each was found. Two columns of percentages are presented. In the first, valid number of cases (those in which a last statement or an indication that the inmate declined to give a statement was identified and collected) is used as a base and the second uses the number of statements given as a base. Both are presented here for descriptive purposes. As an inmate declining to give a last statement can appropriately be interpreted as an absence of any given theme, the percentages based on valid cases are the primary points of analyses here and throughout this chapter.

It should be noted that this is not a typical typology in which categories are mutually exclusive or independent of one another. Rather, each category represents one possible theme among several in any given last statement. In many cases, multiple themes (whether primary or secondary) are expressed in a statement. In fact, it is not uncommon for an individual to express simultaneous (within the same statement), contradictory statements. For example, an inmate may express both contrition and denial or responsibility. Moreover, some secondary themes are used as indicators of more than one primary theme (as is the case with "Gratitude" and "Religion," both of which contain "Gratitude toward God or other deity"). The objective here was not to create a taxonomy of condemned inmates' last statements but to explore the themes commonly expressed in them.

Well-Wishes

The most common theme expressed in the last words of condemned inmates was that of wishing well or expressing love. In 58.6% of cases, an inmate made some form of positive statement toward others usually reflecting love or encouragement. The majority (117 of 171) of these were in the form of statements directed at the condemned's family or friends. In 40.1% of all cases, last statements included an expression of

---

[25] The four that were not used to compose the primary themes are four themes best referred to as "other" or miscellaneous in nature. They are "cheer for a sports team," "an act or statement of defiance," "filibuster," and "recital of song or poem." Although these were each interesting in the context of this study, they did not fit into a broader category nor did they have substantial enough numbers to warrant their own category.

Table 5
Last Statements of Condemned Inmates: Major Themes

Last Statement Theme	N	% of Valid Cases (N = 292)	% of Statements Given (N = 251)
Well-Wishes	**171**	**58.6%**	**68.1%**
Love or Well-Wishes to Family or Friends	117	40.1%	46.6%
Words of Encouragement to Family or Friends	51	17.5%	20.3%
General Expression of Love	50	17.1%	19.9%
Wish Co-Victims Peace or Closure	43	14.7%	17.1%
Words of Encouragement to Fellow Inmates	19	6.5%	7.6%
Wish that Execution Brings Justice	2	0.7%	0.8%
Religion	**141**	**48.3%**	**56.2%**
Afterlife	76	26.0%	30.3%
Proclamation of Faith/Giving Self over to God	70	24.0%	27.9%
Preaching	46	15.8%	18.3%
Prayer for Others	39	13.4%	15.5%
Gratitude Toward God	22	7.5%	8.8%
Prayer-Unspecified	20	6.8%	8.0%
Asks God's Forgiveness	20	6.8%	8.0%
Prayer for Self	19	6.5%	7.6%

Table 5 (continued)

Last Statement Theme	N	% of Valid Cases (N = 292)	% of Statements Given (N = 251)
Contrition	**96**	**32.9%**	**38.2%**
Apology to Co-Victim(s)	62	21.2%	24.7%
Asks for Forgiveness from Co-Victim(s)	32	11.0%	12.7%
Apology to Own Family/Friends	20	6.8%	8.0%
Asks for Forgiveness from God or Other Deity	20	6.8%	8.0%
Apology/Asks Forgiveness-Unspecified	18	6.2%	7.2%
Wish to Turn Back Time	9	3.1%	3.6%
Asks for Forgiveness from Own Family/Friends	8	2.7%	3.2%
Apology to God or Other Deity	2	0.7%	0.8%
Gratitude	**86**	**29.5%**	**34.3%**
Gratitude to Family & Friends	64	21.9%	25.5%
Gratitude to God or Other Deity	22	7.5%	8.8%
Gratitude to Chaplain/Spiritual Advisors	12	4.1%	4.8%
Gratitude to Criminal Justice Staff	10	3.4%	4.0%
Gratitude to Lawyers	9	3.1%	3.6%
Gratitude to Media	4	1.4%	1.6%
Personal Reconciliation	**63**	**21.6%**	**25.1%**
Forgives Others	27	9.2%	10.8%
Found Peace	25	8.6%	10.0%
Personal Transformation	17	5.8%	6.8%
Humanize Self	12	4.1%	4.8%

Table 5 (continued)

Last Statement Theme	N	% of Valid Cases (N = 292)	% of Statements Given (N = 251)
Denial of Responsibility	**57**	**19.5%**	**22.7%**
Claim of Innocence	40	13.7%	15.9%
Externalize Blame	13	4.5%	5.2%
Minimize/Rationalize Actions or Agency	8	2.7%	3.2%
Criticism of Death Penalty	**44**	**15.1%**	**17.5%**
Is Wrong (General)	18	6.2%	7.2%
Hypocritical/Killing is Wrong	16	5.5%	6.4%
Not Justice	14	4.8%	5.6%
Does Not Bring Peace or Closure	13	4.5%	5.2%
Only Creates More Victims	7	2.4%	2.8%
Inhumane	2	0.7%	0.8%
Not a Deterrent	1	0.3%	0.4%
Anger & Resentment	**30**	**10.3%**	**12.0%**
Condemns CJ System or Government in General	16	5.5%	6.4%
Anger or Resentment Toward CJ Officials/CJ System	16	5.5%	6.4%
Condemns Police/CJ Officials	11	3.8%	4.4%
Condemns Co-Victim(s)/Victim(s)	6	2.1%	2.4%
Anger or Resentment Toward Own Lawyers	5	1.7%	2.0%
Anger or Resentment Toward Witnesses at Trial	4	1.4%	1.6%
Anger or Resentment Toward Co-Victims	3	1.0%	1.2%

Table 5 (continued)

Last Statement Theme	N	% of Valid Cases (N = 292)	% of Statements Given (N = 251)
Resignation	**27**	**9.2%**	**10.8%**
Release	16	5.5%	6.4%
Fate	9	3.1%	3.6%
Helplessness	7	2.4%	2.8%
Accountability	**21**	**7.2%**	**8.4%**
Acceptance of Responsibility for the Murder	14	4.8%	5.6%
Acceptance of Responsibility for Other Bad Acts or Crimes	8	2.7%	3.2%

love or well-wishes to family and friends. In most cases, these statements were simple affirmations of love and connection:

> *I would like to tell my family I love them very dearly, and I know they love me.* (Danny Harris, #62).

> *Mom, I just want y'all to know that I love you.* (Tony Chambers, #236).

In some cases these were in the context of a simple "goodbye" to family and friends:

> *I want to say 'bye to my mom--I love her--and my aunt, and my fiance, Regina, in England.* (Jeffery Griffin, #53).[26]

> *I love you, Mom. Goodbye.* (Jeffery Motley, #90).

These expressions of love were often accompanied by words of encouragement to family members and friends. In a somewhat ironic

---

[26] Portions of statement obtained from Dial, J. (1992, November 19). Griffin cheerful in dying. *The Huntsville Item,* p. 8A.

twist, the last statements often reveal the condemned attempting to console his loved ones as he faces his own death:

> *To my family: I love you. When the tears flow, let the smiles grow. Everything is all right.* (Charles Tuttle, #179).

> *I just want to tell my family, everybody I love and I want you to know that I love you, and that God loves you too. Everything is going to be just fine, just fine. I love ya'll.* (Alvin Crane, #190).

> *Be strong, brother. Be strong, my brother. Be strong, Mom. It's going to be alright.* (Jessy San Miguel, #223).

In 17.5% of all cases, such words of encouragement were offered by the condemned. Although less often (6.5% of all cases), condemned inmates also offered words of encouragement or solidarity to their fellow death row inmates:

> *To everyone on death row, keep your heads up and I will see you again.* (Javier Medina, #277).

> *All of the brothers on the row stay strong.* (Patrick Rogers, #124).

Finally, a substantial proportion (14.7%) of condemned inmates expressed a wish for peace or closure for the co-victims:

> *I hope my dropping my appeal has in some way began your healing process...I hope this heals you.* (Charles Tuttle, #179).

> *[I]f my death gives you peace and closure then this is all worthwhile.* (David Herman, #110).

> *My hope is that my death brings you some kind of comfort.* (Michael Lockhart, #144).[27]

---

[27] Portions of statement obtained from Jackson, J. (1997, December 10). Officers hold vigil as cop killer dies. *The Huntsville Item,* pp. 1A, 5A.

It is interesting that the single most predominant theme among the last statements of the condemned is one in which the inmate expresses love, concern, and even sacrifice for others. Perhaps this stems from a need to make their death—a premature and involuntary death—a righteous death. The condemned may, through such expressions, be transforming what is a situation of powerlessness and helplessness into one in which they can feel some level of control. By expressing well-wishes, love, encouragement, and wishes for closure and peace, the condemned effectively transform their execution into something that transcends their otherwise defiled death. By transforming their death into an event that may bring some good to others or by granting their love and encouragement, they exult themselves to a position of beneficence and righteousness—a sort of martyrdom. Whatever the reason, the fact that the majority of condemned inmates use their last statements, at least in part, to express positive feelings of compassion for and connection to other individuals is an astounding reality when you consider the circumstances of their life and death.

Religion

The second most common theme among the last statements of the condemned is that of religion. In nearly half (48.3%) of all cases, the condemned inmate makes some form of religious reference. These references range from simply praying to asking God's forgiveness. Not surprisingly, the most common religious reference is made in regard to the afterlife. In 26% of all cases, the condemned invokes some manifestation of an afterlife. Often these are simply references about "going to a better place" but always suggest a form of transcendence in regard to their present life (and death), that there is something or someplace beyond this life to which they are headed. The most common reference is to heaven or to being with God:

> *Today I'm going home to HEAVEN to live for all eternity with my HEAVENLY FATHER JESUS CHRIST...*(Clifton Belyou, #118).

In many cases, the condemned inmate makes reference to "going home:"

> *Take my hand, Lord Jesus, I'm coming home.* (Steven Renfro, #146).

In some cases, references to an afterlife include a statement in which the condemned indicates he or she will see his or her loved-ones again:

> *...I am going to be face to face with Jesus now. I will see you all when you get there. I will wait for you.* (Karla Faye Tucker, #145).

> *I will wait for you in Heaven. I will be waiting for you.* (Irineo Montoya, #131).

Statements referring to an afterlife are also often accompanied by some form of proclamation of faith or declaration of giving oneself over to God. In 24% of cases, the condemned inmate made such a transformative statement of faith or devotion:

> *I belong to Jesus Christ. I confess my sins. I have been baptised. I am going home with Him.* (Earl Behringer, #128).

The condemned inmate sometimes simply takes an opportunity to offer praise to their God:

> *Yes, I would like to praise Allah and I am praying to Allah. Allah is most gracious. Give praise to Allah.* (Patrick Rogers, #124).

In some cases, the condemned transforms the execution into a positive event allowed for by the grace of God:

> *I would like to give praise to God for the love and grace that he has allowed for all of this to come together.* (Jessel Turner, #134).[28]

Preaching was another common expression of religious faith (15.8% of cases), often accompanying references to the afterlife and proclamations of faith:

> *That's what counts in the end; where you stand with Almighty God. I know that God has used this to change my life. And*

---

[28] Portions of statement obtained from Upshaw, A. (1997, September 23). State executes 27th this year. *The Huntsville Item,* pp. 1A, 7A.

> *it's all been worth it because of that. If I lie here today where I lie, I can say in the face of death, Jesus is Lord. He has changed my life and I know that when I leave this body, I am going home to be with the Lord forever.* (Jason Massey, #245).

In 6.8% of cases, the condemned inmate asked for forgiveness from God (or other deity):

> *I bow down to Allah, most merciful. I ask to seek his forgiveness. If this is what they want to see, this is what they get. I bow down to no man. I bow down to Allah. I will ask Allah for forgiveness because he created me and he will forgive me.* (Patrick Rogers, #124).[29]

Somewhat surprisingly, only 6.8% of condemned inmates actually recited a specific prayer (e.g. a prayer from the Bible, psalm, etc.). Praying, in general, for someone or something was much more common. In these cases, the condemned was much more likely to state that they pray for others (13.4% of all cases) than for themselves (6.5% of all cases).

Again, as with the "well-wishes" category, statements exhibiting these themes offer a sense of transcendence for the condemned. In these cases, religion provides the foundation for this transcendence but the message is similar: there is positive meaning to the otherwise defiled life and death of the condemned individual. These are messages of salvation.

Of course, other factors clearly play a role in the emphasis on religion in the last statements of condemned inmates. First, spiritual guidance is a significant part of an inmate's time on death row. Most prison systems and death rows have chaplains who counsel the inmates often with a focus on (but not limited to) spirituality, spiritual transformation, and spiritual salvation (Pickett & Stowers, 2002). Beyond this, many inmates have other spiritual advisors who visit with them and minister to them (Ingle, 1989). Religion is a particularly powerful source of support and comfort—something condemned inmates may have a difficult time finding elsewhere. Another salient factor to consider is the obvious allure of spiritual transformation in

---

[29] Portions of statement obtained from Jackson, J. (1997, June 3). Killer defiant before death. *The Huntsville Item*, pp. 1A, 5A.

light of the life and impending death of the condemned inmate. It is not at all surprising that religion is a common theme among their last statements; it is a common theme among people who are near death in a variety of forms (Kubler-Ross, 1969).

But, this brings us back to our original point, and that is that there is a strong message that death is not the end for the condemned. Through the religious statements made, and assertion of faith in God and an afterlife, the condemned is able to transcend his or her death. The inmate is indicating that there is something beyond here for them (invariably something *better)* and make positive and meaningful an otherwise defiled life and death.

Contrition

Nearly a third (32.9%) of last statements indicated some form of contrition on the part of the condemned. The most common expression of contrition came in the form of an apology to co-victim(s):

> *To the Weis family, and ah I just want you to know from the bottom of may heart that I am truly sorry. I mean it, I'm not just saying it. Through the years of being in prison I come to hear and respect our life. It was wrong what I did. I know you had to go through a lot of pain and I'm sorry.* (Timothy Gribble, #211).

Such apologies to co-victim(s) were present in 21.2% of cases. Similar to these apologies, yet slightly different were statements in which the condemned asked co-victim(s) for forgiveness. This occurred in 11% of cases and often accompanied an apology:

> *I would like to tell the victims' families that I am sorry, very sorry. I am so sorry. Forgive me if you can. I know it's impossible, but try.* (Steven Renfro, #146).

> *First of all, I want to apologize to the family of Kelly Elizabeth Donovan. I am sorry for what I did to her twelve years ago. I wish they could forgive me for what I did. I am sorry.* (Oliver Cruz, #227).

A much smaller proportion of statements included apologies to the condemned's own family or friends (6.8%) and it was even more rare for the condemned to ask for forgiveness from his or her own family or friends (2.7%):

> *I would like to apologize for all of the hurt, pain and disappointment I caused to my family and all my friends.* (Larry White, #122).

> *Mother, I am sorry for all the pain I've caused you. Please forgive me.* (Anthony Williams, #23).

In 6.8% of the cases, the condemned asked for God's forgiveness and in 6.2% the condemned made a general statement about being sorry or asking forgiveness with no specified individual or individuals to whom the contrition was directed. Interestingly, only 3.1% of condemned inmates indicated a wish to turn back time, to go back and undo what they did or bring their victim back:

> *I know your brother meant a lot to you, and if I could die a hundred times to bring him back, I would do it.* (George Cordova, #168).[30]

The focus, rather, was more likely to be on going forward in time. Moving forward at a the precise time when one is being killed may seem paradoxical, but as was previously indicated in regard to both well-wish and religion themes, the last statements often include attempts to transcend death and provide meaning that will exist beyond the life and death of the condemned inmate. In the case of contrition, the condemned often attempt to accomplish this on behalf of both the co-victims, in the form of apology, and themselves, in the forms of forgiveness and salvation.

Gratitude

Condemned inmates also often (in 29.5% of cases) expressed some form of gratitude or thanks. This was most often directed toward family and friends for their support or commitment (21.9% of cases):

---

[30] Portions of statement obtained from Gideon, L. (1999, February 11). Cordova apologizes, dies for killing. *The Huntsville Item,* pp. 1A, 6A.

> ... *I would also like to thank my mother for standing by me all these years. I would also like to thank my pen pals, Joe and Camille Tilling and JoAnn for helping me stay strong all these years.* (Clarence Lackey, #120).

> *I want to thank my family for their help and moral support and for their struggle. It would have been a lot harder without their love.* (Adolph Hernandez, #243).

Other themes of gratitude were more religious in nature with 7.5% of condemned inmates expressing thanks to God or some other form of deity or religious figure. Below is a particularly lengthy and poignant example:

> *Father, I want to thank you for all of the beautiful people you put in my life. I could not have asked for two greater parents than you gave me. I could just ask for two greater people in their life now. It is a blessing that there are people that they love so much but even more so, people that I love so much. I thank you for all the things you have done in my life, for the ways that you have opened my eyes, softened my heart. The ways that you have taught me. For teaching me how to love, for all of the bad things you have taken out of my life. For all the good things you have added to it. I thank you for all of the beautiful promises that you make us in your word, and I graciously received every one of them. Thank you Heavenly Father for getting me off of death row and for bringing me home out of prison. I love you Heavenly Father, I love you Jesus. Thank you both for loving me.* (Jeffery Dillingham, #233).

Condemned inmates also thanked the prison chaplain or personal spiritual advisors (in 4.1% of cases). These expressions of gratitude were most often in reference to the friendship and support such spiritual guides and advisors had given to the condemned:

> *Jim and Judy Peterson and Chaplain Lopez, I thank you for staying by my side.* (Markum Duff-Smith, #60).

> *Father Walsh my spirit has grown because of you. Father Fitzgerald, thank you for being my friend.* (Jonathan Nobles, #160).[31]

One can surmise that in many cases, these spiritual guides and counselors were the only real source of friendship and support (along with the respective God) the condemned had during his time on death row and in preparing for execution. The following is a statement directed at two spiritual advisors familiar to numerous condemned inmates in Texas and is a good example of the fictive family such spiritual advisors often become to the condemned:

> *To my friends, Jack and Irene Wilcox. Bless you both, you've been my rock. Irene, you have been like a mother and Jack, you have been like a father.* (Jeffery Tucker, #254).

In a similar manner, the condemned's lawyers—the other likely sources of outside support and friendship—were thanked in 3.1% of the cases:

> *... I also thank my two lawyers, Rita and Brent, for fighting to keep me alive.* (Clarence Lackey, #120).

Most surprisingly, perhaps, were statements in which the condemned expressed gratitude toward criminal justice staff (usually, but not always, directed toward correctional administration or staff):

> *Warden Baggett, thank all of you so much. You have been so good to me.* (Karla Faye Tucker, #145).
> *The only thing I want to say is that I appreciate the hospitality that you guys have shown me and the respect; and the last meal was really good.* (James Collier, #289).

In some rare cases, the condemned thanked those responsible for his apprehension and/or prosecution:

> *I want to thank the prosecutor in my case; it took courage for him to do what he did but he did what he did because he believed in the judicial system.* (Raymond Kinnamon, #85).

---

[31] Statement obtained from Sunriver Cartel (2000).

> *I would like to thank one of the arresting officers that I would have killed if I could have. He gave me CPR, saved my life, and gave me a chance to get my life right.* (Larry Hayes, #310).

Again, it is interesting to note the positive, personal connection being made in a substantial proportion of last statements. Some condemned inmates go so far as to portray their time on death row in a transformatively positive light. In this example, the condemned inmate effusively expresses gratitude and connection:

> *I want to thank the Lord, Jesus Christ, for the years I have spent on death row. They have been a blessing in my life. I have had the opportunity to serve Jesus Christ and I am thankful for the opportunity. I would like to thank Father Walsh for having become a Franciscan, and all the people all over the world who have become my friends. It has been a wonderful experience in my life. I would like to thank Chaplain Lopez, and my witnesses for giving me their support and love. I would like to thank the Nuns in England for their support. I want to tell my sons I love them; I have always loved them - they were my greatest gift from God. I want to tell my witnesses, Tannie, Rebecca, Al, Leo, and Dr. Blackwell that I love all of you and I am thankful for your support.* (Hilton Crawford, #306).

It is surprising to see a statement like "It has been a wonderful experience in my life" in this context. The transformative implications of such a statement stand in stark contrast to the event taking place.

Personal Reconciliation

In 21.6% of last statements, the condemned inmate indicated some form of personal reconciliation whether in regard to others or within himself. This was most commonly expressed as forgiveness of others (9.2% of cases), a twist on the previously discussed theme of contrition. In these cases, the condemned was usually making a general statement of forgiveness or that he holds nothing against anyone:

> *I want everybody to know that I hold nothing against them. I forgive them all.* (Thomas Barefoot, #4).

Others specifically addressed their forgiveness to those they held responsible for their execution:

> *I would forgive all who have taken part in any way in my death.* (Ronald O'Brien, #3).

Sometimes the statement even further specified the forgiveness by directing it at the co-victim(s):

> *To the victim's family: I hope you will find it in your heart to forgive me as I have forgiven you.* (Willis Barnes, #187).

In this latter case (and in several others), transformation (or restoration) seems to be the primary focus. The condemned is expressing the hope for mutual reconciliation through apology and forgiveness.

Other more individualized expressions of personal reconciliation were statements indicating that the condemned had found peace or come to peace with the events and circumstances of his or her life (and death) or had otherwise made a personal transformation (8.6% and 5.8% of cases, respectively):

> *If you don't see peace in my eyes you don't see me.* (Jeffery Doughtie, #251).

> *I have no animosity; I am at peace and invite you all to my funeral.* (Toronto Patterson, #279).

Not surprisingly, these statements were often accompanied by religious references and references to God:

> *I want you to know I'm at peace with myself and with my God.* (Jay Pinkerton, #13).

> *I have found everlasting peace with God. I wish the guys on the row peace. I have everlasting peace now and I am ready.* (Harold Lane, #100).

> *I thank the Lord for the past 14 years that have allowed me to grow as a man and mature spiritually enough to accept what is happening to me tonight.* (Kenneth Gentry, #113).

Finally, several (4.1%) condemned inmates made statements asserting their humanity or humanizing themselves. These statements were most often simple statements refuting any notion that one was evil or a bad person:

> *I would like to say to the world, I have always been a nice person. I have never been mean-hearted or cruel.* (Granville Riddle, #295).

> *I was not a monster like they said I was.* (Richard Williams, #298).

Given the dehumanizing circumstances of the condemned's recent life and immediately impending death, it is not surprising that they would make statements reasserting their humanity. What is surprising is that only a small proportion of them do so.

The theme of personal reconciliation reflects another attempt, among those already discussed, to highlight the positive realities of the condemned's life and to transform the negative events and circumstances into something meaningful and transcendent. By forgiving others, acknowledging their personal transformations, evoking a state of peace and asserting their humanity, they effectively reconcile themselves with the world they are leaving.

Denial of Responsibility

In contrast to many of the themes discussed above (especially contrition), some condemned inmates used their last statements to deny personal responsibility. In 19.5% of all cases, the condemned made a statement in some way denying his or her responsibility for the act for which he or she is about to be executed. These statements varied in the degree of responsibility being denied. Not surprisingly, the most common form of denial of responsibility was that of claiming innocence (13.7% of cases). In these cases, the condemned contends that he or she did not commit the murder and thus was wrongfully convicted and is being wrongfully executed. These often accompany broader outcries about wrongful executions and calls for protection of the wrongfully convicted:

> *I am innocent, innocent, innocent. Make no mistake about this; I owe society nothing. Continue the struggle for human*

> *rights, helping those who are innocent, especially Mr. Graham. I am an innocent man, and something very wrong is taking place tonight.* (Leonel Herrera, #58).
>
> *I would like to say that I see there are a number of you gathered here tonight to see an execution by the state of Texas; however, I have news for you. There is not going to be an execution. This is premeditated murder by the appointed district attorney and the State of Texas. I am not guilty of this crime. I hope that my death will snowball an avalanche that will stop all executions in the State of Texas and elsewhere. If my death serves this purpose, then maybe it will be worthwhile.* (Jesse Jacobs, #86).[32]

Of course, there is no way of knowing which, if any, of the condemned inmates who make such claims in their last statements are actually innocent. In such cases, a denial of responsibility would be completely legitimate. In cases in which the condemned actually committed the offense, it means something very different; it represents either a lie, an unwillingness to take responsibility, or a deeper psychological mechanism by which the condemned may be able to reduce feelings of guilt and shame (Cohen, 2001). The latter two functions also manifest themselves in attempts to externalize the blame (4.5% of cases), usually by blaming other individuals, forces, or circumstances, or by minimizing or rationalizing their actions or their personal agency (2.7% of cases). Whether making a statement as one who is actually innocent or one who committed the murder but denies it, it is interesting to note that the condemned inmates sometimes (as illustrated in the two examples above) express the hope that their (wrongful) death will bring about positive change (awareness about wrongful executions; abolition of the death penalty) in the future. Again, we see the statements reflect the condemned inmates' desires to give transcendent meaning to their lives and death.

Criticism of Death Penalty

Some condemned inmates take the opportunity in their last statements to criticize the death penalty. In 15.1% of all cases, condemned inmates made some kind of statement against the death penalty. The

---

[32] Statement obtained from Sunriver Cartel (2000).

most common statement was a general one, one simply proclaiming the death penalty to be wrong (6.2% of cases). More specific statements focused on the hypocritical nature of the death penalty often simply noting (perhaps ironically) that killing of any kind is wrong or that the death penalty equates to murder (5.5% of cases):

> *It was horrible and inexcusable for me to take the life of your loved one and to hurt so many mentally and physically. I am here because I took a life and killing is wrong by an individual and by the state.* (David Herman, #110).

> *GOD help you, because what you're doing here today and what's in your hearts here today makes you no better than any man or woman on death-rows across this country. Today you're committing murder too!!!* (Clifton Belyou, #118).

> *I'm not only saddened, but disappointed that a system that is supposed to protect and uphold what is just and right can be so much like me when I made the same shameful mistake.* (Napoleon Beazley, #270).

Others argue that the death penalty does not bring justice (4.8% of cases) and will not bring peace or closure for the co-victims (4.5%) of cases:

> *I would like to say to the victim's family, if this goes on record, that I know they have gotten grief and I know with this execution, it will not be any relief for them. That with my death, it will just remind them of their loved one.* (Bobby Cook, #299).

> *Politicians say that this brings closure. But my death doesn't bring your son back - it doesn't bring closure.* (Emerson Rudd, #255).

Anger & Resentment

Contrary to what might be expected given the circumstances, relatively few condemned inmates use their last statements to express anger or resentment (only 10.3% of all cases). When they did, it was most likely directed at the criminal justice or governmental system (5.5% of cases) or at criminal justice officials (5.5% of cases). The most common form of anger & resentment to these groups was expressed as condemnation. Sykes and Matza (1964) identified "condemnation of condemners" as one technique of neutralization internalized by individuals allowing them to more easily justify or rationalize their own condemnable acts (crimes). In this case, it appears that condemned inmates utilize this technique after the fact and thus attempt to lighten the burden of their own condemnation. In some cases, condemned inmates go so far as to condemn (2.1% of cases) or express anger & hostility toward (1% of cases) the victims or co-victims, usually when also claiming innocence:

> *But get to church and get right with God. Jane, you know damn well I did not molest that kid of yours. You are murdering me and I feel sorry for you. Get in church and get saved.* (William Chappell, #287).

In another case, an inmate expressed extreme hostility toward a co-victim:

> *I hope you rot in hell, Bitch; I hope you fucking rot in hell, Bitch. You Bitch; I hope you fucking rot, cunt.* (Cameron Willingham, #320).

Without knowing for certain whether or not the condemned inmate was actually innocent, and thus justified in his anger and hostility, it is hard to draw conclusions about such statements. What can be concluded, however, is that these negativistic statements are more the exception than the rule whatever the circumstances.

Resignation

As we have seen in relation to many of the previously discussed themes, resignation does not appear to be a dominant response to facing execution (only 9.2% of all cases). Instead, it appears that condemned inmates assert themselves against their impending death by applying meaning to their lives and deaths and attempting to transcend their fate. The largest proportion of statements indicating resignation involved the condemned expressing release or readiness to be released or freed from this life:

> *I'm ready to be released. Release me.* (Kenneth McDuff, #161).

> *Thank you for setting me free.* (Javier Cruz, #159).
> *I'm fixin' to be free.* (Jeffery Griffin, #53).

Such themes of release also often accompany religious statements:

> *I wanted to let you know that the Lord Jesus is my life and I just want to go. I'm gonna fall asleep and I'll be in his presence shortly.* (Johnny Pyles, #154).

Other themes of resignation include fate (3.1% of cases) and helplessness (2.4% of cases). Fate and helplessness seem to be manifested in statements about the inevitability of death (generally or in specific regard to the condemned's own death):

> *I'm an African warrior, born to breathe, and born to die.* (Carl Kelly, #65).

> *Everybody's got to go sooner or later and sooner or later everyone of ya'll will be along behind me.* (Thomas Mason, #219).

Some even frame their fatalistic perspective in a positive light, suggesting that their execution is happening for a reason or that something good must come from their fated death:

> *Uh, look at this as a learning experience. Everything happens for a reason. We all know what really happened, but there are some things you just can't fight. Little people always seem to get squashed. It happens. Even so, just got to take the good with the bad.* (David Castillo, #158).

> *Life has not been that good to me, but I believe that now, after meeting so many people who support me in this, that all things will come to an end, and may this be fruit of better judgements for the future.* (Odell Barnes, Jr., #209).

Given the complete lack of power and control on the part of the condemned and the mix of force and bureaucratic sterility on the part of the state, it is not surprising that helplessness and fatalistic attitudes would be expressed in final statements. What is surprising is that they are not expressed very often.

Accountability

In spite of the high proportion of condemned inmates who express contrition in their last statements, only a small proportion (7.2%) explicitly own their responsibility for the capital murder or for other criminal acts. To be sure, this does not mean that they don't take responsibility for these acts (as such may be strongly implied in statements of contrition), but simply that they do not go to the length of making a statement specifically indicating that they do. In 4.8% of cases the condemned specifically indicate their responsibility for the capital murder for which they are being executed. In 2.7% of cases, the condemned inmate accepts responsibility for other crimes or bad acts, sometimes even confessing to murders previously unsolved:

> *I am the sinner of all sinners. I was responsible for the '75 and '79 cases.* (David Markum-Smith, #60).

> *I would like to clear some things up if I could. Tommy Perkins, the man that got a capital life sentence for murdering Kinslow -- he did not do it. I did it. He would not even have had anything to do with it if he had known I was going to shoot the man. He would not have gone with me if he had known. I was paid to shoot the man...A boy on Eastham doing a life sentence for killing Jamie Kent - I did not do it, but I was with his daddy when it was done. I was there with him and down through the years there were several more that I had done or had a part of. And I am sorry and I am not sure how many - there must be a dozen or 14 I believe all total. One I would like to clear up is Cullen Davis - where he was charged with shooting his wife. And all of these it was never nothing personal. It was just something I did to make a living.* (Billy Vickers, #317).

These were rare cases, to be sure. In fact, it is extremely rare that a condemned inmate specifically refers directly to his responsibility for his acts or holds himself accountable. Indeed, even in the last statement cited above, the inmate mitigates his responsibility by indicating that "it was never nothing personal" and "just something I did to make a living." Again, in light of the earlier discussed themes of contrition and religion expressed so often in last statements, this finding is somewhat astounding.

LAST STATEMENTS AND CHARACTERISTICS OF THE CONDEMNED

In an attempt to identify differences or similarities in themes based on factors related to the individual condemned inmate, last statements were examined across several demographic categories. For each of the ten major themes previously discussed, percentages were computed within each demographic category and chi-square statistics were obtained to ascertain statistical significance in differences among these groups. Table 6 presents the findings for each of the ten major themes of last statements.

Although sex of inmate is presented among the descriptive statistics in Table 6, the low number of executed women does not allow for meaningful statistical analyses. In regard to race, three groups were examined: Whites, Blacks, and Hispanics. No significant differences were found for any of the ten thematic categories. However, some interesting substantively significant findings are identified[33]. Surprisingly, there is very little difference between white and black inmates in statements expressing criticism of the death penalty with 15.9% of Whites and 16.3% of Blacks making such statements. Perhaps most surprisingly, only 9.8% of Hispanic inmates made statements criticizing the death penalty. Whites were nearly twice as likely as Black or Hispanic inmates to express anger and resentment (13.2% versus 7.1% and 7.3%, respectively). Black inmates, on the other hand, were more likely to express personal reconciliation (26.5% as compared to 19.9% of Whites and 17.1% of Hispanics) and resignation (12.2% versus 7.9% of Whites and 7.3% of Hispanics).

---

[33] It is important to note that reported differences not found to be statistically significant should be analyzed with some reservation as the differences may be explained by chance. However, given the qualitative nature of this study, it is this researcher's belief that substantive significance is important and valid even in the absence of statistical significance. Although drawing inferences to other populations or to the broader population of condemned inmates may not be appropriate, the (non-statistically significant) descriptive percentages tell us important things about these inmates and the essence of their expressed perspectives.

Overall, there is very little difference in statement themes by education level. The only statistically significant difference is on the theme of accountability with 10.7 % of inmates with a high school education or GED and only 3.9% of inmates with less than a high school education making a statement indicating personal accountability ($\chi^2 = 4.92$, $p < .05$). Non-statistically significant, but substantively interesting findings include the facts that those with more education were more likely to express contrition (36.9% versus 29.7%) but less likely to make a religious statement (44.5% versus 53.3%).

The offender's age at the time of the crime had some modest impact on statements of the condemned. Although those who were under the age of 18 at the time of their offense exhibited some distinct differences in several of the statement themes, conclusion regarding this population should be made with caution as only nine such offenders were among those in this study. Nevertheless, those who were under the age of 18 at the time of the crime were significantly more likely to express contrition ($\chi^2 = 11.20$, $p < .05$) and to claim accountability ($\chi^2 = 10.37$, $p < .05$) for their actions (77.8% and 33.3%, respectively). Although not a significant difference, they were also more likely to express resignation (22.2%) than those who were adults at the time of their offense. Interestingly, it appears that the older an offender was at the time of his offense, the more likely he was to invoke religion in his last statement. Conversely, offenders who were older at the time of their crime were less likely to indicated personal reconciliation. Although neither of these findings is statistically significant, they are distinctive patterns worth noting.

Offenders who were older at the time of execution (aged 45 or higher) were significantly less likely to express well-wishes or love toward others ($\chi^2 = 7.73$, $p < .05$) or to make statements of contrition ($\chi^2 = 6.71$, $p < .05$). Although not reaching a level of statistical significance, other findings show that those who were older at the time of execution were more likely to deny responsibility (24.2% vs. 19.1% of those between the ages of 35 and 44 and 16.8% of those 34 or younger) and express anger or resentment (15.2% as compared to 8.4% and 9.5% of the other two groups). They were less likely to make a statement indicating accountability for their crimes (3.0% vs. 6.9% and 10.5% of the other two groups).

Table 6
Last Statement Themes by Characteristics of the Condemned

		% within Characteristic Category		
Characteristic	N	Well-Wishes	Religion	Contrition
Total Sample	292	58.6%	48.3%	32.9%
Sex				
Male	290	58.6	48.3	32.8
Female	2	50.0	50.0	50.0
Race				
White	151	55.0	50.3	39.1
Black	98	65.3	40.8	28.6
Hispanic	41	56.1	56.1	22.0
Education				
High School or GED	122	58.2	44.5	36.9
Less than High School	155	61.3	53.3	29.7
Age at Time of Crime				
Under 18	9	66.7	33.3	77.8**
18-24	119	62.2	48.7	32.8
25-34	106	61.3	52.8	34.9
35 or Older	53	43.4	41.5	22.6
Age at Time of Execution				
24-34	95	61.1	50.5	36.8
35-44	131	64.1	50.4	36.6
45 or Older	66	43.9**	40.9	19.7**
Evidence of MR?				
Yes	3	0.0	66.7	66.7
No	289	59.2	48.1	32.5
Texas Native?				
Yes	166	57.2	44.6*	31.3
No	101	62.4	56.4	33.7
Foreign National?				
Yes	6	66.7	66.7	33.3
No	286	58.4	47.9	32.9
Prior Prison Record				
Yes	157	59.2	51.0	31.2
No	119	58.8	49.6	37.0

*Significant at $p < .10$
**Significant at $p < .05$

Table 6 (continued)

Characteristic	N	% within Characteristic Category: Gratitude	Personal Reconcil-iation	Denial of Responsib-ility
Total Sample	292	29.5%	21.6%	19.5%
Sex				
Male	290	29.3	21.7	19.7
Female	2	50.0	0.0	0.0
Race				
White	151	31.8	19.9	18.5
Black	98	26.5	26.5	21.4
Hispanic	41	26.8	17.1	19.5
Education				
High School or GED	122	27.9	21.3	18.9
Less than High School	155	31.6	21.9	20.6
Age at Time of Crime				
Under 18	9	22.2	44.4	33.3
18-24	119	31.1	24.4	16.0
25-34	106	30.2	17.9	22.6
35 or Older	53	24.5	15.1	18.9
Age at Time of Execution				
24-34	95	27.4	25.3	16.8
35-44	131	32.8	19.8	19.1
45 or Older	66	25.8	19.7	24.2
Evidence of MR?				
Yes	3	33.3	0.0	66.7**
No	289	29.4	21.8	19.0
Texas Native?				
Yes	166	28.3	20.5	22.3
No	101	32.7	20.8	15.8
Foreign National?				
Yes	6	33.3	16.7	0.0
No	286	29.4	21.7	19.9
Prior Prison Record				
Yes	157	28.7	24.2	19.7
No	119	31.9	19.3	21.8

*Significant at $p < .10$

**Significant at $p < .05$

Table 6 (continued)

Characteristic	N	% within Characteristic Category: Criticism of Death Penalty	Anger & Resentment
Total Sample	292	15.1%	10.3%
Sex			
Male	290	15.2	10.3
Female	2	0.0	0.0
Race			
White	151	15.9	13.2
Black	98	16.3	7.1
Hispanic	41	9.8	7.3
Education			
High School or GED	122	16.4	9.0
Less than High School	155	14.8	11.6
Age at Time of Crime			
Under 18	9	33.3	11.1
18-24	119	11.8	8.4
25-34	106	21.7**	11.3
35 or Older	53	7.7	11.3
Age at Time of Execution			
24-34	95	14.7	9.5
35-44	131	17.6	8.4
45 or Older	66	10.6	15.2
Evidence of MR?			
Yes	3	33.3	33.3
No	289	14.9	10.0
Texas Native?			
Yes	166	15.1	11.4
No	101	13.9	6.9
Foreign National?			
Yes	6	16.7	0.0
No	286	15.0	10.5
Prior Prison Record			
Yes	157	14.0	9.6
No	119	18.5	12.6

*Significant at $p < .10$

**Significant at $p < .05$

Table 6 (continued)

		% within Characteristic Category	
Characteristic	N	Resignation	Accountability
Total Sample	292	9.2%	7.2%
Sex			
Male	290	9.3	7.2
Female	2	0.0	0.0
Race			
White	151	7.9	8.6
Black	98	12.2	6.1
Hispanic	41	7.3	4.9
Education			
High School or GED	122	12.3	10.7**
Less than High School	155	7.1	3.9
Age at Time of Crime			
Under 18	9	22.2	33.3**
18-24	119	7.6	7.6
25-34	106	9.4	6.6
35 or Older	53	11.3	3.8
Age at Time of Execution			
24-34	95	9.5	10.5
35-44	131	8.4	6.9
45 or Older	66	10.6	3.0
Evidence of MR?			
Yes	3	33.3	0.0
No	289	9.0	7.3
Texas Native?			
Yes	166	10.8	6.6
No	101	7.9	6.9
Foreign National?			
Yes	6	0.0	0.0
No	286	9.4	7.3
Prior Prison Record			
Yes	157	10.2	5.7
No	119	7.6	9.2

*Significant at $p < .10$

**Significant at $p < .05$

Although the numbers are too low to really make any determination of significance, it is worth noting that chi-square analyses revealed offenders for whom there was evidence of mental retardation were more likely to deny responsibility for the capital offense ($\chi^2 = 4.29$, p <.05). Although the base number of those cases in which evidence of mental retardation is too low to be confident in this finding, two out of the three mentally retarded offenders denied responsibility in comparison to only 19 percent of the other 289 condemned inmates.

Finally, one of the more interesting findings indicates that Texas natives are significantly less likely to make a statement pertaining to religion than those who were from other states or countries ($\chi^2 = 3.53$, p < .10). Only 44.6% of Texas natives invoked God or religion in their statement as compared to 56.4% of those from outside of Texas. This is interesting in light of the common claim that religion plays a significant role in the cultural attitudes and sentiments regarding the death penalty in Texas (See, for example, Halmari, 1998). Although religion did indeed have a place in a substantial proportion of native Texans' last statements, it was significantly less prevalent than among the last statements of those from outside of Texas.

LAST STATEMENTS AND CHARACTERISTICS OF THE OFFENSE

Characteristics of the offense were also examined in regard to the themes of last statements of the condemned. Table 7 displays the percentages of statements containing each of the major themes across eight specific factors related to the offense. Included among these factors are characteristics of the victim or victims of the condemned inmate's capital murder.

Factors related to the crime event which were examined included whether or not there was a codefendant, whether the murder was committed in the act of a felony and whether a concurrent offense (a separate offense committed during the same criminal event) was committed. The findings suggest that in those cases in which there was one or more codefendants, the condemned was less likely to express contrition ($\chi^2 = 3.12$, p < .10) and less likely to express any form of personal reconciliation ($\chi^2 = 3.38$, p < .10).

Table 7
Last Statement Themes by Characteristics of the Offense

		% within Characteristic Category		
Characteristic	N	Well-Wishes	Religion	Contrition
Total Sample	292	58.6%	48.3%	32.9%
Codefendant(s)?				
Yes	125	60.0	52.0	27.2*
No	159	57.9	45.9	37.1
Related to Victim?				
Yes	30	50.0	43.3	30.0
No	262	59.5	48.9	33.2
Victim a Police Officer?				
Yes	22	63.6	45.5	40.9
No	270	58.1	48.5	32.2
Multiple Victims?				
Yes	73	49.3	45.2	34.2
No	219	61.6	49.3	32.4
Race of Victim(s)†				
White	277	57.0	48.4	33.6
Black	39	64.1	35.9	25.6
Hispanic	35	60.0	48.6	40.0
Sex of Victim(s)†				
Male	184	60.9	46.7	32.1
Female	179	53.6	48.6	34.1
Murder in Act of a Felony?				
Yes	229	60.3	47.6	31.4
No	63	52.4	50.8	38.1
Concurrent Offense				
Yes	242	59.9	46.7	30.6*
No	50	52.0	56.0	44.0

† These are multiple response variables. Due to multiple victims in some cases, their sum is larger than total number of cases.

* Significant at $p < .10$

** Significant at $p < .05$

Table 7 (continued)

		% within Characteristic Category		
Characteristic	N	Gratitude	Personal Reconc-iliation	Denial of Respons-ibility
Total Sample	292	29.5%	21.6%	19.5%
Codefendant(s)?				
Yes	125	28.8	16.8*	16.8
No	159	49.6	25.2	22.6
Related to Victim?				
Yes	30	30.0	10.0	26.7
No	262	29.4	22.9	18.7
Victim a Police Officer?				
Yes	22	27.3	27.3	22.7
No	270	29.6	21.1	19.3
Multiple Victims?				
Yes	73	32.9	17.8	26.0
No	219	28.3	22.8	17.4
Race of Victim(s)†				
White	277	30.7	20.9	21.3
Black	39	30.8	28.2	28.2
Hispanic	35	22.9	17.1	17.1
Sex of Victim(s)†				
Male	184	31.0	21.7	20.1
Female	179	29.1	20.1	21.8
Murder in Act of a Felony?				
Yes	229	27.9	20.5	16.2**
No	63	34.9	25.4	31.7
Concurrent Offense				
Yes	242	27.3*	20.7	16.9**
No	50	40.0	26.0	32.0

† These are multiple response variables. Due to multiple victims in some cases, their sum is larger than total number of cases.

* Significant at $p < .10$

** Significant at $p < .05$

Table 7 (continued)

Characteristic	N	% within Characteristic Category Criticism of Death Penalty	Anger & Resentment
Total Sample	292	15.1%	10.3%
Codefendant(s)?			
Yes	125	17.6	12.0
No	159	13.2	9.4
Related to Victim?			
Yes	30	13.3	13.3
No	262	9.1	9.9
Victim a Police Officer?			
Yes	22	36.4**	27.3**
No	270	13.3	8.9
Multiple Victims?			
Yes	73	13.7	8.2
No	219	15.5	11.0
Race of Victim(s)†			
White	277	15.2	11.2
Black	39	20.5	7.7
Hispanic	35	11.4	2.9
Sex of Victim(s)†			
Male	184	18.5	11.4
Female	179	11.2	7.8
Murder in Act of a Felony?			
Yes	229	12.7**	8.3**
No	63	23.8	17.5
Concurrent Offense			
Yes	242	12.8**	8.7**
No	50	26.0	18.0

† These are multiple response variables. Due to multiple victims in some cases, their sum is larger than total number of cases.

* Significant at $p < .10$

** Significant at $p < .05$

Table 7 (continued)

		% within Characteristic Category	
Characteristic	N	Resignation	Accountability
Total Sample	292	9.2%	7.2%
Codefendant(s)?			
Yes	125	8.8	7.2
No	159	8.8	6.9
Related to Victim?			
Yes	30	10.0	6.7
No	262	9.2	7.3
Victim a Police Officer?			
Yes	22	4.5	9.1
No	270	9.6	7.0
Multiple Victims?			
Yes	73	13.7	8.2
No	219	7.8	6.8
Race of Victim(s)†			
White	277	9.4	6.9
Black	39	20.5	10.3
Hispanic	35	8.6	8.6
Sex of Victim(s)†			
Male	184	9.8	6.0
Female	179	10.6	8.4
Murder in Act of a Felony?			
Yes	229	8.7	7.0
No	63	11.1	7.9
Concurrent Offense			
Yes	242	8.3	6.6
No	50	14.0	10.0

† These are multiple response variables. Due to multiple victims in some cases, their sum is larger than total number of cases.

* Significant at $p < .10$

** Significant at $p < .05$

Only 27.2% of those who had accomplices (as compared to 37.1% of those acting alone) indicated that they were sorry or were in any way contrite. In a related manner, although not statistically significant, a higher percentage of condemned inmates who had accomplices made statements denying responsibility for the crime (26.7% vs. 18.7% of those acting alone). This is not that surprising given the greater ability to externalize blame or diffuse responsibility when multiple actors are involved in an offense (See Bandura, 1990, 1999). It would be expected, then, that those with accomplices would be less likely to make a statement of personal accountability in regard to the capital offense; yet, no significant findings in regard to accountability were found.

Those who committed the capital murder in the act of a felony (e.g. robbery, kidnapping, rape) were significantly less likely to deny responsibility ($\chi^2 = 7.64$, $p < .05$), criticize the death penalty ($\chi^2 = 4.80$, $p < .05$) or express anger and resentment ($\chi^2 = 4.50$, $p < .05$). Similarly, condemned inmates who had committed concurrent offenses (offenses which occurred during the same criminal event other than the felony elevating the murder to a capital offense) were less likely to express gratitude ($\chi^2 = 3.23$, $p < .10$), deny responsibility ($\chi^2 = 5.98$, $p < .05$), criticize the death penalty ($\chi^2 = 5.63$, $p < .05$), or express anger or resentment ($\chi^2 = 3.91$, $p < .05$). It's almost as if in these cases, the condemned is more apt to accept the circumstances in which they find themselves and the punishment they are receiving. Of course, one would then also expect them to be more likely to express resignation which is not the case (although not statistically significant, both those who committed the capital murder in the act of a felony and those who had concurrent offenses were less likely to express resignation).

In regard to characteristics of the victims, very few statistically significant distinctions were found in the thematic messages of the last statements of the condemned. However, in cases in which the victim was a police officer, last statements were significantly more likely to include criticism of the death penalty ($\chi^2 = 8.43$, $p < .05$) and expressions of anger or resentment ($\chi^2 = 7.46$, $p < .05$). Condemned inmates who had been sentenced to death for killing a police officer were nearly three times more likely (36.4% vs. 13.3%) to make statements criticizing the death penalty and over three times more likely (27.3% vs. 8.9%) to express anger and resentment.

Statistical significance was unable to be determined for the race of victim and sex of victim categories because these were multiple response variables (i.e. variables for which there could be more than one value—more than one victim), so examinations of these variables in the context of the major themes of last statements are purely descriptive. That being said, there are some interesting findings in regard to race and sex of the victim or victims. As regards race, cases in which the victim is a minority (Black or Hispanic) seem to differ from those in which the victim is White. In cases with Black victims, statements expressing well-wishes or love, personal reconciliation, and denial of responsibility are more prevalent and statements expressing religious themes and contrition are less prevalent. Those in cases with Hispanic victims are less likely to express gratitude, criticize the death penalty or express anger and resentment. It's hard to make sense of all of this, but it should be noted that most executions in which a minority was the victim are intra-racial murders. Therefore, it is likely that these particular findings are just as much about the race of the offender as they are about the race of the victim. In regard to the sex of the victim, statements by those convicted of killing a female were less likely to exhibit well-wishes or love toward others, criticism of the death penalty and anger or resentment and more likely to express accountability for their crimes.

LAST STATEMENTS AND CHARACTERISTICS OF THE EXECUTION

The final points of analysis regarding the major themes of the last statements of condemned inmates are those factors related to or directly relevant to the execution. Most salient among these factors are those related to witnesses at the execution. Whether or not witnesses on behalf of the condemned and witnesses on behalf of the victims were present at the execution are examined in relation to the major themes of last statements. Other factors considered are whether the condemned was a "volunteer" (waived appeals so that the execution would be carried out), whether the condemned and co-victim(s) had engaged in victim-offender mediation (VOM), whether the capital trial occurred when victim impact statements were allowed (after June, 1991), and the time period during which the execution took place. Table 8 presents the percentages of condemned inmates within these categories who made statements categorized into each of the ten major themes.

One of the factors which would be most expected to have an impact on the condemned's last statement is the witnesses who are present at his execution and while he is making that last statement. Not surprisingly, when witnesses for the condemned (including most often family members, attorneys, and spiritual advisors) were present, the condemned inmate was significantly more likely to make statements expressing well-wishes and love toward others ($\chi^2 = 3.41$, $p < .10$), contrition ($\chi^2 = 3.16$, $p < .10$), and gratitude ($\chi^2 = 3.08$, $p < .10$). In the cases of well-wishes and gratitude, these are themes most often expressed toward the condemned's own family or friends, so it is not surprising that such a directed monologue would occur when they are present. It is a bit surprising that contrition is more prevalent in these cases as such statements are most often directed at co-victims. Although not supported by statistical significance, condemned inmates who had witnesses attending their executions were more likely to make a religious statement (53.1% vs. 28.3%) and deny responsibility (20.8% vs. 15.1%) but less likely to express anger and resentment (8.8% vs. 13.2%) or resignation (8.8% vs. 13.2%). These findings seem to suggest that personal connection at the time of execution is an important factor in whether the condemned inmate expresses positive or negative sentiments in his last statement, with the presence of family or friends potentially evoking more positive feelings and thoughts.

There are two variables related to the presence of witnesses on behalf of the victim(s). One makes the distinction between executions that occurred prior to the policy enactment allowing victim witnesses at the execution and those that occurred after this policy was put in place. The other indicates the cases in which victim witnesses were actually present at the execution. Although these are similar and seemingly redundant variables, the former is included more as a temporal marker examining historical policy change and the latter is a more specific indicator of witness presence. The only statistically significant finding for either of these variables was on the theme of contrition. Condemned inmates were significantly more likely to express contrition in their last statements when witnesses for the victim(s) were present at the execution ($\chi^2 = 10.17$, $p < .05$). In 41.2% of the cases in which victims' witnesses were present, the condemned made a statement either apologizing or asking forgiveness for his crime.

Table 8
Last Statement Themes by Characteristics of the Execution

		% within Characteristic Category		
Characteristic	N	Well-Wishes	Religion	Contrition
Total Sample	292	58.6%	48.3%	32.9%
Witnesses for Condemned?				
Yes	226	61.1*	53.1	35.4*
No	53	47.2	28.3	22.6
Witnesses for Victim Allowed?				
Yes	212	59.4	50.5	37.7**
No	80	56.3	42.5	20.0
Witnesses for Victim?				
Yes	153	59.5	50.3	41.2**
No	129	57.4	46.5	23.3
Volunteer?				
Yes	20	35.0**	55.0	35.0
No	272	60.3	47.8	32.7
Victim-Offender Mediation				
Yes	3	66.7	33.3	66.7
No	286	58.4	48.6	32.5
Requested by Co-Victim; Denied by Condemned	2	50.0	0.0	0.0
Requested by Condemned; Denied by Co-Victim or TDCJ Officials	1	100.0	100.0	100.0
VIS Allowed?				
Pre-Payne	219	60.3	48.4	30.6
Post-Payne	73	53.4	47.9	39.7
Time Period of Execution				
1982-1989	28	57.1	39.3	35.7
1990-1995	52	55.8	44.2	11.5**
1996-2000	130	62.3	50.8	34.6
2001-2004	82	54.9	50.0	42.7

*Significant at $p < .10$

**Significant at $p < .05$

Table 8 (continued)

Characteristic	N	% within Characteristic Category Gratitude	Personal Reconciliation	Denial of Responsibility
Total Sample	292	29.5%	21.6%	19.5%
Witnesses for Condemned?				
Yes	226	31.0*	21.7	20.8
No	53	18.9	20.8	15.1
Witnesses for Victim Allowed?				
Yes	212	30.2	19.8	21.2
No	80	27.5	26.3	15.0
Witnesses for Victim?				
Yes	153	27.5	20.3	22.9
No	129	31.0	24.0	16.3
Volunteer?				
Yes	20	15.0	20.0	10.0
No	272	30.5	21.7	20.2
Victim-Offender Mediation				
Yes	3	66.7	0.0	0.0
No	286	29.0	22.0	19.9
Requested by Co-Victim; Denied by Condemned	2	0.0	0.0	0.0
Requested by Condemned; Denied by Co-Victim or TDCJ Officials	1	100.0	0.0	0.0
VIS Allowed?				
Pre-Payne	219	31.5	23.3	19.2
Post-Payne	73	23.3	16.4	20.5
Time Period of Execution				
1982-1989	28	21.4	35.7	10.7
1990-1995	52	30.8	21.2	17.3
1996-2000	130	30.8	20.8	21.5
2001-2004	82	29.3	18.3	20.7

*Significant at $p < .10$

**Significant at $p < .05$

Table 8 (continued)

		% within Characteristic Category	
Characteristic	N	Criticism of Death Penalty	Anger & Resentment
Total Sample	292	15.1%	10.3%
Witnesses for Condemned?			
Yes	226	14.6	8.8
No	53	11.3	13.2
Witnesses for Victim Allowed?			
Yes	212	15.1	9.0
No	80	15.0	13.8
Witnesses for Victim?			
Yes	153	15.0	9.2
No	129	13.2	10.9
Volunteer?			
Yes	20	15.0	5.0
No	272	15.1	10.7
Victim-Offender Mediation			
Yes	3	33.3	0.0
No	286	14.7	10.5
Requested by Co-Victim; Denied by Condemned	2	0.0	0.0
Requested by Condemned; Denied by Co-Victim or TDCJ Officials	1	100.0	0.0
VIS Allowed?			
Pre-Payne	219	15.1	10.5
Post-Payne	73	15.1	9.6
Time Period of Execution			
1982-1989	28	17.9	14.3
1990-1995	52	13.5	13.5
1996-2000	130	13.1	6.2
2001-2004	82	18.3	13.4

*Significant at $p < .10$

**Significant at $p < .05$

Table 8 (continued)

Characteristic	N	% within Characteristic Category	
		Resignation	Accountability
Total Sample	292	9.2%	7.2%
Witnesses for Condemned?			
Yes	226	8.8	7.1
No	53	13.2	5.7
Witnesses for Victim Allowed?			
Yes	212	9.9	6.6
No	80	7.5	8.8
Witnesses for Victim?			
Yes	153	11.1	7.2
No	129	7.8	6.2
Volunteer?			
Yes	20	5.0	15.0
No	272	9.6	6.6
Victim-Offender Mediation			
Yes	3	0.0	0.0
No	286	9.4	7.3
Requested by Co-Victim; Denied by Condemned	2	0.0	0.0
Requested by Condemned; Denied by Co-Victim or TDCJ Officials	1	0.0	0.0
VIS Allowed?			
Pre-Payne	219	8.7	6.4
Post-Payne	73	11.0	9.6
Time Period of Execution			
1982-1989	28	7.1	14.3
1990-1995	52	7.7	5.8
1996-2000	130	10.8	5.4
2001-2004	82	8.5	8.5

*Significant at $p < .10$

**Significant at $p < .05$

This is in comparison to only 23.3% of cases in which no victims' witnesses were present and to 32.9% of all cases. This is not surprising, but highlights the potential value of victim-offender encounters in evoking contrition and other forms of empathic sensibilities on the part of the offender and catharsis through apology and/or forgiveness for co-victims. However, in these same cases (in which witnesses for the victim were present), a higher percentage of statements contained denials of responsibility (22.9% vs. 16.3%) and resignation (11.1% vs. 7.8%) too. Although these are not statistically significant findings, they are worth noting for the potential contradiction they introduce. The specific quality of the evocation of the presence of witnesses on behalf of the victim is not completely clear.

In some instances, condemned inmates abandon their appeals and become what are referred to as "volunteers." By this is meant that they volunteer to forego further appeals and go forward with their execution without further legal contest. Although only 20 volunteers were identified among the condemned inmates in this study, some interesting findings in regard to the major themes of their last statements in relation to volunteer status were yielded. However, the only statistically significant relationship was found between volunteer status and statements expressing well-wishes or love. Volunteers were far less likely (35.0% vs. 60.3%) to express well-wishes and love than their non-volunteer counterparts ($\chi^2 = 4.91$, $p < .05$). Non-statistically significant but substantively notable findings are also interesting. Not surprisingly, volunteers were much less likely to deny responsibility (10.0% vs. 20.2% of non-volunteers) or anger and resentment (5.0% vs. 10.7%); and, they were much more likely to claim accountability (15.0% vs. 6.6%). Somewhat perplexing is the finding that volunteers are less likely than non-volunteers to express resignation in their last statements (5.0% vs. 9.6%). This seems counter to the nature of volunteers given that the very act of "volunteering" appears to be a form of resignation.

Factors related to victim participation in the capital punishment process include participation during trial in which they present victim impact statements (VIS) and the more recent and rare participation in victim-offender mediation (VOM) in which they meet with the offender in an attempt at reconciliation and healing. In regard to the latter, cases in which VOM took place were identified for this study. In only three cases was VOM carried out. In two other cases, it had been requested by a co-victim but refused by the condemned (VOM is voluntary on the part of both co-victims and offenders); in one other case it was requested by the condemned but denied by the co-victim(s) and TDCJ officials. Because of these low numbers, meaningful analyses across the major thematic messages of last statements were not possible. Nevertheless, for illustrative purposes these findings have been included in Table 8.

Analyses related to VIS were conducted simply in regard to the temporal distinction between trials that occurred prior to the allowance of VIS (pre-*Payne*[34]) and those that occurred after VIS became allowed in capital trials (post-*Payne*). This allowed for an examination of differences in last statement themes across these two distinct time periods in regard to victim participation in capital trials. However, no statistically significant differences between the pre-*Payne* and post-*Payne* time periods were found. But, some interesting substantive differences in percentages are worth noting. Most notable are the findings that the condemned who were convicted in the post-*Payne* time-period were more likely to express contrition (39.7% vs. 30.6% from the pre-*Payne* period) and accountability (9.6% vs. 6.4% from the pre-*Payne* period). This potentially indicates that VIS has not only an impact on the jury (as is its intent) but also on the condemned.

For a more general look at change over time, the ten major statement themes were examined across four broad time periods. Although little significant change over time was detected, some trends can be noted. Figure 1 exhibits trend lines over these time-periods. As can be seen in Figure 1, trends vary widely across major thematic categories. For example religiously themed statements steadily increased in the late 1980s and early 1990s but leveled off after that whereas messages of personal reconciliation have declined since the 1980s with the steepest decline occurring prior to 1990. The only statistically significant change over time was detected for the theme of contrition. Statements in which the condemned expressed contrition declined sharply after the early executions in the 1980s and then rose just as sharply in the late 1990s. Also in the early decade of post-*Furman* executions in Texas, statements in which the condemned denied responsibility for the crime increased. Conversely, statements expressing accountability declined.

---

[34] The Supreme Court decided the case of *Payne v. Tennessee* in June of 1991 and held that victim impact statements and testimony may be presented in the sentencing phase of capital trials.

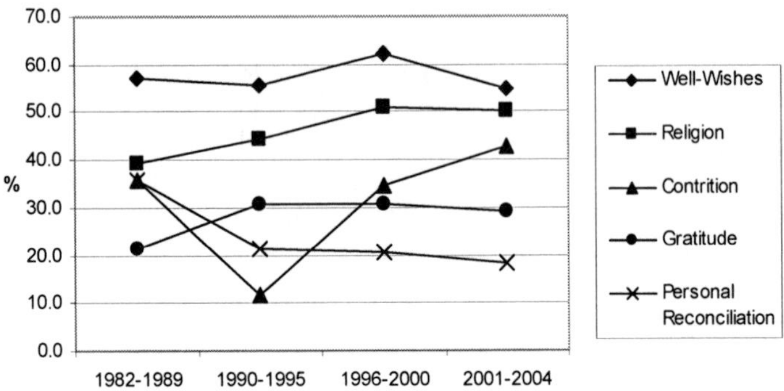

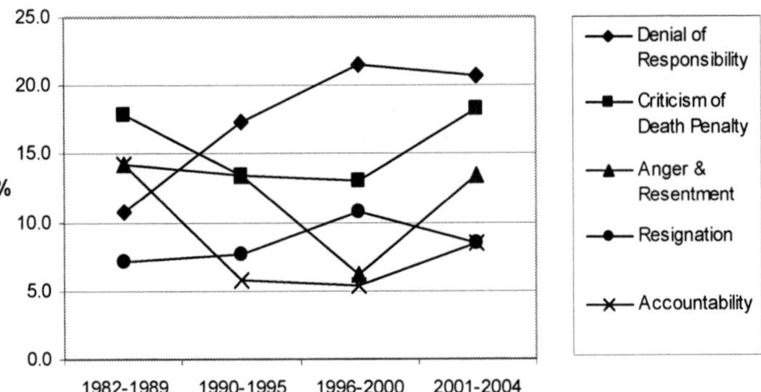

Figure 1. **Last Statement Themes, Percentage of Statements over Time**

Not surprisingly, the last decade (a decade that has seen increasing criticism of the death penalty and exposure of its failures) has seen a sharp increase in statements expressing criticism of the death penalty and anger or resentment. This is a potential indication that condemned inmates are well in-touch with outside sentiments about the punishment they are receiving and that their statements may be, at least in part, reflective of broader social trends and sensibilities.

RESTORATIVE JUSTICE AND LAST STATEMENTS OF THE CONDEMNED

As discussed in Chapter III, principles of restorative justice have begun to be considered and applied in the context of the death penalty. Although an execution is far from restorative for the condemned, the death penalty process is a potentially transformative one for many inmates. Being faced with death at the hands of the state and being forced to await and anticipate that death on death row, needless to say, are extreme human circumstances. These circumstances inevitably evoke reflection and bring about unique social connections and unique personal perspectives. The psychic, emotional and spiritual transformative power of this process and these circumstances is hard to deny. The time spent on death row and unique interaction with others including family, friends, correctional staff, media, attorneys, spiritual advisors, other inmates, and even co-victims place the condemned inmate at the center of what Arrigo and Fowler (2001) call the "death row community." In one of the many ironies of capital punishment, condemned inmates often experience connection and transformation which are inherently restorative in nature at the same time that they are preparing to be killed. This "restorative" reality of the death penalty process is illustrated well in their last statements.

Table 9 shows that an overwhelming majority (74.0%) of the last statements of the condemned included some restorative element or theme and that only a small proportion (18.2%) included a non-restorative theme. Themes were identified as restorative if they reflected any of the major principles or characteristics of restorative justice or restorative processes. Expressions of connection to others such as love, well-wishes, and encouragement were included as were expressions of contrition, responsibility, and gratitude. Finally, any expressions of personal transformation, growth, peace, humanity or spirituality were also included as restorative. Non-restorative statements were those containing themes counter to restorative justice such as refusing to take responsibility for actions or otherwise denying accountability, and expressing anger, resentment or condemnation toward others. Also, expressions of helplessness or a sense of being "wronged" by capital punishment were included as non-restorative. Table 9 presents all specific themes that made up the restorative and non-restorative categories.

Restorative-themed statements most often involved statements directed at the condemned's family and loved ones, with general expressions of love and well-wishes toward them the most common (40.1% of cases). But, statements of contrition or apology directed at co-victims were also among the most common restorative messages (20.1%). In cases in which non-restorative statements were made, the most common theme was one of innocence (overt denial of responsibility). This may actually exaggerate the proportion of statements which contained non-restorative themes as there may be cases in which the condemned was actually innocent. It can hardly be considered non-restorative for an innocent inmate to deny responsibility for the crime. Since actual innocence cannot be known, however, all claims of innocence were included as denials of responsibility and thus non-restorative.

Table 10 presents the percentages of restorative and non-restorative statement themes by characteristics of the condemned. Those condemned inmates who were older (45 years of age or older) at the time of execution were less likely to make a statement with restorative themes ($\chi^2 = 5.06$, $p < .10$). Similarly, those offenders who were older at the time of the offense appear less likely to make restorative statements at the time of their execution.[35] Although these findings in regard to age may leave us wondering about the relationship between time spent on death row and restorative themes of last statements, subsequent analyses reveal that length of time on death row and restorative or non-restorative themes are unrelated. The other statistically significant finding in regard to characteristics of the condemned and restorative or non-restorative last statement themes is that Texas natives are much more likely than inmates originally from other states to make overtly non-restorative statements ($\chi^2 = 3.26$, $p < .10$). Although not statistically significant, differences based on race were also detected. Whites were more likely to express non-restorative sentiments than Blacks and Hispanics (20.5% vs. 17.3% of Blacks and 12.2% of Hispanics). There was no discernable difference among these racial groups on restorative sentiments, however.

In Table 11 the restorative and non-restorative last statement themes are examined in relation to characteristics of the offense, including factors related to the victim(s). The most striking finding is

---

[35] This finding is not statistically significant most likely due to the inclusion of the category of offenders who were under the age of 18 at the time of crime. The small number within this category (N = 9) results in small cell sizes and thus inadequate chi square computations. However, the pattern is similar to that for age at the time of execution and is thus substantively significant.

that last statements of the condemned were much more likely to include non-restorative messages when the victim was a police officer (χ^2 = 2.99, p < .10). In nearly one-third (31.8%) of cases in which the victim was a police officer, condemned inmates made statements that were non-restorative (in comparison to only 17% of cases where the victim was not a police officer). Given that anger, resentment and condemnation of criminal justice officials or the criminal justice system comprise some of the aspects of non-restorative themes, this is not a surprising finding. But, it does highlight the contentious nature of cases in which a police officer is the victim. Condemned inmates were also much more likely to make non-restorative statements when the capital murder was committed without the presence of another offense. In 25.4% of cases in which the murder was not committed in the act of a felony (vs. 16.2% of cases in which it was), the condemned inmate expressed non-restorative sentiments (χ^2 = 4.91, p < .10). Other findings, although not statistically significant, indicate that restorative statements were less likely in cases in which the condemned was related to the victim and in which the victim was White or female.

Finally, Table 12 presents percentages of restorative and non-restorative themes across categories of factors related to the execution and death penalty process. The most striking finding pertains to the presence of witnesses on behalf of the condemned at the execution. Condemned inmates were significantly more likely to make restoratively themed statements when they had family or friends present at the execution. This is not surprising given the human connection that such presence allows for the condemned in his last moments. Interestingly, however, there was no discernable difference in non-restorative messages between cases in which witnesses for the condemned were present and cases in which they were not. Also, it appears that presence of witnesses on behalf of the victim(s) had little if any effect on the restorative or non-restorative nature of the condemned's last statement. Nor does it seem that the allowance of victim impact statements at trial had any discernible impact on the restorative nature of the last statements of the condemned. Finally, Figure 2 presents trends in both restorative and non-restorative themes across time periods. Restorative statements were slightly more common in the 1980s than any time after that and non-restorative statements were more common in the early 1990s and again in the early 2000s.

Table 9
Last Statements of Condemned Inmates: Restorative and Non-Restorative Themes

Last Statement Theme	N	% of Valid Cases (N = 292)	% of Statements Given (N = 251)
Restorative	**216**	**74.0%**	**86.1%**
Love or Well-Wishes to Family or Friends	117	40.1%	46.6%
Gratitude to Family & Friends	64	21.9%	25.5%
Apology to Co-Victim(s)	62	21.2%	24.7%
Words of Encouragement to Family or Friends	51	17.5%	20.3%
General Expression of Love	50	17.1%	19.9%
Wish Co-Victims Peace or Closure	43	14.7%	17.1%
Prayer for Others	39	13.4%	15.5%
Asks for Forgiveness from Co-Victim(s)	32	11.0%	12.7%
Forgives Others	27	9.2%	10.8%
Found Peace	25	8.6%	10.0%
Apology to Own Family/Friends	20	6.8%	8.0%
Asks for Forgiveness from God or Other Deity	20	6.8%	8.0%
Words of Encouragement to Fellow Inmates	19	6.5%	7.6%
Prayer for Self	19	6.5%	7.6%
Apology/Asks Forgiveness-Unspecified	18	6.2%	7.2%
Personal Transformation	17	5.8%	6.8%
Release	16	5.5%	6.4%
Acceptance of Responsibility for The Capital Murder	14	4.8%	5.6%
Humanize Self	12	4.1%	4.8%
Gratitude to Chaplain/Spiritual Advisors	12	4.1%	4.8%

Table 9 (continued)

Last Statement Theme	N	% of Valid Cases (N = 292)	% of Statements Given (N = 251)
Gratitude to Criminal Justice Staff	10	3.4%	4.0%
Wish to Turn Back Time	9	3.1%	3.6%
Gratitude to Lawyers	9	3.1%	3.6%
Asks for Forgiveness from Own Family/Friends	8	2.7%	3.2%
Acceptance of Responsibility for Other Bad Acts or Crimes	8	2.7%	3.2%
Wish that Execution Brings Justice	2	0.7%	0.8%
Apology to God or Other Deity	2	0.7%	0.8%
Non-Restorative	**53**	**18.2%**	**21.1%**
Claim of Innocence	40	13.7%	15.9%
Condemns CJ System or Government in General	16	5.5%	6.4%
Anger or Resentment Toward CJ Officials/CJ System	16	5.5%	6.4%
Externalize Blame	13	4.5%	5.2%
Condemns Police/CJ Officials	11	3.8%	4.4%
Minimize/Rationalize Actions or Agency	8	2.7%	3.2%
Death Penalty Only Creates More Victims	7	2.4%	2.8%
Helplessness	7	2.4%	2.8%
Condemns Co-Victim(s)/Victim(s)	6	2.1%	2.4%
Anger or Resentment Toward Own Lawyers	5	1.7%	2.0%
Anger or Resentment Toward Witnesses at Trial	4	1.4%	1.6%
Anger or Resentment Toward Co-Victims	3	1.0%	1.2%
Death Penalty is Inhumane	2	0.7%	0.8%

Table 10
Restorative and Non-Restorative Last Statement Themes by Characteristics of the Condemned

		% within Characteristic Category	
Characteristic	N	Restorative	Non-Restorative
Total Sample	292	74.0%	18.2%
Sex			
Male	290	74.1	18.3
Female	2	50.0	0.0
Race			
White	151	73.5	20.5
Black	98	75.5	17.3
Hispanic	41	73.2	12.2
Education			
High School or GED	122	74.6	16.4
Less than High School	155	74.2	20.6
Age at Time of Crime			
Under 18	9	88.9	33.3
18-24	119	77.3	14.3
25-34	106	75.5	21.7
35 or Older	53	62.3*	17.0
Age at Time of Execution			
24-34	95	78.9	12.6
35-44	131	75.6	20.6
45 or Older	66	63.6*	21.2
Evidence of MR?			
Yes	3	66.7	66.7
No	289	74.0	17.6
Texas Native?			
Yes	166	72.9	21.7*
No	101	74.3	12.9
Foreign National?			
Yes	6	66.7	0.0
No	286	74.1	18.5
Prior Prison Record			
Yes	157	73.9	18.5
No	119	74.8	20.2

*Significant at $p < .10$

**Significant at $p < .05$

Table 11
Restorative and Non-Restorative Last Statement Themes by Characteristics of the Offense

		% within Characteristic Category	
Characteristic	N	Restorative	Non-Restorative
Total Sample	292	74.0%	18.2%
Codefendant(s)?			
Yes	125	72.0	17.6
No	159	75.5	19.5
Related to Victim?			
Yes	30	66.7	26.7
No	262	74.8	17.2
Victim a Police Officer?			
Yes	22	81.8	31.8*
No	270	73.3	17.0
Multiple Victims?			
Yes	73	69.9	19.2
No	219	75.3	17.8
Race of Victim(s)†			
White	277	72.2	19.9
Black	39	76.9	12.8
Hispanic	35	80.0	14.3
Sex of Victim(s)†			
Male	184	78.3	20.1
Female	179	68.2	16.2
Murder in the Act of a Felony?			
Yes	229	74.7	16.2*
No	63	71.4	25.4
Concurrent Offense			
Yes	242	74.8	16.5
No	50	70.0	26.0

† These are multiple response variables. Due to multiple victims in some cases, their sum is larger than total number of cases.

* Significant at $p < .10$

** Significant at $p < .05$

Table 12
Restorative and Non-Restorative Last Statement Themes by Characteristics of the Execution

		% within Characteristic Category	
Characteristic	N	Restorative	Non-Restorative
Total Sample	292	74.0%	18.2%
Witnesses for Condemned?			
Yes	226	77.9**	17.7
No	53	58.5	18.9
Witnesses for Victim Allowed?			
Yes	212	72.6	17.5
No	80	77.5	20.0
Witnesses for Victim?			
Yes	153	73.2	19.6
No	129	76.0	16.3
Volunteer?			
Yes	20	65.0	10.0
No	272	74.6	18.8
Victim-Offender Mediation			
Yes	3	66.7	33.3
No	286	74.1	18.2
Requested by Co-Victim; Denied by Condemned	2	50.0	0.0
Requested by Condemned; Denied by Co-Victim or TDCJ Officials	1	100.0	0.0
Prior VIS?			
Pre-Payne	219	74.9	18.3
Post-Payne	73	71.2	17.8
Time Period of Execution			
1982-1989	28	85.7	14.3
1990-1995	52	73.1	23.1
1996-2000	130	73.1	15.4
2001-2004	82	72.0	20.7

*Significant at $p < .10$

**Significant at $p < .05$

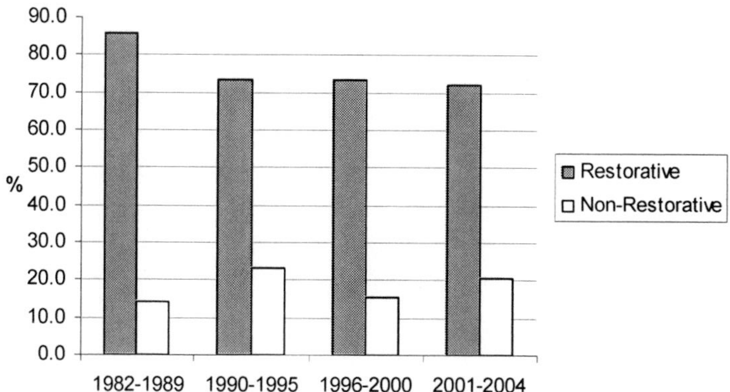

Figure 2. **Restorative and Non-Restorative Last Statements of the Condemned by Time Period during Which the Execution was Carried Out.**

CONCLUSION

By reproducing and analyzing the last statements of the condemned in this chapter, it is my hope that the voices of these men and women resonate with the reader. The diversity and depth of these statements are overwhelming, but the humanity at their core is rather simple and clear. By "giving voice" to the condemned, I have shed light on this humanity—humanity asserted against a backdrop of violence and dehumanization. In reclaiming humanity at the point of death, the condemned often seeks to transcend this defiled life. This leaves us to wonder: How might these individuals have achieved such transcendence or transformation in life rather than death? Perhaps some of the answers are there in their statements. The overwhelmingly restorative nature of the sentiments expressed in these last statements offers some hope for change and transformation.

CHAPTER VII:

Co-Victim Statements

Offering an important and intriguing counterpart to the last statements of the condemned, statements made by the condemned's co-victims at the time of execution were gathered from the local newspaper (*The Huntsville Item*) stories on each execution. Much as with the last statements of the condemned, the objective here is to "give voice" to a population whose voice often goes unheard. In this chapter the focus turns to those who have been victimized by the acts of the condemned—the co-victims of capital murder. Just as the perspectives and thoughts of condemned inmates were gleaned from their last statements, so can thoughts and perspectives of co-victims be gleaned from the statements they make at the time of execution. Toward this end, the major themes of these statements are examined primarily qualitatively and descriptively. First, the major themes are identified and discussed at length, offering examples from the actual statements. Then, these themes are examined in the context of the offender, offense and execution characteristics previously examined in relation to the last statements of the condemned. Finally, an analysis of the restorative nature of co-victim statements is conducted. It is the hope of the researcher that this analysis will not only shed light on the thoughts and perspectives of this all-too-often neglected population, but will also offer a salient counterpart to the last statements of the condemned.[36]

Of the 321 executions included in this study, co-victim statements were present for 159 (49.5%) of them. As can be seen in Table 13, the majority of co-victim statements were given by immediate family members with mothers by far being the most likely to give a statement

[36] Portions of this chapter were previously published in the journal *Violence and Victims* (See Vollum & Longmire, 2007).

and be quoted. However, statements did come from a wide variety of family members and friends.

Table 13
Co-Victim Statements at the Time of Execution: Relationship to Victim

	# of Statements	% of All Statements (N = 253)	% of Cases With Statements (N = 159)
Mother	46	18.2%	28.9%
Brother	27	10.7%	17.0%
Father	26	10.3%	16.4%
Sister	25	9.9%	15.7%
Son	21	8.3%	13.2%
Daughter	18	7.1%	11.3%
Wife	14	5.5%	8.8%
Collective Family Statement	12	4.7%	7.5%
Husband	8	3.2%	5.0%
Survivor, Not related	6	2.4%	3.8%
Niece	6	2.4%	3.8%
Friend	6	2.4%	3.8%
Uncle	5	2.0%	3.1%
Co-worker	5	2.0%	3.1%
Cousin	4	1.6%	2.5%
Aunt	4	1.6%	2.5%
Step-son	2	0.8%	1.3%
Nephew	2	0.8%	1.3%
Granddaughter	2	0.8%	1.3%
Friend of Co-victim	2	0.8%	1.3%
Brother-in-law	2	0.8%	1.3%
Unspecified Family Member	1	0.4%	0.6%
Step-mother	1	0.4%	0.6%
Step-father	1	0.4%	0.6%
Step-daughter	1	0.4%	0.6%
Step-brother	1	0.4%	0.6%
Sister-in-law	1	0.4%	0.6%
Grandmother	1	0.4%	0.6%
Grandfather	1	0.4%	0.6%
Fiance or other partner	1	0.4%	0.6%
Daughter-in-law	1	0.4%	0.6%

MAJOR THEMES

As with the last statements of the condemned, statements made by co-victims at the time of execution express a wide variety of sentiments and perspectives. With the diversity of messages among these statements comes some very interesting insight into what executions and the death penalty mean to co-victims. As with the major themes, there is much diversity and contrast in this meaning. Upon examining the words of co-victims in this context, one is struck by the divergent and sometimes conflicting messages expressed in these statements.

Open coding was again used in examining and categorizing the major themes found among co-victim statements. Ten major thematic categories of statements were identified and examined. These major (primary) themes were each composed of more specific statement themes (secondary themes), sometimes even containing divergent or contrasting sub-themes. For example, under the major thematic category of "Healing and Closure," there are the divergent statement themes of "Brought Healing and Closure" and "Did Not Bring Healing and Closure." For subsequent analyses, it is these broad sub-themes which are the point of analysis (as they represent a more singular conceptual theme). The original open coding process yielded 58 specific secondary themes (See Appendix B), several of which were grouped together into more meaningful specific thematic categories for the sake of these analyses.

Table 14 presents each of these statement themes, broken down into categories and sub-categories, and the percentages of cases and statements in which they were found. The first column of percentages presents percentages of the total number of valid cases (cases in which copies of *The Huntsville Item* were obtained[37]). The second column presents percentages of the total number of cases in which statements were actually found. Because the researcher cannot confidently conclude that a lack of statement found in *The Huntsville Item* equates to "no statement," and thus a null response on the identified themes, the total number of cases in which a statement was given (159) was determined to be a more appropriate base. The simple fact of not finding a statement in *The Huntsville Item* does not equate to an absence of any given identified theme. Rather, it is unknown as to

[37] Although there are 321 cases included in this study, there was one case in which no copies of *The Huntsville Item* were available for the dates surrounding the execution. Therefore, the researcher has determined this case to be missing in regard to co-victim statements leaving 320 valid cases.

whether the co-victim(s) made any such statements to other sources, media or otherwise. Therefore, the total number of cases in which statements were given (159) is used as the primary base for percentages in analyses here and throughout the chapter. For descriptive purposes, however, both are presented in Table 14.

Healing and Closure

In a strong majority of cases (72.3%), healing and closure were focal points of co-victim statements. In 40.9% of cases, the co-victim indicated that the execution brought some form of healing or closure. Although in only a very few cases did co-victims state that the execution brought them actual closure (2.5%, or 4 cases), it was common to observe themes related to such closure and the broader notion of healing. For example, in 22.6% of the cases, co-victims indicated that the execution was a form of conclusion, usually referring to it as a conclusion to a particularly difficult and traumatizing time in their lives:

> *I guess we're just glad to have this part over.* (Victim's husband in case of Earl Heiselbetz, #200).[38]

Often the conclusion was depicted as the closing or end of a chapter in the co-victims' lives:

> *This is a time of closing a chapter in my life and the lives of other victims of murdered children.* (Victim's father in case of Ricky McGinn, #232).[39]

---

[38] Lyons, M. C. (2000, January 13). Texas executes first inmate of the year for 1991 murder. *The Huntsville Item*, pp. 1A, 3A.

[39] Lyons, M. C. (2000, September 28). Man executed after DNA tests find him guilty. *The Huntsville Item*, p. 1A.

Table 14
Co-Victim Statements at the Time of Execution: Major Themes

Co-Victim Statement Theme	N	% of Total Valid Cases (N=320)	% of Cases in Which Statements Given (N=159)
Healing and Closure	**115**	**35.9%**	**72.3%**
Brought Healing or Closure	*65*	*20.3%*	*40.9%*
Conclusion	36	11.3%	22.6%
Peace and/or Relief	27	8.4%	17.0%
Beginning	16	5.0%	10.1%
No More Appeals, Trials, or Hearings	13	4.1%	8.2%
Closure	4	1.3%	2.5%
Did Not Bring Healing or Closure	*46*	*14.4%*	*28.9%*
No Healing or Closure	32	10.0%	20.1%
Won't Bring Victim Back	20	6.3%	12.6%
Execution was Traumatizing	6	1.9%	3.8%
Already Experienced Prior Reconciliation	8	2.5%	5.0%
Satisfaction/Dissatisfaction	**105**	**32.8%**	**66.0%**
Satisfied	*65*	*20.3%*	*40.9%*
Happy to be Present at Execution	25	7.8%	15.7%
Satisfaction with Death	24	7.5%	15.1%
Looking/Looked Forward to Execution	18	5.6%	11.3%
Gratitude to State of Texas/CJ System	12	3.8%	7.5%
Grateful for Apology	12	3.8%	7.5%
General Satisfaction with Last Statement of Condemned	2	0.6%	1.3%
Dissatisfied	*76*	*23.8%*	*47.8%*
Delay/Length of Time	41	12.8%	25.8%
Related to Condemned	39	12.2%	24.5%
With Execution Itself	13	4.1%	8.2%
Media	2	0.6%	1.3%

Table 14 (continued)

Co-Victim Statement Theme	N	% of Total Valid Cases (N=320)	% of Cases in Which Statements Given (N=159)
Justice/Revenge	**98**	**30.6%**	**61.6%**
Justice for Society	36	11.3%	22.6%
Just Deserts	36	11.3%	22.6%
Comparison of Suffering of Victim & Condemned	29	9.1%	18.2%
Execution Not Harsh Enough	28	8.8%	17.6%
Justice for Victim	19	5.9%	11.9%
Desire to See or Inflict Suffering or Harm	15	4.7%	9.4%
Memorialize/Honor Victim	**53**	**16.6%**	**33.3%**
Speaks to Qualities of Victim	26	8.1%	16.4%
Memorializes or Honors Victim	23	7.2%	14.5%
Wishes Peace/Release for Deceased Victim	11	3.4%	6.9%
Reference (Specific) to Victim's Murder	7	2.2%	4.4%
Removal of Condemned	**43**	**13.4%**	**27.0%**
No Longer Presents Threat to Others/Society	30	9.4%	18.9%
No Longer Presents Threat to Co-Victim(s)	11	3.4%	6.9%
Extermination	11	3.4%	6.9%
Forgiveness	**41**	**12.8%**	**25.8%**
No Forgiveness	*23*	*7.2%*	*14.5%*
Does Not Forgive Condemned	13	4.1%	8.2%
Rejects Condemned's Apology	12	3.8%	7.5%
Forgives Condemned	19	5.9%	11.9%

Table 14 (continued)

Co-Victim Statement Theme	N	% of Total Valid Cases (N=320)	% of Cases in Which Statements Given (N=159)
Sympathy	**36**	**11.3%**	**22.6%**
Sympathy for Condemned's Family	22	6.9%	13.8%
Sympathy for Condemned	14	4.4%	8.8%
Prayer for Condemned	6	1.9%	3.8%
Prayer for Condemned's Family	3	0.9%	1.9%
Rationalization	**29**	**9.1%**	**18.2%**
Dehumanization of Condemned	17	5.3%	10.7%
Denial of Personal Malevolence	10	3.1%	6.3%
Disparages Condemned	9	2.8%	5.7%
Death Penalty Support/Opposition	**24**	**7.5%**	**15.1%**
Support of Death Penalty	*16*	*5.0%*	*10.1%*
General/Abstract Death Penalty Support	9	2.8%	5.7%
Criticism of Death Penalty Protestors	7	2.2%	4.4%
Personalized Death Penalty Support	3	0.9%	1.9%
Opposition of Death Penalty	*8*	*2.5%*	*5.0%*
Opposition of Death Penalty or Execution	7	2.2%	4.4%
Death Penalty Doesn't Solve Anything	2	0.6%	1.3%
Religion	**22**	**6.9%**	**13.8%**
Proclamation of Faith	9	2.8%	5.7%
God's Judgment	7	2.2%	4.4%
Prayer for Condemned	6	1.9%	3.8%
Prayer for Victim(s)/Co-Victim(s)	4	1.3%	2.5%
Prayer for Family of Condemned	3	0.9%	1.9%
Death Penalty in the Bible	3	0.9%	1.9%

Another father referred to the execution of his daughter's killer as "the end of a long road" (Victim's Father in case of Jermarr Arnold, #258[40]). In a similar manner, some co-victims depicted the execution as a beginning to a new phase in their lives, often referring to moving forward or getting on with their lives:

> *And now the family can get on with our lives and know that my brother is resting in peace. We can all be happy once again.* (Victim's sister in case of Larry Smith, #17).[41]

These messages of conclusion and beginning were often presented without further qualification that might indicate any actual psychic closure or healing, but in some cases were accompanied by such sentiments:

> *We are here together as a family, not in celebration, but as a closing to a horrible chapter in our lives. Perhaps, and only perhaps, this phase of justice will hopefully remove the scab of pain as we move toward the final steps of healing.* (Victim's daughter in case of John Burks, #220).[42]

The lack of real psychic or emotional closure is best represented in the following, seemingly paradoxical, co-victim statement:

> *It's not going to bring closure as far as inside me, but it does bring closure.* (Victim's daughter in case of Glen McGinnis, #205).[43]

It was more likely that themes of conclusion or beginning were accompanied by references to the lengthy wait for execution while having to experience appeals, hearings and sometimes new trials for the

---

[40] Bell, D. (2002, January 17). Inmate executed for jewelry store killing. *The Huntsville Item*, p. 3A.

[41] Sister: Execution brings peace. (1986, August 22). *The Huntsville Item*, p. 1A.

[42] Lyons, M. C. (2000, June 15). Inmate executed for 1989 slaying. *The Huntsville Item*, p. 7A.

[43] Lyons, M. C. (2000, January 26). Inmate executed for gun slaying. *The Huntsville Item*, p. 7A.

person who killed their loved one. Referring to the impact such a lengthy process of appeals and hearings has on co-victims, one co-victim put it this way:

> *You're trying to move on with your life but you keep being dragged back into it…[t]he one positive about this…is that we can move on. We can go on with our lives and not have to worry about what tomorrow will bring.* (Victim's daughter in case of Stacey Lawton, #235).

Clearly, the process that follows a capital murder and death sentence takes its toll on co-victims. In 8.2% of cases, co-victims commented that they were glad there would be no more trials, hearings or appeals.

Although co-victims rarely indicated that they experienced closure from the execution, they did often (in 17% of the cases) express feelings of peace or relief:

> *Tonight, we have finally obtained peace.* (Victim's family's statement in case of Randall Hafdahl, Sr., #250).[44]

> *I didn't know that I would feel this relief. I really didn't know. It was not just because of the death of another human being, but that now there is some hope in this society for victims.* (Victim's mother in case of Charlie Brooks, Jr., #1).[45]

Although a substantial proportion of co-victims' statements include messages of healing or closure, these messages are usually in reference to the transitional aspect of executions—that the execution simply represents a temporal marker in a long road of trauma and grief. The messages in this regard were much more likely to be related to the simple fact that a part or one stage of a difficult and tragic set of circumstances was either coming to an end or beginning. What was, for the most part, missing from these messages was a sense of real psychic or emotional healing and closure.

In contrast to those expressing healing or closure, a substantial proportion of co-victims (in 28.9% of cases) indicated that the

---

[44] Bell, D. (2002, February 1). Hafdahl executed for 1985 slaying. *The Huntsville Item*, p. 5A.

[45] Victim's widow, mother are relieved. (1982, December 8). *The Huntsville Item,* p. 1A.

execution did not provide healing or closure and in some cases impeded it. In 20.1% of cases, co-victims explicitly stated that the execution did not bring healing or closure:

> *This is not really closure to an event...we still have to deal with this daily.* (Victim's son in case of Javier Cruz, #159).[46]

> *I wouldn't want to call it relief...[n]othing can ever ease that pain completely.* (Victim's mother in case of Ricky Blackmon, #181).[47]

In some cases this sentiment was accompanied by alternative justifications for the execution in spite of the lack of closure:

> *There will be no closure, but we thank God that the individual was taken off the street where he can't do this again. The main thing is that it was over and done.* (Victim's brother in case of Gerald Tigner, #262).[48]

In 12.6% of cases, co-victims referred to the fact that the execution would not bring back the victim:

> *This execution tonight will do nothing to restore our family as it was with her love, her laughter, her caring support for each of us and her joy in it.* (Victim's family's statement in case of Charles Boyd, #182).[49]

Some co-victims (3.8% of cases) even indicated that the execution would impede their healing, just further adding to their trauma:

---

[46] Lyons, M.C. (1998, October 2). Cruz executed for '91 murders. *The Huntsville Item*, p. 1A.

[47] Gideon, L. (1999, August 5). Blackmon executed, asked people to view Internet site, *The Huntsville Item*, p. 3A.

[48] Bell, D. (2002, April 8). Waco man put to death for killings, *The Huntsville Item*, p. 3A.

[49] Gideon, L. (1999, August 6). Boyd denies committing crime, *The Huntsville Item*, p. 3A.

> *Killing Kenneth Brock will not ease my suffering or my wife's suffering ...[t]wo wrongs don't make a right. I could not be at peace if Kenneth Brock dies.* (Victim's father in case of Kenneth Brock, #15).[50]

It is clear that there exists some ambivalence among co-victims in regard to the execution of the person responsible for their loss. Although many co-victims express a sense of transition in regard to the execution, they rarely express a true sense of emotional catharsis or what would often be considered personal healing or closure. Instead, the focus tends to be on relief that a difficult time and process has come to an end or can be put behind the co-victims. Additionally, co-victims tend to identify alternative instrumental connotations of the execution in lieu of the more emotionally-oriented healing and closure often sought for co-victims. Although a very large proportion of co-victim statements mention healing and closure (whether regarding the presence of it, presence of some form of it, or the absence of it), very few indicate that the execution provided such an emotional catharsis for them.

Satisfaction/Dissatisfaction

The second most common focus among co-victim statements was on the co-victims' satisfaction with the execution (66% of cases in which co-victim statements were given). Co-victims were more likely to express dissatisfaction (47.8% of cases) than satisfaction (40.9% of cases). At first glance this may seem somewhat surprising given that the sample of statements is biased toward those who were more likely to be present at the execution and/or available to the press for comments. As previously mentioned, it would be expected that this sample would be more inclined to support the execution of the condemned and be pleased that it is being carried out (see Gross & Matheson, 2003). Indeed, the dissatisfaction does not appear to be in regard to the fact that the condemned is being executed but that the death penalty system and execution does not live up to the co-victims' expectations or standards.

The most commonly expressed point of dissatisfaction was in regard to the length of time between the conviction and the execution.

---

[50] Convicted killer awaits execution on Thursday. (1986, June 18). *The Huntsville Item*, p. 1A.

As previously mentioned, in Texas condemned inmates spend an average of just over ten years on death row before being executed. In 25.8% of cases, co-victims pointed to the length of time they had to wait before the condemned was executed as frustrating and dissatisfying:

> *Cooks needed killing and it took the state almost 14 years to do it. That's too long.* (Victim's friend in case of Vincent Cooks, #256).[51]

> *Justice has been delayed, you bet. Our system provides for Checks and balances which take a lot of time and although that time is painful, it really is appropriate. That takes four or five years. In our case, there's another 12 that should never have happened.* (Victim's father in case of James Russell, #41).[52]

> *I resent the fact that he got so many chances. He's been in prison for killing her for 15 years. I resent it when someone gets all those chances, one after another after another.* (Victim's mother in case of Robert West, Jr., #132).[53]

It's important to note that in many of these cases, the co-victim did express satisfaction that the execution was carried out but dissatisfaction that it took so long. However, it was not always clear whether the satisfaction came from the execution itself or from the end of the lengthy process during which the co-victim may have had to "re-live" the traumatic event over and over again. It was clear that the latter was present in a majority of statements, but it was not clear in most of these cases as to whether the execution provided satisfaction or catharsis outside of this context.

Dissatisfaction with the execution also frequently focused on factors specifically related to the condemned (24.5% of cases), usually

---

[51] Bell, D. (2001, December 13). Execution numbers down in 2001. *The Huntsville Item*, p. 5A.

[52] No stay expected in Russell execution. (1991, September 19). *The Huntsville Item*, p. 1A.

[53] Duncan, T. (1997, July 30). Killer apologizes before execution. *The Huntsville Item*, pp. 1A, 8A.

in regard to his last statement or demeanor at the execution. Co-victims often expressed disappointment stemming from the condemned's last statement. This included factors such as a lack of remorse or apology, lack of acknowledgment of co-victims or a claim of innocence:

> *It would have meant a world of difference. It would have made it a little bit lighter on me, but he didn't say he was sorry.* (Victim's uncle in case of James Davis, #133).[54]

> *I think we felt cheated. We were cheated out of any remorse or any kind of admission.* (Victim's niece in case of Andrew Cantu, #170).[55]

> *I think we all wanted to hear an apology. We deserved it.* (Victim's mother in case of Jessy San Miguel, #223).[56]

> *I think he should have acknowledged me, but he never did during the trial, so I did not expect it.* (Victim's wife in case of Cedric Ransom, #308).[57]

Co-victims who attend the execution seem to have certain expectations regarding the interaction that will occur between them and the condemned. However, the condemned is not obliged to conform to these expectations and when he doesn't, co-victims may be left dissatisfied with the experience.

In 8.2% of the cases, co-victims expressed a lack of satisfaction with the execution itself, often simply indicating that they received no joy or pleasure from the execution:

> *You don't get a big charge of satisfaction. There's no pleasure in this.* (Victim's son in case of Javier Cruz, #159).[58]

---

[54] Duncan, T. (1997, September 10). Defiant inmate executed. *The Huntsville Item*, pp. 1A, 7A.

[55] Gideon, L. (1999, February 17). Cantu dies for triple murder. *The Huntsville Item*, pp. 1A, 7A.

[56] Lyons, M.C. (2000, June 30). Inmate put to death for 1991 killing. *The Huntsville Item*, p. 3A.

[57] Lacy, B. (2003, July 24). Fort Worth man executed for killing gun dealer. *The Huntsville Item*, p. 3A.

> *He's a victim of our society--our failures. When we get to this point where we have to execute somebody, we have failed as a society. I saw him as a human being. Secondly, not only did I see him as a human being, but he looked like me and how can I take pleasure in watching the death of someone who looks like me?* (Victim's brother in case of Emerson Rudd, #255).[59]

In some cases, the co-victims' statements went further, lambasting the execution as malignant or wrong:

> *It's a total farce as far as the justice system is concerned. She was a perfect example of how rehabilitation in the penal system is supposed to work. And what did they do? They executed her. What I witnessed today was an atrocity.* (Victim's brother in case of Karla Faye Tucker, #145).[60]

Although co-victims expressed some level of dissatisfaction in nearly half of the cases, a substantial proportion (in 40.9% of cases) also expressed satisfaction. The most common themes of satisfaction were expressions of happiness to be present at the execution and general satisfaction with the death of the condemned (15.7% and 15.1% of cases, respectively):

> *I needed to be here because of what he did to my daughter. It's not the same pain my daughter went through but to see him take his last breath made me feel better.* (Victim's mother in case of Jack Clark, #240).[61]

---

[58] Lyons, M.C. (1998, October 2). Cruz executed for '91 murders. *The Huntsville Item,* p. 1A.

[59] Lyons, M.C. (2001, November 16). Rudd becomes 16th Texas inmate executed this year. *The Huntsville Item*, p. 3A.

[60] The execution of Karla Faye Tucker. (1998, February 4). *The Huntsville Item*, p. 4A.

[61] Lyons, M.C. (2001, January 10) Lubbock man put to death in Texas' first execution of 2001. *The Huntsville Item*, p. 1A.

> *I would go to the end of the earth to see this end.* (Victim's father in case of Rex Mays, #283).[62]

> *I wanted to see him pay for what he did to my daughter.* (Victim's mother in case of Larry Hayes, #310).[63]

> *It made me feel good, real good.* (Victim's uncle in case of Edward Lagrone, #318).[64]

> *I wanted him to see me. I wanted him to see me there. I'm glad I was there.* (Victim's mother in case of Robert West, Jr., #132).[65]

> *[I]t is a satisfaction to see it has finally been taken care of.* (Victim's father in case of Excell White, #173).[66]

Other co-victims indicated that they had been looking forward to the execution, sometimes referring to the interval of time during which the co-victim(s) awaited the execution with anticipation:

> *I've seen him die many times in my dreams, and it was exactly what I expected. I have lived for this moment. I hope he was terrified as they were strapping him down. I've counted every hour.* (Wife and mother of victims in case of Robert Madden, #123).[67]

---

[62] Passwaters, M. (2002, September 25). Man executed for double murder. *The Huntsville Item*, p. 3A.

[63] Lindblade, T. (2003, September 11). Conroe man executed for 1999 killings. *The Huntsville Item*, p. 5A.

[64] Rowe, T. (2004, February 12). Fort Worth man executed for killing pregnant 10-year-old. *The Huntsville Item*, p. 3A.

[65] Duncan, T. (1997, July 30). Killer apologizes before execution. *The Huntsville Item*, pp. 1A, 8A.

[66] Gideon, L. (1999, March 31). Quarter-century on death row ends for White. *The Huntsville Item*, p. 9A.

[67] Jackson, J. (1997, May 29). Murderer executed for father/son killing. *The Huntsville Item*, pp. 1A, 5A.

> *I've waited half my life for this.* (Victim's daughter in case of James Richardson, #215).[68]

> *I was looking forward to it, as any family member should...I went through eight years to get here.* (Victim's brother in case of Jeffrey Williams, #274).[69]

These messages reaffirm the previous notion of apparent trauma and grief caused by the time period between the murder and the execution (previously identified as a source of dissatisfaction). Just the very notion of looking forward to an execution or even seeing it "many times in my dreams" suggests some extension of grief and suffering during this interval. At the least, it appears to potentially interfere with normal grieving and healing processes.

Other statements indicating co-victim satisfaction were expressed as gratitude. In 7.5% of cases, co-victims thanked either the criminal justice system or the state of Texas for having the death penalty or carrying out the execution:

> *I want to take this opportunity to thank everyone who had a part in bringing this man to justice. I wanted to show support for law enforcement, for the death penalty, for the system.* (Victim's father in case of David Holland, #64).[70]

> *I believe in the death penalty and I'm going to tell you right now, thank God for George Bush.* (Victim's mother in case of Garry Miller, #237).[71]

In some cases, co-victims thanked the Texas criminal justice system for their support of victims:

---

[68] Lyons, M.C. (2000, May 24). Texas executes man for robbery, fatal shooting. *The Huntsville Item*, p. 7A.

[69] Passwaters, M. (2002, June 27). Williams executed for 1994 killing of Houston woman. *The Huntsville Item*, p. 5A.

[70] LeFebvre, J. (1993, August 12). Victim's family expressing relief after man executed. *The Huntsville Item*, p. 1A.

[71] Lyons, M.C. (2000, December 6). 38th execution this year sets record. *The Huntsville Item*, pp. 1A, 12A.

> *We are grateful for the support of our friends and families, the community and the Texas Department of Criminal Justice victim services division.* (Victim's family's statement in case of Larry Robison, #203).[72]

Other messages of gratitude were directed toward an apology made by the condemned in his or her last statement (7.5% of cases). In these cases, the co-victim was comforted by the condemned's expression of remorse and grateful for it:

> *I'm glad to hear Mr. Goss say what he said because I needed to hear that. I'm glad to see that he apologized...*(Victim's son in case of Cornelius Goss, #207).[73]

> *I was very thankful that he apologized. He had never given any indication he would do so. I do appreciate him doing that.* (Victim's wife in case of T.J. Jones, #276).[74]

As was the case with messages related to healing and closure, there appears to be some ambivalence among co-victims in regard to satisfaction with the death penalty and executions. In fact, in 29.2% of the cases in which co-victims indicated that they were satisfied with the execution, they also simultaneously indicated some level of dissatisfaction. The meaning of the death penalty and execution for co-victims, if we are to judge from statements regarding satisfaction and healing or closure, is complex and often conflicting.

Justice and Revenge

Co-victims tend to be a bit less equivocal when it comes to their sentiments about justice and revenge. In 61.6% of cases, co-victims made statements associated with justice or revenge. The most common themes of justice were general statements about executions or the death

---

[72] Towery, A. (2000, January 22). Inmate dies by injection amid protests. *The Huntsville Item*, p. 3A.

[73] Lyons, M.C. (2000, February 24). Inmate dies for killing Dallas man. *The Huntsville Item*, p. 3A.

[74] Passwaters, M. (2002, August 9). Victim apologizes for 1994 murder before being executed. *The Huntsville Item*, p. 3A.

penalty representing a broad sense of justice for society (22.6% of cases) or "just deserts" or equitably deserved punishment for the crime (22.6% of cases). The former often referred to "justice being done" or "justice being served:"

> *This was justice in a big way. Believe me, it was served in a big way tonight.* (Victims' mother in case of Leo Jenkins, #105).[75]

The latter sometimes referred to the common "eye for an eye" call for retributive justice but more generally related to the condemned getting what he deserved or paying for his crime:

> *I feel like he was paying for a crime he committed. If you do wrong, I am a firm believer that you have to be punished.* (Victim's aunt in case of James Davis, #133).[76]

In some cases both themes were present:

> *Justice is being done. He should go ahead and die. That is what he rightfully deserves.* (Victim's sister in case of Richard Andrade, #20).[77]

In 11.9% of cases, co-victims made similar statements regarding justice but specified that the execution provided justice for the victim.

Justice was certainly an important theme among co-victim statements. In many cases, the death penalty served this end. In other cases, the reaction of co-victims was a more visceral one—one of revenge. And, in yet other cases, executions were not enough to satisfy desires for justice or revenge. In a substantial proportion of cases, co-victims expressed the feeling that the death penalty and/or execution were not enough to satisfy their desire for justice or revenge. In 18.2% of the cases, co-victims made a direct comparison between the death of

---

[75] Jackson, J. (1996, February 10). Victims' mom says witnessing "was easy." *The Huntsville Item*, pp. 1A, 3A.

[76] Duncan, T. (1997, September 10). Defiant inmate executed. *The Huntsville Item*, pp. 1A, 7A.

[77] Graczyk, M.L. (1986, December 18). Victim's dream turned to tragedy with murder. *The Huntsville Item*, pp. 1A, 8A.

the condemned and the death of the victim, usually referring to the fact that the condemned suffered no where near as much as the victim did:

> *Lethal injection is a luxury that Martin Vega did not extend to his victims who died in pain, helplessness and fear as they took their last breaths.* (Victim's brother in case of Martin Vega, #167).[78]

> *He did not die with multiple skull fractures and a butcher knife through his heart as did my mother. His punishment was much less painful.* (Victim's daughter in case of Joseph Faulder, #178).[79]

The related message that the execution was not harsh enough or should have been more painful was present in 17.6% of cases:

> *I'm going to say it like this: If a guy set out to kill the way he did, he shouldn't die that easy.* (Victim's brother in case of Jeffrey Williams, #274).[80]

> *It was still a little bit too humane for me after what I watched him do.* (Surviving victim in case of David Herman, #110).[81]

Finally, in 9.4% of cases, co-victims went even further, indicating that they desired to see or even directly inflict more suffering and harm on the condemned, in some cases referring to other methods of execution (whether actual past methods or imaginary proposed methods):

> *Mr. Powell should be thankful he has gone so quietly into the night. Were I to have had the opportunity, his due process*

---

[78] Gideon, L. (1999, January 27). Vega claims innocence until his final breath. *The Huntsville Item*, p. 6A.

[79] Gideon, L. (1999, June 18). Faulder executed for 1975 killing. *The Huntsville Item,* pp. 1A, 5A.

[80] Passwaters, M. (2002, June 27). Williams executed for 1994 killing of Houston woman. *The Huntsville Item*, p. 5A.

[81] Jackson, J. (1997, April 3). Family members, witnesses have mixed reactions to execution. *The Huntsville Item*, p. 5A.

> *would have been very unpleasant indeed.* (Victim's father in case of James Powell, #285).[82]
>
> *It was too easy. I would at least like to watch a little more, even if it's the IV starting. It was too long to wait for a moment. Yes, I wanted to see him suffer.* (Victim's mother in case of Gerald Casey, #265).[83]
>
> *He should have been staked down to a fire ant bed, as far as I'm concerned, for two or three days and let them eat away at him until he died.* (Victim's brother in case of Excell White, #173).[84]
>
> *I thought that there should have been more suffering. The electric chair would have been nice enough for me.* (Victim's step-brother in case of Steven Renfro, #146).[85]

As these statements make clear, the hurt and anger in the wake of a tragic loss of a loved one to murder, even after many years, are powerful and often accompanied by overwhelming desires for revenge. Given the apparent length of time in which such emotions have persisted, one must wonder what else could be done during that interval to help such co-victims move forward toward healing. One also wonders what role, if any, the death penalty process and execution (whether looming and anticipated or actually carried out) play in perpetuating or extending these emotions.

Memorializing or Honoring Victim

In 33.3% of the cases, co-victims made specific references to the victim, usually in an attempt to memorialize, honor or otherwise

---

[82] Passwaters, M. (2002, October 2). Man executed for 1990 rape, murder of 10-year-old. *The Huntsville Item*, p. 3A.

[83] Passwaters, M. (2002, April 19). Montgomery County man executed for 1989 murder. *The Huntsville Item*, pp. 1A, 6A.

[84] Gideon, L. (1999, March 31). Quarter-century on Death Row ends for White. *The Huntsville Item*, p. 9A.

[85] Gideon, L. (1998, February 10). Execution sees smaller crowd. *The Huntsville Item*, pp. 1A, 7A.

remember them and their qualities. In 16.4% of cases, co-victims recollected the good qualities of the victim and highlighted what was lost in the victim's tragic death:

> *She was not just a woman, but a lady. She was almost an innocent, and her biggest adventure in a week was probably ladies bible class.* (Victim's family's statement in case of Joe Trevino, Jr., #185).[86]

> *She was on call 24 hours a day. She was a shoulder to cry on, somebody to listen to. She gave Christian advice. Now, it's just thinking about the nice things. It's something I deal with every day. There's not a day I don't think about her.* (Victim's daughter in case of Jeffery Barney, #12).[87]

> *Our mother and father were beloved, healthy, energetic people, looking forward after years of hard work to their retirement to travel together, to see the weddings of their grandchildren and the long-awaited births of their great-grandchildren. They were deprived of this and we have been deprived of them.* (Victim's family's statement in case of John Thompson, #25).[88]

> *This victim was someone's daughter, someone's mother, someone's wife and someone's sister. This victim was a beautiful person with an artistic soul. This victim never got the chance to see her small boy grow into the wonderful young man he is today. This victim never got the chance to be the great, fun-loving aunt we all know she would have been. This victim never got the chance to paint any more pictures, take any more photographs or spend any more time with her family and friends. This victim had these and all the other things she*

---

[86] Gideon, L. (1999, August 19). Trevino dies for strangling, raping 80-year-old woman. *The Huntsville Item*, pp. 1A, 3A.

[87] Murderer's victim "didn't deserve to die." (1986, April 16). *The Huntsville Item*, pp. 1A, 9A.

[88] Spring bitter for victim's family. (1987, July 8). *The Huntsville Item*, pp. 1A, 3A.

> *loved to do brutally taken from her.* (Victim's family's statement in case of Caruthers Alexander, #242).[89]

Other co-victims more specifically memorialized the victim by claiming the execution and/or their presence at the execution as a tribute to the victim:

> *I am here out of the remembrance of my sister.* (Victim's brother in case of Pedro Muniz, #152).[90]

> *Today I am here to represent my daughter Pamela Miller who was murdered 10 years ago. May you now rest in peace my precious one, I love you still.* (Victim's mother in case of Genaro Camacho, Jr., #156).[91]

As this last example indicates, co-victims also sometimes wished peace or release for the deceased victim (6.9% of cases). In rare cases, co-victims made specific references to the details of the victim's murder.

There is apparent desire on the part of co-victims, in many cases, to reclaim the execution event in the name of the victim. From the apprehension of the murderer to the trial and subsequent appeals, to the time on death row, and ultimately to the deathwatch and execution, the process is almost solely focused on the condemned. Often, and especially from the perspective of co-victims, the victims get forgotten in this process. The words of the co-victims clearly indicate a desire (if not a need) to rectify this and to claim some part of the process on behalf of, or in memory of, the victim.

Removal of Condemned

In over a quarter of the cases (27%), the co-victims made statements about the execution being a positive form of removal of the condemned from society. In most cases the co-victims highlighted the fact that the

---

[89] Lyons, M.C. (2001, January 30). Alexander executed for killing. *The Huntsville Item*, p. 1A.

[90] Gideon, L. (1998, May 20). Victim's brother speaks at execution. *The Huntsville Item*, pp. 1A, 6A.

[91] Gideon, L. (1998, August 27). Camacho runs out of appeals. *The Huntsville Item*, pp. 1A, 8A.

condemned would no longer be a threat or future danger. This was most often stated in regard to the fact that the condemned could no longer potentially harm any others or be a threat to society, generally (18.9% of cases):

> *[Lockhart] told me personally that if he ever got out, he would do it again. He said a feeling came over him, that he couldn't control it. He needed to go to stop him from ever hurting anyone else again.* (Victim's step-mother in case of Michael Lockhart, #144).[92]

In some cases the removal of a potentially dangerous person seemed to be a rationalization to mitigate dissonance over the taking of the condemned's life:

> *I don't wish him ill. But by the same token I don't wish him free. I don't want him to be able to do this to anybody else. And that's the bottom line.* (Victim's mother in case of Ronald Allridge, #95).[93]

In one case, such rationalizations for the death penalty were taken further and were more deeply informed by policies and actual behavior of the condemned:

> *There's no life sentence in Texas. That's just not even an acceptable alternative. As we all know, at the time Soria was convicted, had we agreed to a life sentence, it would have been 20 years flat time and he would have been out, so five years from now, he would have been out. If he was willing to attack a chaplain at this prison, then he would have been able to attack anybody if given his freedom. Until the state of Texas decides that we're going to incarcerate for lifetimes--true*

[92] Jackson, J. (1997, December 10). Officers hold vigil as cop killer dies. *The Huntsville Item*, pp. 1A, 5A.

[93] Sturrock, P. (1995, June 8). Man executed for slaying of 19-year-old. *The Huntsville Item*, pp. 1A, 3A.

> *lifetimes--I don't find a life sentence acceptable.*[94] (Victim's father in case of Juan Soria, #225).[95]

Such rationales based on incapacitation are common among supporters of the death penalty, in general (Vollum et al., 2004). Moreover, the potential threat of future danger is one of the central factors required to secure a death sentence in Texas (del Carmen et al., 2005). It is not surprising to see the same sentiments expressed by those whose lives have been most directly affected by the individuals who are the source of this danger.

Similar sentiments were sometimes stated in regard to the threat the condemned represented to the co-victims, themselves (6.9% of cases). In some cases this threat was, at least in part, imaginary or based on irrational fear (although experienced as real fear). Referring to her sister, the mother of the victims of John Wheat (#247), one co-victim wrote: "she doesn't have to have any more nightmares about him coming to get her."[96] In other cases, this threat was perceived to be much more real:

> *There's no chance of an appeal now; it's over and done with. I'm relieved. If he had ever escaped, I would have gone into hiding. I would have probably been the second person, after his ex-wife, who he would have come after.* (Victim's mother in case of William Chappell, #287).[97]

A more vitriolic form of removal was manifested in statements reflecting what I term "extermination." These statements, which occurred in 6.9% of the cases, did not specifically focus on removing the condemned out of safety or protection concerns. Rather, the focus here was simply on eradicating the condemned from the earth:

---

[94] The Texas legislature recently (in 2005) passed legislation allowing for true life sentences in capital cases—sentences in which the inmate may never be released on parole.

[95] Lyons, M.C. (2000, July 27) Inmate put to death for '85 murder. *The Huntsville Item*, pp. 1A, 5A.

[96] Lyons, M.C. (2001, June 14) Wheat dies for murder of toddler. *The Huntsville Item*, p. 1A.

[97] Passwaters, M. (2002, November 21). Fort Worth man put to death for 1988 killings. *The Huntsville Item*, p. 6A.

> *He was nothing but a child predator. He needed to be removed.* (Victim's father in case of Rex Mays, #283).[98]

> *I thought it was going to be a waste of human life, but it's not...I'm glad it's done. I'm glad it's over, and I'm glad he is off this Earth.* (Victims' mother in case of Leo Jenkins, #105).[99]

Although fear may play a role in the cultivation of these sentiments (as it does in the prior two forms of removal-themed statements), these statements were often framed in anger, hatred, and dehumanization of the condemned (a theme to be discussed in greater detail later). From one co-victim's perspective, execution is a way of making sure there is "one less weirdo"[100] in the world.

Forgiveness

Contrition was among the most prevalent themes of the last statements of the condemned, with many specifically apologizing or asking for forgiveness. On the part of co-victim statements, forgiveness is indeed a common theme, found in 25.8% of the cases. However, the most common message regarding forgiveness among co-victims is that they *do not* forgive the condemned (14.5% of cases). In 8.2% of cases, co-victims explicitly state that they do not forgive the condemned and in 7.5% of cases, they make a statement indicating that they reject the condemned's apology. In the latter cases, the rejections are sometimes based on simply dismissing the condemned's apology and other times on perceived lack of sincerity:

> *I cannot forgive him. He took away too much.* (Victim's father in case of Miguel Flores, #234).[101]

---

98 Passwaters, M. (2002, September 25). Man executed for double murder. *The Huntsville Item*, p. 3A.

99 Jackson, J. (1996, February 10). Victims' mom says witnessing "was easy." *The Huntsville Item*, pp. 1A, 3A.

100 Victim's sister in case of Benjamin Boyle, #114; Trow, L. (1997, April 22). Truck driver put to death Monday. *The Huntsville Item*, pp. 1A, 3A.

101 Lyons, M.C. (2000, November 10). Execution protesters seek justice. *The Huntsville Item*, p. 6A.

> *Forgiveness is not even in my vocabulary, one way or the other.* (Victim's father in case of Michael Lockhart, #144).[102]

> *He offered it (an apology), but it's not going to do him no good.* (Victim's sister in case of Daniel Corwin, #162).[103]

> *My religion says to forgive. Turn a cheek. I still cannot do it. I've heard her words. I don't think they are heartfelt.* (Victim's husband in case of Karla Faye Tucker, #145).[104]

Given the severity of the offense and the lengthy and adversarial nature of the capital trial and death penalty process, it is no surprise that forgiveness is not forthcoming in many cases. Nevertheless, forgiveness was granted by several co-victims (in 11.9% of the cases):

> *I forgive her, I ask God to forgive her and that's just the way I feel in my heart.* (Victim's son in case of Betty Lou Beets, #208).[105]

> *I think we as a whole accept his apology because we are Christians and being of Christian faith, we believe we should forgive. He's a victim--he's just as much a victim.* (Victim's brother in case of Emerson Rudd, #255).[106]

Often, however, forgiveness was qualified with statements supporting the execution or statements about not forgetting what the condemned did to put himself in these circumstances:

---

[102] Jackson, J. (1997, December 10). Officers hold vigil as cop killer dies. *The Huntsville Item*, pp. 1A, 5A.

[103] Gideon, L. (1998, December 6). Family finds some peace. *The Huntsville Item*, p. 5A.

[104] The execution of Karla Faye Tucker. (1998, February 4). *The Huntsville Item*, p. 4A.

[105] Lyons, M.C. (2000, February 25). Beets put to death for 1983 killing. *The Huntsville Item*, p. 5A.

[106] Lyons, M.C. (2001, November 16). Rudd becomes 16th Texas inmate executed this year. *The Huntsville Item*, p. 3A.

> You can forgive, but you can't forget. (Victim's father in case of Eddie Johnson, #130).[107]

> Although forgiven, he is not exempt from being held accountable for his actions. (Victim's brother-in-law in case of Kenneth Harris, #125).[108]

Although completely understandable, the overall lack of forgiveness and, in many cases, outright resistance to forgiveness in the statements of co-victims is troubling. The healing and restorative powers of forgiveness are well documented (Cose, 2004; Enright, 2001; Enright & North, 1998; Ransley & Spy, 2004). These appear to be opportunities lost in the death penalty process.

Sympathy

In 22.6% of cases, co-victims expressed some level of sympathy for either the condemned or his or her family. This was most often directed at the condemned's family (13.8% of cases), often with some indication that the co-victims could understand and relate to the loss they were experiencing:

> *We have already been down that road for 12 years, and we have great empathy for his family for the pain that they are suffering at this time.* (Jonathan Nobles, #160).[109]

> *I think everybody is at a loss, (including) his family. Of course, we have been for the last 10 years. His family is going through our minds.* (Victim's niece in case of Andrew Cantu, #170).[110]

---

[107] Jackson, J. (1997, June 18). Murderer executed for triple slayings. *The Huntsville Item*, pp. 1A, 6A.

[108] Jackson, J. (1997, June 4). Murderer apologizes before being executed. *The Huntsville Item*, pp. 1A, 5A.

[109] Gideon, L. (1998, October 8). "Silent night:" Nobles executed Wednesday for two 1986 stabbing deaths. *The Huntsville Item*, pp. 1A, 3A.

[110] Gideon, L. (1999, February 17). Cantu dies for triple murder. *The Huntsville Item*, p. 7A.

> *His mother lost a son tonight.* (Victim's father in case of Jerry McFadden, #191).[111]

> *My heart really goes out to his family. I lost my daughter, and I know today is a terrible day for them.* (Victim's mother in case of Harold Lane, #100).[112]

> *On behalf of the family of Jesse Contreras, we wish to express our sincere condolences to the survivors of John Albert Burks. We too know how devastating the unnecessary and premature loss of one that we greatly love.* (Victim's family's statement in case of John Burks, #220).[113]

In several cases (8.8%), co-victims even offered sympathy to the condemned inmate who killed their loved one:

> *I felt compassion. I think it is a waste of life--he was so young--but it just had to be.* (Victim's niece in case of Andrew Cantu, #170).[114]

> *I feel sorry for him.* (Victim's cousin in case of Edward Lagrone, #318).[115]

A particularly striking element of co-victims' expressions of sympathy is the seeming connection they feel toward the family of the condemned. As Arrigo and Fowler (2001), in their discussion of the "death row community" and Eschholz et al. (2003), in their discussion of the restorative needs of both the families of victims and offenders, point out, this is a connection that should not be ignored. In the death

---

[111] Gideon, L. (1999, October 15). Notorious killer McFadden dies for rape, murder. *The Huntsville Item*, pp. 1A, 3A.

[112] Lightsey, J. (1995, October 5). "Europe thinks you're uncivilized." *The Huntsville Item*, pp. 1A, 5A.

[113] Lyons, M.C. (2000, June 15). Inmate executed for 1989 slaying. *The Huntsville Item*, p. 7A.

[114] Gideon, L. (1999, February 17). Cantu dies for triple murder. *The Huntsville Item*, pp. 1A, 7A.

[115] Rowe, T. (2004, February 12). Fort Worth man executed for killing pregnant 10-year-old. *The Huntsville Item*, p. 3A.

penalty process, these are two groups who are too often polarized or pitted against one another (Arrigo & Williams, 2003). This polarization not only impedes healing for both groups, it also appears, according to the co-victim statements discussed here as well as other accounts, to violate the natural inclinations for connection on the part of both groups.

Rationalization

Some co-victim statements include what I refer to as "rationalizations" regarding the killing of the condemned. These rationalizations are attempts to separate oneself from an act that generally violates one's values or moral sensibilities. For many, killing of another human being is an act that falls into this category (Bandura, 1990, 1999). In 18.2% of cases, co-victims' statements included some form of rationalization. The most common was dehumanization of the condemned (10.7% of cases). By making a dehumanizing statement about the condemned, the co-victim effectively denies the condemned's humanity and thus rationalizes his or her killing as not the same as killing a human being:

> *He's just got to be an animal.* (Victim's aunt in case of Jay Pinkerton, #13).[116]

> *To me, as a human being he doesn't even exist.* (Victim's husband in case of Robert Streetman, #27).[117]

> *[He was an] animal; I think everybody who knew anything about him knew that.* (Victim's brother in case of Daniel Corwin, #162).[118]

> *I feel sorry for his family and hate that it comes down to this, that we have to do away with evil like this, but he was just like*

---

[116] Trow, L. (1986, May 15). Murder victim's aunt hopes for end to ordeal. *The Huntsville Item*, pp. 1A, 8A.

[117] Victim's husband forever changed by murder. (1988, January 17), *The Huntsville Item*, pp. 1A, 6A.

[118] Gideon, L. (1998, December 6). Family finds some peace. *The Huntsville Item*, p. 5A.

an animal that goes bad. You have to put them to sleep. (Victim's daughter in case of Danny Barber, #169).[119]

In 6.3% of the cases, other disparaging characterizations of the condemned were used in a similar manner with references to the condemned being evil, a predator or not worthy of living.

The other identified form of rationalization was a denial of personal malevolence on the part of the co-victim. In these cases, the co-victim expressed that, although they were taking part in the killing of another human being, they were not a bad or malicious person:

I am not an unfeeling person, but with our present system of legal jurisprudence as it is--all for the assailant and with no consideration for the victim--life imprisonment as an alternative in this case is clearly absurd. (Victim's daughter in case of John Thompson, #25).[120]

It's not that we're bloodthirsty. They put themselves in this position. (Victim's mother in case of Leo Jenkins, #105).[121]

All I wanted was justice. I am not an evil man. (Victim's son in case of Javier Medina, #277).[122]

In these cases, the co-victims are separating themselves from the act that is being carried out. They are rationalizing their involvement, whether active or passive, in the death of another human being.

Death Penalty Support

Some co-victims took the opportunity in their statements to register their opinion about the death penalty. Not surprisingly, support for the

---

[119] Gideon, L. (1999, February 12). Family members of victims confront death penalty protesters at execution. *The Huntsville Item*, p. 5A.

[120] Spring bitter for victim's family. (1987, July 8). *The Huntsville Item*, pp. 1A, 3A.

[121] Jackson, J. (1996, February 10). Victims' mom says witnessing "was easy." *The Huntsville Item*, pp. 1A, 3A.

[122] Passwaters, M. (2002, August 15). Mexican national put to death. *The Huntsville Item*, p. 5A.

death penalty was more prevalent than opposition among co-victims making statements. In 10.1% of cases, co-victims made some statement in support of the death penalty. Most statements in this regard indicated general or abstract support for the death penalty (5.7% of cases) in comparison to only 1.9% of cases in which more personalized statements of support for the death penalty were expressed. In the former cases, co-victims simply expressed their support for the death penalty with no specific reference to their murdered loved one or the associated execution. In the latter, by contrast, the co-victims gave very personal reasons for their support of the death penalty, usually referring to their loss as the reason they had come to support the death penalty:

> *I used to think it was terrible to see somebody die. I said I wouldn't want to sit on a jury and decide that. I don't think that way anymore.* (Victim's wife in case of Elliot Johnson, #24).[123]

Co-victims also sometimes expressed support for the death penalty by criticizing protesters:

> *It irritated me. I think that foreign countries should mind their own business. They need to worry about their own problems and leave Texas Death Row alone.* (Victim's husband in case of Glen McGinnis, #205).[124]

> *This was about justice...those people who are against the death penalty, good for them. But they've never walked in our shoes.* (Co-victim-relation to victim unknown in case of John Elliot, #296).[125]

Opposition to the death penalty was a lot less likely to be found in the statements of co-victims. In only 5% of the cases did co-victims

---

[123] Graczyk, M.L. (1987, June 24). Victim had been looking forward to his retirement. *The Huntsville Item*, pp. 1A, 10A.

[124] Lyons, M.C. (2000, January 26). Inmate executed for gun slaying. *The Huntsville Item*, p. 7A.

[125] Passwaters, M. (2003, February 5). British-American executed for 1982 murder. *The Huntsville Item*, p. 3A.

make statements in opposition of the death penalty. Usually, their opposition was directed at the execution occurring on their behalf (4.4% of cases) and, in several cases, included statements indicating that the death penalty doesn't solve anything (1.3% of cases):

> *Killing Kenneth Brock is wrong. It will not change what has happened to my son. Killing Kenneth Brock will not ease my suffering or my wife's suffering or the loss of Michael. Two wrongs don't make a right. I could not be at peace if Kenneth Brock dies.* (Victim's father in case of Kenneth Brock, #15).[126]

Religion

In contrast to the last statements of the condemned, in which religion was one of the more common themes, religion was the least common among identified themes in co-victim statements. In only 13.8% of cases did co-victims make a religious or religion-oriented statement, the most common being a simple proclamation of faith (5.7% of cases). Others referred to God's judgment of the condemned (4.4% of cases):

> *We realize that our system for dealing with those who choose to kill others is not exactly the right answer but we know in our hearts that Charles Boyd will have to face the perfect justice of God.* (Victim's family's statement in case of Charles Boyd, #182).[127]

> *Robert Carter will suffer a real and true punishment after death by the hand of God.* (Victim's family's statement in case of Robert Carter, #218).[128]

Other co-victims offered prayers. In 3.8% of the cases co-victims said they had prayed or were praying for the condemned and in 1.9% they offered prayers for the family of the condemned. In only 2.5% of cases

---

[126] Convicted killer awaits execution on Thursday. (1986, June 18). *The Huntsville Item*, p. 1A.

[127] Gideon, L. (1999, August 6). Boyd denies committing crime. *The Huntsville Item*, p. 3A.

[128] Lyons, M.C. (2000, June 1). Former correctional officer executed for 1992 murders. *The Huntsville Item*, p. 3A.

did co-victims explicitly state that they were praying for themselves, other co-victims or the deceased victim.

In rare but interesting cases (1.9%), co-victims cited the bible in respect to the justifiability of the death penalty. As can be seen, there were conflicting interpretations:

> *The Bible says 'an eye for an eye'...we just feel it was the Biblical thing to do.* (John Burks, #220).[129]

> *We killed a man. We killed a person. He was a terrible person, and he deserved it, but still the Bible says it is not right. But to be honest with you, I'm glad we did.* (Victim's brother in case of Kenneth McDuff, #161).[130]

Again, conflicting sentiments and ambivalence regarding the death penalty and the execution of the condemned are inherent in many of the co-victims' statements. This is true both across the diverging themes of co-victim statements and within individual co-victim statements. These last two statements illustrate this well.

CO-VICTIM STATEMENTS AND CHARACTERISTICS OF THE CONDEMNED

Differences and similarities in themes were examined across the same offender demographic categories as with the last statement analyses. For each of the ten major thematic categories of co-victim statements, percentages were computed within each demographic category and chi-square statistics were obtained to ascertain statistical significance in differences among these groups. However, several of the broad thematic categories were broken down further for these analyses. The category of healing and closure is split into two separate groups: those indicating that the execution brought them healing and closure and those indicating that it did not. Similarly, satisfaction/dissatisfaction is split into separate satisfied and dissatisfied categories. Distinctions are also made between those who indicated forgiveness and those who

---

[129] Lyons, M.C. (2000, June 15). Inmate executed for 1989 slaying. *The Huntsville Item*, p. 7A.

[130] Gideon, L. (1998, November 17). Victims' families find relief. *The Huntsville Item*, p. 11A.

specifically indicated that they did not forgive. Finally, death penalty support is broken down into support and opposition categories. This makes for fourteen specific thematic categories which are analyzed in the context of the various offender, offense and execution characteristics. Table 15 presents the findings for each of the fourteen themes of co-victim statements.

As was the case when examining the last statements of the condemned, the first demographic category of sex of offender is difficult to adequately analyze due to the low number of women executed (N = 2). For race of offender, however, some significant findings are revealed. For example, in cases in which the condemned was White, co-victims were more likely to state that the execution brought them healing or closure ($\chi^2 = 10.35$, $p < .05$). Similarly, co-victims were significantly more likely to express satisfaction with the execution when the condemned was White ($\chi^2 = 5.84$, $p < .10$). Co-victims were also more likely to make a statement in opposition of the death penalty when the person being executed was White ($\chi^2 = 3.40$, $p < .10$). Although not reaching a level of statistical significance, there were some other interesting findings in regard to race of offender. Co-victims were much more likely to express forgiveness when the condemned was Black (15.4%) than when he was White (10.1%). Likewise, they were twice as likely to make a statement explicitly indicating that they do not forgive or refuse to forgive the condemned when he was White (18.0% as compared to 9.6% when Black). Perhaps the most interesting finding is that co-victims were more than twice as likely to rationalize the killing of the condemned when he was not Black. In only 9.6% of cases in which the condemned inmate was Black did co-victims make statements rationalizing the execution, in comparison to 22.5% and 22.2% of cases in which the condemned was White or Hispanic, respectively.

In regard to offender education, the only statistically significant finding is that in cases in which the offender has a high school education or GED, co-victims are more likely to specifically state that they do not forgive the offender ($\chi^2 = 3.51$, $p < .10$). In fact, co-victims were more than twice as likely to make non-forgiving statements when the offender was high school educated (21.4% as compared to 10.3% in cases in which the offender has less than a high school education). This may perhaps be due to the higher degree of culpability being associated with more educated offenders.

Table 15
Co-Victim Statement Themes by Characteristics of Condemned Offender

		% within Characteristic Category	
		Healing and Closure	
Characteristic	N	Brought Healing or Closure	Did Not Bring Healing or Closure
Total Sample	159	40.9%	28.9%
Sex			
Male	157	40.1	29.9
Female	2	50.0	0.0
Race			
White	89	46.1**	29.2
Black	52	42.3	26.9
Hispanic	18	5.6	38.9
Education			
High School/GED	70	42.9	31.4
Less than High School	78	38.5	28.2
Time on Death Row			
Less than 5 Yrs.	18	44.4	27.8
5 to 10 Yrs.	72	45.8	33.3
11 to 15 Yrs.	53	32.1	28.3
More than 15 Yrs.	15	33.3	20.0
Juvenile at Time of Crime?			
Yes	4	75.0	50.0
No	155	39.4	29.0
Texas Native?			
Yes	77	46.8	29.9
No	63	34.9	27.0
Foreign National?			
Yes	5	20.0	0.0
No	154	40.9	30.5
Prior Prison Record			
Yes	78	37.2	26.9
No	71	46.5	31.0

*Significant at $p < .10$
**Significant at $p < .05$

Table 15 (continued)

		% within Characteristic Category	
		Satisfaction/Dissatisfaction	
Characteristic	N	Satisfied	Dissatisfied
Total Sample	159	40.9%	47.8%
Sex			
Male	157	39.5	47.1
Female	2	100.0	100.0
Race			
White	89	46.1*	46.1
Black	52	38.5	53.8
Hispanic	18	16.7	38.9
Education			
High School/GED	70	45.7	51.4
Less than High School	78	39.7	46.2
Time on Death Row			
Less than 5 Yrs.	18	27.8	27.8
5 to 10 Yrs.	72	37.5	51.4
11 to 15 Yrs.	53	47.2	49.1
More than 15 Yrs.	15	40.0	46.7
Juvenile at Time of Crime?			
Yes	4	50.0	75.0
No	155	40.0	47.1
Texas Native?			
Yes	77	45.5	45.5
No	63	42.9	55.6
Foreign National?			
Yes	5	20.0	20.0
No	154	40.9	48.7
Prior Prison Record			
Yes	78	42.3	56.4
No	71	42.3	45.1

*Significant at $p < .10$
**Significant at $p < .05$

Table 15 (continued)

Characteristic	N	% within Characteristic Category Justice and Revenge	Memorialize or Honor Victim	Removal
Total Sample	159	61.6%	33.3%	27.0%
Sex				
Male	157	61.1	32.5	26.1
Female	2	50.0	100.0	50.0
Race				
White	89	61.8	34.8	28.1
Black	52	57.7	32.7	28.8
Hispanic	18	66.7	27.8	11.1
Education				
High School/GED	70	64.3	30.0	27.1
Less than High School	78	53.8	34.6	29.5
Time on Death Row				
Less than 5 Yrs.	18	72.2	33.3	16.7
5 to 10 Yrs.	72	58.3	30.6	29.2
11 to 15 Yrs.	53	62.3	30.2	28.3
More than 15 Yrs.	15	53.3	53.3	20.0
Juvenile at Time of Crime?				
Yes	4	25.0	75.0*	25.0
No	155	61.9	32.3	26.5
Texas Native?				
Yes	77	59.7	31.2	28.6
No	63	63.5	30.2	28.6
Foreign National?				
Yes	5	100.0*	40.0	0.0
No	154	59.7	33.1	27.3
Prior Prison Record				
Yes	78	60.3	28.2	29.5
No	71	59.2	35.2	23.9

*Significant at $p < .10$

**Significant at $p < .05$

Table 15 (continued)

		% within Characteristic Category			
		Forgiveness			
Characteristic	N	Yes	No	Symp-athy	Rationaliz-ation
Total Sample	159	11.9%	14.5%	22.6%	18.2%
Sex					
Male	157	11.5	14.0	20.4	18.5
Female	2	50.0	50.0	0.0	0.0
Race					
White	89	10.1	18.0	18.0	22.5
Black	52	15.4	9.6	21.2	9.6
Hispanic	18	11.1	11.1	27.8	22.2
Education					
High School/GED	70	8.6	21.4*	22.9	21.4
Less than High School	78	14.1	10.3	19.2	15.4
Time on Death Row					
Less than 5 Yrs.	18	5.6	27.8	27.8	16.7
5 to 10 Yrs.	72	8.3	12.5	18.1	18.1
11 to 15 Yrs.	53	17.0	13.2	20.8	18.9
More than 15 Yrs.	15	20.0	13.3	20.0	20.0
Juvenile at Time of Crime?					
Yes	4	0.0	14.2	25.0	25.0
No	155	12.3	25.0	20.0	18.1
Texas Native?					
Yes	77	11.7	11.7	22.1	14.3
No	63	14.3	20.6	19.0	19.0
Foreign National?					
Yes	5	0.0	20.0	0.0	40.0
No	154	12.3	14.3	20.8	17.5
Prior Prison Record					
Yes	78	9.0	12.8	24.4	19.2
No	71	15.5	18.3	15.5	14.1

*Significant at $p < .10$

**Significant at $p < .05$

Table 15 (continued)

		% within Characteristic Category		
Characteristic	N	Religion	Support DP	Oppose DP
Total Sample	159	13.8%	10.1%	5.0%
Sex				
Male	157	12.7	9.6	4.5
Female	2	100.0	50.0	50.0
Race				
White	89	15.7	10.1	7.9*
Black	52	13.5	11.5	1.9
Hispanic	18	5.6	5.6	0.0
Education				
High School/GED	70	12.9	12.9	2.9
Less than High School	78	14.1	7.7	5.1
Time on Death Row				
Less than 5 Yrs.	18	16.7	11.1	5.6
5 to 10 Yrs.	72	12.5	9.7	2.8
11 to 15 Yrs.	53	15.1	9.4	9.4
More than 15 Yrs.	15	13.3	13.3	0.0
Juvenile at Time of Crime?				
Yes	4	0.0	25.0	0.0
No	155	14.2	9.7	5.2
Texas Native?				
Yes	77	14.3	10.4	6.5**
No	63	15.9	9.5	0.0
Foreign National?				
Yes	5	0.0	20.0	0.0
No	154	14.3	9.7	5.2
Prior Prison Record				
Yes	78	10.3	5.1*	5.1
No	71	18.3	14.1	2.8

*Significant at $p < .10$

**Significant at $p < .05$

There were no statistically significant findings in regard to the length of time on death row, but one substantively interesting finding should be highlighted. It appears that as the length of time the offender has spent on death row increases, the likelihood of forgiveness rises. For each of the examined time increments, the percentage of co-victims expressing forgiveness in their statements increased. In cases in which the condemned has spent less than five years on death row, only 5.6% of co-victims made statements of forgiveness. For those cases in which the condemned was on death row between five to ten years, this percentage is 8.3%, for those with tenures between ten and fifteen, it's 17.0% and for those in which offenders were on death row more than fifteen years, 20.0% of co-victims expressed forgiveness! In spite of the lack of statistical significance, this is a noteworthy finding, indicating that with time forgiveness may be forthcoming even in these most traumatic and tragic situations. It also potentially indicates the necessity of time for forgiveness to be attained (on the part of both the co-victim and the offender).

Analyses regarding whether or not the offender was a juvenile at the time of the crime or a foreign national were not adequate in looking at co-victim statements due to small numbers. However, they are included in Table 15 for illustrative purposes. Analyses regarding whether or not the offender was a Texas native and had a prior prison record are more tenable but reveal few meaningful findings. Co-victims were significantly more likely to state that they oppose the death penalty in cases in which the condemned was a Texas native ($\chi^2 = 4.24$, $p < .05$) and, paradoxically, almost three times less likely to make a statement in support of the death penalty when the condemned had a prior record ($\chi^2 = 3.50$, $p < .10$).

CO-VICTIM STATEMENTS AND CHARACTERISTICS OF THE OFFENSE

Table 16 displays the percentages of statements containing each of the major themes across the eight specific factors related to the offense. These include particularly salient factors in regard to victim and co-victims. For example, whether the offender was related to the victim, whether there were multiple victims and whether the victim was a police officer are examined in relation to the major themes of co-victim statements. It is expected that each of these factors would have an impact on the perspectives of the co-victims and thus on their statements. Other factors such as whether there were co-victims, whether the murder occurred in the act of a felony or alongside other offenses and the race and sex of the victim(s) are also examined.

Factors related to the condemned inmate's victim or victims are the most interesting in the analysis of co-victim statements given the direct relevance to co-victims. Although small numbers of condemned offenders who were related to their victims preclude statistical significance, some interesting findings were yielded. First, in cases in which the offender and victim were related, co-victims were more likely to state that the execution brought them closure or healing (53.3% vs. 38.9% in cases in which offender and victim were not related). Similarly, co-victims were more likely to state that the execution brought them satisfaction in cases in which the offender and victim were related (53.3% vs. 38.9% in cases where they are not related). Moreover, co-victims were significantly less likely to indicate any dissatisfaction in such cases ($\chi^2 = 2.96$, $p < .10$) with only 26.7% reporting dissatisfaction in cases in which the offender and victim were related (as compared to 50.0% in other cases). Co-victims were also less likely to express sympathy in such cases (6.7% vs. 21.5% when offender and victim were unrelated). Finally, co-victims were significantly more likely to provide rationalizations in cases in which the offender and victim were not related ($\chi^2 = 3.70$, $p < .10$). We can only speculate, but it may be the case that the co-victim is more likely to be familiar with the condemned offender and thus more connected to their actions or their life. Their existence may cause more direct unrest for co-victims and thus their death may provide more satisfaction, closure and healing and evoke less sympathy. Potential feelings of betrayal and the shock of being victimized by someone you know (and possibly trust or rely on) might explain the apparently greater potency of the execution for co-victims.

Again, statistical significance was unable to be determined for the race of victim and sex of victim categories because these were multiple response variables. Therefore, examinations of these variables in the context of the major themes of last statements are purely descriptive. Moreover, due to low numbers of cases with Black (N = 23) or Hispanic (N =11) victims in which co-victim statements were reported, these findings should be interpreted with caution. In spite of these potential inferential problems, some interesting results in regard to victim race and sex were found. Satisfaction with the execution was less likely to be reported by co-victims in cases in which there was

Table 16
Co-Victim Statement Themes by Characteristics of the Offense

		% within Characteristic Category	
		Healing and Closure	
Characteristic	N	Brought Healing or Closure	Did Not Bring Healing or Closure
Total Sample	159	40.9%	28.9%
Codefendant(s)?			
Yes	63	42.9	19.0**
No	91	39.6	37.4
Related to Victim?			
Yes	15	53.3	20.0
No	144	38.9	30.6
Victim a Police Officer?			
Yes	16	43.8	31.3
No	143	39.9	29.4
Multiple Victims?			
Yes	44	56.8**	31.8
No	115	33.9	28.7
Race of Victim(s)†			
White	167	44.3	32.3
Black	23	47.8	26.1
Hispanic	11	27.3	9.1
Sex of Victim(s)†			
Male	89	44.9	28.1
Female	113	42.5	31.9
Murder in Act of Felony?			
Yes	119	37.8	26.9
No	40	47.5	37.5
Concurrent Offense			
Yes	126	39.7	28.6
No	33	42.4	33.3

† These are multiple response variables. Due to multiple victims in some cases, their sum is larger than total number of cases.

* Significant at p < .10

** Significant at p < .05

Table 16 (continued)

		% within Characteristic Category	
		Satisfaction/Dissatisfaction	
Characteristic	N	Satisfied	Dissatisfied
Total Sample	159	40.9%	47.8%
Codefendant(s)?			
Yes	63	38.1	60.3**
No	91	44.0	41.8
Related to Victim?			
Yes	15	53.3	26.7*
No	144	38.9	50.0
Victim a Police Officer?			
Yes	16	18.8*	43.8
No	143	42.7	48.3
Multiple Victims?			
Yes	44	61.4**	52.3
No	115	32.2	46.1
Race of Victim(s)†			
White	167	42.5	46.7
Black	23	56.5	56.5
Hispanic	11	54.5	45.5
Sex of Victim(s)†			
Male	89	40.5	50.6
Female	113	47.8	46.0
Murder in Act of Felony?			
Yes	119	38.7	48.7
No	40	45.0	45.0
Concurrent Offense			
Yes	126	37.3	48.4
No	33	51.5	45.5

† These are multiple response variables. Due to multiple victims in some cases, their sum is larger than total number of cases.

* Significant at $p < .10$

** Significant at $p < .05$

Table 16 (continued)

		% within Characteristic Category		
Characteristic	N	Justice and Revenge	Memorialize or Honor Victim	Removal
Total Sample	159	61.6%	33.3%	27.0%
Codefendant(s)?				
Yes	63	65.1	28.6	20.6
No	91	58.2	36.3	31.9
Related to Victim?				
Yes	15	53.3	26.7	20.0
No	144	61.8	34.0	27.1
Victim a Police Officer?				
Yes	16	62.5	50.0	31.3
No	143	60.8	31.5	25.9
Multiple Victims?				
Yes	44	75.0**	27.3	34.1
No	115	55.7	35.7	23.5
Race of Victim(s)†				
White	167	64.7	33.5	28.7
Black	23	47.8	17.4	26.1
Hispanic	11	72.7	36.4	27.3
Sex of Victim(s)†				
Male	89	60.7	33.7	23.6
Female	113	65.5	30.1	31.9
Murder in Act of Felony?				
Yes	119	61.3	36.1	24.4
No	40	60.0	25.0	32.5
Concurrent Offense				
Yes	126	62.7	35.7	25.4
No	33	54.5	24.2	30.3

† These are multiple response variables. Due to multiple victims in some cases, their sum is larger than total number of cases.

* Significant at $p < .10$

** Significant at $p < .05$

Table 16 (continued)

		% within Characteristic Category			
		Forgiveness			
Characteristic	N	Yes	No	Symp-athy	Rationaliz-ation
Total Sample	159	11.9%	14.5%	22.6%	18.2%
Codefendant(s)?					
Yes	63	7.9	12.7	19.0	19.0
No	91	15.5	16.5	22.0	17.6
Related to Victim?					
Yes	15	6.7	6.7	6.7	0.0
No	144	12.5	15.3	21.5	20.1*
Victim a Police Officer?					
Yes	16	12.5	6.3	12.5	31.3
No	143	11.9	15.4	21.0	16.8
Multiple Victims?					
Yes	44	11.4	15.9	22.7	25.0
No	115	12.2	13.9	19.1	15.7
Race of Victim(s)†					
White	167	10.8	15.6	18.0	19.2
Black	23	21.7	8.7	30.4	8.7
Hispanic	11	9.1	18.2	27.3	36.4
Sex of Victim(s)†					
Male	89	13.5	12.4	14.6	15.7
Female	113	10.6	16.8	24.8	21.2
Murder in Act of Felony?					
Yes	119	13.4	15.1	20.2	18.5
No	40	7.5	12.5	20.0	17.5
Concurrent Offense					
Yes	126	12.7	15.9	19.8	19.8
No	33	9.1	9.1	21.2	12.1

† These are multiple response variables. Due to multiple victims in some cases, their sum is larger than total number of cases.

* Significant at $p < .10$

** Significant at $p < .05$

Table 16 (continued)

Characteristic	N	% within Characteristic Category: Religion	Support DP	Oppose DP
Total Sample	159	13.8%	10.1%	5.0%
Codefendant(s)?				
Yes	63	19.0	12.7	4.8
No	91	11.0	7.7	4.4
Related to Victim?				
Yes	15	20.0	6.7	0.0
No	144	13.2	10.4	5.6
Victim a Police Officer?				
Yes	16	6.3	12.5	0.0
No	143	14.7	9.8	5.6
Multiple Victims?				
Yes	44	20.5	9.1	6.8
No	115	11.3	10.4	4.3
Race of Victim(s)†				
White	167	15.0	10.2	6.6
Black	23	21.7	4.3	0.0
Hispanic	11	9.1	18.2	0.0
Sex of Victim(s)†				
Male	89	14.6	10.1	3.4
Female	113	15.9	9.7	7.1
Murder in Act of Felony?				
Yes	119	15.1	11.8	5.0
No	40	10.0	5.0	5.0
Concurrent Offense				
Yes	126	15.1	11.9	4.8
No	33	9.1	3.0	6.1

† These are multiple response variables. Due to multiple victims in some cases, their sum is larger than total number of cases.

* Significant at $p < .10$

** Significant at $p < .05$

a White victim (42.5% vs. 56.5% and 54.5% of cases with Black and Hispanic victims, respectively). Additionally, co-victims were far less likely to express sympathy toward the condemned or the condemned's family in cases with White victims than in cases with minority victims (18.0% vs. 30.4% and 27.3% with Black and Hispanic victims, respectively). On the other hand, in cases in which there was a Black victim, co-victims were much more likely to express forgiveness toward the offender (21.7% compared to 10.8% when victim was White) and less likely to express support for the death penalty (4.3% compared to 10.2% when victim was White). Given prior research showing that Black victims appear to be "devalued" as victims in the death penalty process (Baldus, Pulaski et al., 1986; Baldus, Woodworth et al., 1998; Blume, 2003; Longmire, 2000), these findings, although striking, are not that surprising. What is surprising is that these sentiments are coming from co-victims—those who, in most cases, are related to the victim. Thus, what appears to be potential relative devaluation at first glance is more likely to be a relic of the fact that sentiments among Black populations tend to be less in favor of the death penalty (Bohm, 2007; Britt, 1998; Vollum et al., 2005) and that co-victims in cases with Black victims are probably more likely to be Black themselves. Further muddying the waters of these findings is the fact that condemned inmates who had Black victims are predominantly Black themselves (DPIC, 2007a). What can be concluded is that race plays a role in the co-victim sentiments surrounding executions; but, further, more in-depth research is needed to shed real light on what this role is and in whom the distinctions are inhabited.

Less distinctive differences were detected between cases in regard to sex of victim, but the differences that did exist are more difficult to explain away than those for race of victim and, in some cases, are a bit more perplexing. In cases with female victims, co-victims were more likely to express satisfaction with the execution (47.8% of cases as compared to 40.5% of cases with male victims), make statements regarding the "removal" of the offender (31.9% vs. 23.6% of cases with male victims), and rationalize the execution (21.2% vs. 15.7% of cases with male victims). These findings are not surprising given the greater potential fear for women when it comes to victimization—fear being a primary factor in sentiments about removal or extermination of the condemned. This fits with the often cited paternalism that exists in the context of criminal justice and punishment (Belknap, 1996). Much more surprising were the findings that co-victims were more likely to express sympathy toward the condemned or his family in cases with female victims (24.8% vs. 14.6% of cases with male victims) and to express opposition to the death penalty (7.1% vs. 3.4% of cases with male victims).

Factors more germane to the actual offense were also examined across the major themes of co-victim statements, revealing some interesting findings. Not surprisingly, co-victims were significantly less likely to state that the execution brought them closure or healing when the condemned had codefendants ($\chi^2 = 5.96$, $p < .05$). Similarly, co-victims were more likely to make statements indicating dissatisfaction with the execution in cases in which the condemned did not act alone ($\chi^2 = 5.13$, $p < .05$). Given that an accomplice may still be alive and potentially even in free society, it is easy to understand how an execution of one of the people responsible for the co-victim's loss would evoke few feelings of closure or healing or leave the co-victim dissatisfied with the execution.

CO-VICTIM STATEMENTS AND CHARACTERISTICS OF THE EXECUTION

The final set of variables analyzed across the major themes of co-victim statements are the factors related to the execution or the execution event, in which many of the co-victims in this study to some degree took part. Factors particularly salient to the analysis of co-victim statements are whether the condemned was a "volunteer" (waived appeals so that the execution would be carried out), whether the condemned and co-victim(s) had engaged in victim-offender mediation (VOM), whether the capital trial occurred when victim impact statements (VIS) were allowed, and the time period during which the execution took place. Other important factors are those regarding witnesses being present at the execution. Whether or not witnesses on behalf of the condemned and witnesses on the behalf of the victims were present at the execution are examined in relation to the major themes of co-victim statements, nearly all of which were given by co-victims who had been present at the execution. Table 17 presents the percentages of co-victims within these categories who made statements categorized into each of the ten major themes.

Whether or not co-victims witnessed the execution is a crucial factor in examining the nature of their statements at or around the time of execution. Although not all co-victims who made statements witnessed the execution, the majority of those whose statements were recorded in *The Huntsville Item* were available to make a statement because of their presence at the execution. Whether they themselves witnessed or not, the fact of co-victims witnessing the execution seems to be related to co-victim statements. For example, co-victims were much more likely to report satisfaction ($\chi^2 = 7.87$, $p < .05$) and less likely to report dissatisfaction ($\chi^2 = 3.75$, $p < .05$) with executions when witnesses for the victim were present at the execution. Perhaps more interestingly, co-victims were significantly more likely to make a statement expressing justice or revenge in cases in which victim witnesses were present at the execution ($\chi^2 = 4.59$, $p < .05$); although this is likely more a result of the fact that those who choose to be present at an execution may be already more inclined toward justice or revenge orientations. Presenting something of a paradox, co-victims were both more likely to express forgiveness ($\chi^2 = 5.77$, $p < .05$) and make statements indicating no forgiveness ($\chi^2 = 5.23$, $p < .05$) in cases in which witnesses were present at the execution on behalf of the victim. Although it is unclear exactly what to make of these contradictory findings, it is clear that forgiveness, in general, was more likely a statement theme in such cases. Finally, religion was more likely to be invoked in co-victim statements when witnesses for the victim were present at the execution ($\chi^2 = 2.81$, $p < .10$). Although not statistically significant, it is interesting to note that in cases where witnesses for the *condemned* were present at the execution, co-victims were less likely to express satisfaction (38.4% vs. 53.8% where witnesses for the condemned were not present) and more likely to express dissatisfaction (50.4% vs. 42.3% where witnesses for the condemned were not present). This seems to indicate that the very presence of the loved ones of the condemned has an important impact on or evokes some emotional response from co-victims.

We would expect the level of co-victim participation in the death penalty process and interaction with the offender to play a major role in the themes of co-victim statements. One possible form of interaction is VOM. Unfortunately, the number of cases in which VOM was conducted is extremely small (N = 3) and thus analyses based on this variable are difficult to interpret with any confidence. Nevertheless, the purely descriptive findings should be noted. For example, in all three cases in which VOM was conducted, co-victims (not necessarily the ones who participated in VOM) made statements that the execution did not bring them closure or healing and in two of the three cases, co-victims made statements indicating dissatisfaction with the execution (as compared to satisfaction being reported in none of the three cases).

Table 17
Co-Victim Statement Themes by Characteristics of the Execution

		% within Characteristic Category	
		Healing and Closure	
Characteristic	N	Brought Healing or Closure	Did Not Bring Healing or Closure
Total Sample	159	40.9%	29.9%
Witnesses for Condemned?			
Yes	125	42.4	29.6
No	26	30.8	19.2
Witnesses for Victim Allowed?			
Yes	123	41.5	30.9
No	36	36.1	25.0
Witnesses for Victim?			
Yes	110	44.5	29.1
No	44	31.8	27.3
Volunteer?			
Yes	11	36.4	45.5
No	148	40.5	28.4
Victim-Offender Mediation			
Yes	3	66.7	100.0
No	153	40.5	28.8
Requested by Co-Victim; Denied by Condemned	2	0.0	0.0
Requested by Condemned; Denied by Co-Victim or TDCJ Officials	1	0.0	0.0
Prior VIS?			
Pre-Payne	124	37.9	29.0
Post-Payne	35	48.6	31.4
Time Period of Execution			
1982-1989	21	42.9	28.6
1990-1995	15	26.7	20.0
1996-2000	85	41.2	34.1
2001-2004	38	42.1	23.7

*Significant at $p < .10$

**Significant at $p < .05$

Table 17 (continued)

		% within Characteristic Category	
		Satisfaction/Dissatisfaction	
Characteristic	N	Satisfied	Dissatisfied
Total Sample	159	40.9%	47.8%
Witnesses for Condemned?			
Yes	125	38.4	50.4
No	26	53.8	42.3
Witnesses for Victim Allowed?			
Yes	123	44.7**	49.6
No	36	25.0	41.7
Witnesses for Victim?			
Yes	110	47.3**	53.6*
No	44	22.7	36.4
Volunteer?			
Yes	11	18.2	36.4
No	148	41.9	48.6
Victim-Offender Mediation			
Yes	3	0.0	66.7
No	153	40.5	47.1
Requested by Co-Victim; Denied by Condemned	2	50.0	100.0
Requested by Condemned; Denied by Co-Victim or TDCJ Officials	1	100.0	0.0
Prior VIS?			
Pre-Payne	124	54.3*	48.6
Post-Payne	35	36.3	47.6
Time Period of Execution			
1982-1989	21	19.0**	38.1
1990-1995	15	33.3	46.7
1996-2000	85	40.0	48.2
2001-2004	38	55.3	52.6

*Significant at $p < .10$

**Significant at $p < .05$

Table 17 (continued)

Characteristic	N	Justice and Revenge	Memorialize or Honor Victim	Removal
		% within Characteristic Category		
Total Sample	159	61.6%	33.3%	27.0%
Witnesses for Condemned?				
Yes	125	62.4	34.4	24.0
No	26	57.7	26.9	30.8
Witnesses for Victim Allowed?				
Yes	123	65.0*	32.5	28.5
No	36	47.2	36.1	19.4
Witnesses for Victim?				
Yes	110	66.4**	34.5	25.5
No	44	47.7	29.5	22.7
Volunteer?				
Yes	11	63.6	27.3	9.1
No	148	60.8	33.8	27.7
Victim-Offender Mediation				
Yes	3	66.7	33.3	33.3
No	153	60.1	34.0	26.1
Requested by Co-Victim; Denied by Condemned	2	100.0	0.0	50.0
Requested by Condemned; Denied by Co-Victim or TDCJ Officials	1	100.0	0.0	0.0
Prior VIS?				
Pre-Payne	124	60.5	20.0*	31.4
Post-Payne	35	62.9	37.1	25.0
Time Period of Execution				
1982-1989	21	52.4	52.4**	14.3
1990-1995	15	40.0	13.3	26.7
1996-2000	85	67.1	40.0	29.4
2001-2004	38	60.5	15.8	26.3

*Significant at $p < .10$

**Significant at $p < .05$

Table 17 (continued)

		% within Characteristic Category			
		Forgiveness			
Characteristic	N	Yes	No	Symp-athy	Rational-ization
Total Sample	159	11.9%	14.5%	22.6%	18.2%
Witnesses for Condemned?					
Yes	125	13.6	16.0	20.8	17.6
No	26	7.7	7.7	23.1	19.2
Witnesses for Victim Allowed?					
Yes	123	14.6*	17.1*	20.3	17.1
No	36	2.8	5.6	19.4	22.2
Witnesses for Victim?					
Yes	110	16.4**	19.1**	21.8	18.2
No	44	2.3	4.5	18.2	18.2
Volunteer?					
Yes	11	9.1	27.3	18.2	9.1
No	148	12.2	13.5	20.3	18.9
Victim-Offender Mediation					
Yes	3	66.7	33.3	66.7	33.3
No	153	11.1	13.1	19.6	17.6
Requested by Co-Victim; Denied by Condemned	2	0.0	100.0	0.0	0.0
Requested by Condemned; Denied by Co-Victim or TDCJ Officials	1	0.0	0.0	0.0	100.0
Prior VIS?					
Pre-Payne	124	13.7	12.9	17.1	21.0*
Post-Payne	35	5.7	20.0	21.0	8.6
Time Period of Execution					
1982-1989	21	0.0	9.5	19.0	28.6
1990-1995	15	6.7	0.0	20.0	13.3
1996-2000	85	18.8**	16.5	23.5	14.1
2001-2004	38	5.3	18.4	13.2	23.7

*Significant at $p < .10$

**Significant at $p < .05$

Table 17 (continued)

		% within Characteristic Category		
Characteristic	N	Religion	Support DP	Oppose DP
Total Sample	159	13.8%	10.1%	5.0%
Witnesses for Condemned?				
Yes	125	15.2	8.8	5.6
No	26	11.5	11.5	3.8
Witnesses for Victim Allowed?				
Yes	123	15.4	9.8	4.1
No	36	8.3	11.1	8.3
Witnesses for Victim?				
Yes	110	17.3*	9.1	4.5
No	44	6.8	9.1	6.8
Volunteer?				
Yes	11	18.2	0.0	0.0
No	148	13.5	10.8	5.4
Victim-Offender Mediation				
Yes	3	0.0	0.0	66.7**
No	153	14.4	9.8	3.9
Requested by Co-Victim; Denied by Condemned	2	0.0	50.0	0.0
Requested by Condemned; Denied by Co-Victim or TDCJ Officials	1	0.0	0.0	0.0
Prior VIS?				
Pre-Payne	124	14.5	14.3	6.5
Post-Payne	35	11.4	8.9	0.0
Time Period of Execution				
1982-1989	21	14.3	14.3	14.3*
1990-1995	15	0.0	6.7	0.0
1996-2000	85	16.5	8.2	5.9
2001-2004	38	13.2	13.2	0.0

*Significant at $p < .10$

**Significant at $p < .05$

Finally, in two of the three cases with VOM, co-victims expressed forgiveness of the condemned and sympathy for either the condemned or his family. All of this seems to potentially illustrate the power connection to the condemned holds for co-victims.

The other primary form of co-victim participation in the death penalty process is through victim impact statements presented at trial. In cases in which victim impact statements were allowed during the trial (not necessarily meaning that such statements were presented), co-victims were significantly less likely to express satisfaction with the execution ($\chi^2 = 3.68$, $p < .10$). Not surprisingly, co-victims were also more likely to make statements at the time of the execution memorializing or honoring the victim in cases in which victim impact statements were allowed at trial ($\chi^2 = 3.59$, $p < .10$). Finally, in those cases prior to the policy allowing victim impact statements, co-victims were significantly more likely to rationalize the use of the death penalty by making statements dehumanizing or disparaging the condemned or denying their own personal malevolence ($\chi^2 = 2.81$, $p < .10$).

The final point of analysis in regard to characteristics of the execution is the time period in which the execution occurred. In addition to the percentages reported in Table 17, Figure 3 presents the trends over time in regard to each of the fourteen co-victim statement themes. The most consistent significant trend across the four time periods is in regard to statements expressing satisfaction with the execution, with satisfaction increasing steadily from 19% in the 1980s to 55.3% in the early years of the new century ($\chi^2 = 7.79$, $p < .05$). From this it might be surmised that as co-victim participation in the death penalty process (whether through VIS or witnessing of executions) has increased so has their satisfaction. There were also significant variations by time period for statements memorializing and honoring victims, forgiveness, and death penalty opposition. Co-victim statements memorializing or honoring co-victims were significantly higher during the 1980s and then again during the late 1990s than during the early 1990s or the early years of the 2000s ($\chi^2 = 13.09$, $p < .05$). Although it is difficult to know exactly what to make of this, it is possible that focus on, or sensitivity toward, victims in the death penalty process were heightened during the earlier time periods. This is particularly likely during the 1996 to 2000 time-period as it was in 1996 that co-victims began being allowed to witness executions. There was also a sharp and significant increase in statements expressing forgiveness during the 1996 to 2000 period ($\chi^2 = 8.68$, $p < .05$) whereas statements expressing opposition to the death penalty were significantly more likely during the 1980s than during any other time-period ($\chi^2 = 6.70, p < .10$).

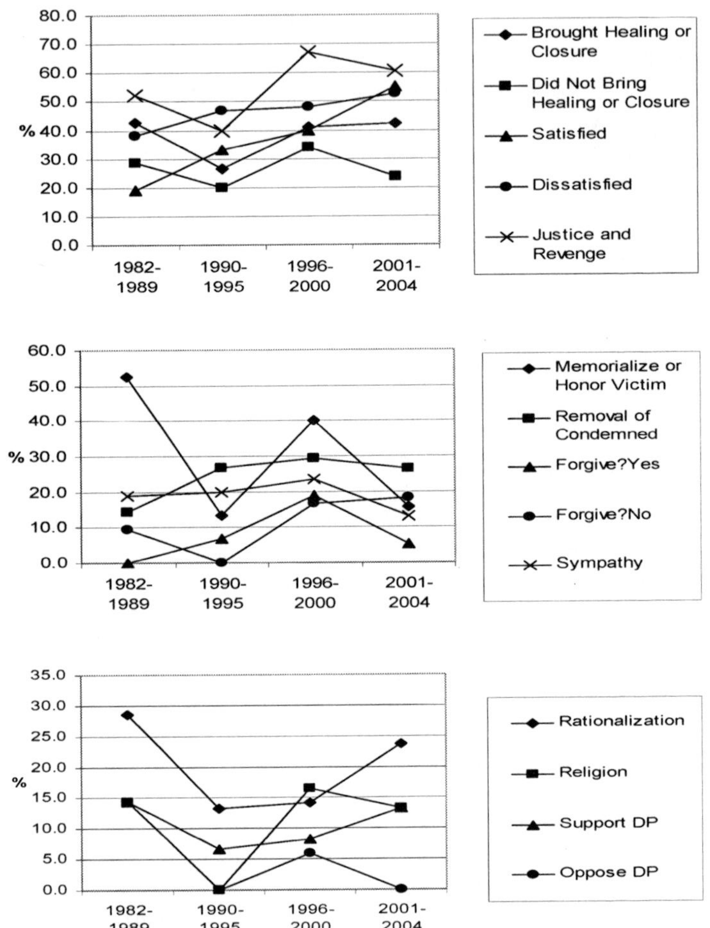

Figure 3. **Co-Victim Statement Themes, Percentages over Time**

NEEDS OF HOMICIDE CO-VICTIMS AND THEMES OF RESTORATIVE JUSTICE

One cannot examine the co-victim statements without thinking about the humanity and underlying needs of the co-victims in these particularly tragic cases of murder. As discussed in Chapter II, homicide co-victims experience especially acute trauma in the loss of their loved one. From this loss and trauma comes a long process of grieving and the associated need to seek healing and closure. These needs align well with many of the elements of restorative justice which, as indicated in Chapter III, asserts that the needs of victims must be drawn into the justice process. With a focus on reconciliation and making things right, restorative justice offers an avenue toward meeting some of the most essential needs of homicide co-victims. Through attempts to facilitate healing, closure, transformation, and forgiveness, restorative justice holds the promise of a salve on the wounds left behind by murder. While this promise typically goes unfulfilled, the death penalty is often held out instead as the necessary form of justice for the co-victims and the appropriate mechanism by which to bring them the much needed healing and closure. The statements made by co-victims at the time of execution offer a valuable opportunity to examine whether and to what degree the death penalty indeed provides these things.

Table 18 shows that in a majority (59.1%) of cases, co-victims do indeed make some form of restorative-oriented statement. However, in a much larger proportion (75.5%) of cases, co-victims made statements that were explicitly non-restorative. Themes were identified as restorative if they reflected any of the major principles or characteristics of restorative justice or restorative processes. Expressions of some form of closure such as the execution being a form of conclusion to pain and suffering or bringing healing, peace or relief were paramount among the themes considered restorative. Similarly, references to the execution as a transitional or transformative event toward a better state were considered restorative. Finally, expressions of forgiveness, sympathy or other connection to the condemned or his family were included in the broad category of restorative statements. Non-restorative statements were those containing themes contrary to restorative justice. These included explicit statements that the execution did not bring the desired healing or closure as well as more indirect statements of frustration or dissatisfaction with the death penalty process or execution itself.

Statements in which the co-victim expresses anger toward or a disconnection from the condemned or a denial of his humanity also fall into this category. Table 18 presents all specific themes of co-victim statements that made up the restorative and non-restorative categories.

Table 18
Co-Victim Statements: Restorative and Non-Restorative Themes

Co-Victim Statement Theme	N	% of Valid Cases (N=320)	% of Cases in Which Statements Given (N=159)
Restorative	**94**	**29.4%**	**59.1%**
Conclusion	36	11.3%	22.6%
Execution Brings Peace &/or Relief	26	8.1%	16.4%
Sympathy for Condemned's Family	22	6.9%	13.8%
Forgive	19	5.9%	11.9%
Beginning	16	5.0%	10.1%
Sympathy for Condemned	14	4.4%	8.8%
Grateful for Apology	12	3.8%	7.5%
Prayer for Condemned	6	1.9%	3.8%
Execution Brings Healing &/or Closure	4	1.3%	2.5%
Prayer for Family of Condemned	3	0.9%	1.9%
General Satisfaction w/ Last Statement	2	0.6%	1.3%
Non-Restorative	**120**	**37.5%**	**75.5%**
Frustration with Delays/CJ System	41	12.8%	25.8%
No Healing or Closure	32	10.0%	20.1%
Won't Bring Loved-One Back	20	6.3%	12.6%
Dehumanization of Condemned	17	5.3%	10.7%
Frustration with Last Statement	14	4.4%	8.8%
Frustration with Lack of Remorse	13	4.1%	8.2%
Question Truthfulness of Statement	13	4.1%	8.2%

Table 18 (continued)

Co-Victim Statement Theme	N	% of Valid Cases (N=320)	% of Cases in Which Statements Given (N=159)
Non-Restorative (continued)			
No Happiness/Joy/Satisfaction from Execution	13	4.1%	8.2%
Does Not Forgive	13	4.1%	8.2%
Rejects Apology	12	3.8%	7.5%
Dismisses Condemned's Words/Sentiments	11	3.4%	6.9%
Extermination	10	3.1%	6.3%
Maligns/Demeans Character of Condemned	9	2.8%	5.7%
Execution was Traumatizing	5	1.6%	3.1%
Frustration with Acknowledgement	3	0.9%	1.9%
Frustration with Lack of Claim of Responsibility	3	0.9%	1.9%
Frustration with Claim of Innocence	2	0.6%	1.3%
Frustration with Media	2	0.6%	1.3%

Restorative themes among co-victim statements fall into two different broad categories: self-oriented statements and other-oriented statements. The most common restorative elements among co-victim statements were self-oriented and related to a form of ending or conclusion to a difficult time in the co-victim's life. Specifically, conclusion was a theme in 22.6% of the cases and an indication that the execution brings peace or relief was expressed in 16.4% of all cases. However, a good proportion of restorative statements were other-oriented, directed toward the condemned and/or the condemned's family. Sympathy for the condemned's family was the third most common restorative theme of co-victim statements, occurring in 13.8% of all cases. Forgiveness of the condemned was expressed in 11.9% of cases (the fourth most common restorative theme).

Non-restorative themes among co-victim statements were most commonly expressed toward the death penalty process itself. Frustration with the lengthy process and the seemingly endless delays was expressed in over a quarter (25.8%) of all cases. In 20.1% of cases, co-victims explicitly stated that the execution did not bring any personal healing or closure and in 12.6% of cases they made reference to the fact that the execution does not bring back the victim. Other common non-restorative statements were directed at the condemned. In 10.7% of cases, co-victims made statements dehumanizing the condemned inmate. Other non-restorative statements directed at the condemned related directly to the last statement given by the condemned at the execution. 8.8% expressed general frustration with the condemned's last statement and 8.2% indicated frustration with the lack of remorse expressed by the condemned. The same proportion (8.2%) questioned the truthfulness of the condemned's last statement. Other common non-restorative statements addressed the issue of forgiveness; in 8.2% of cases, co-victims stated that they did not forgive the condemned and in 7.5% of cases they stated that they rejected an apology offered by the condemned. Again, non-restorative themes were more prevalent than restorative themes among co-victim statements at the time of execution. Overall, co-victim statements seem to be characterized more by pain, anger and frustration than anything else.

In Table 19 the restorative and non-restorative themes of co-victim statements are examined in the context of characteristics of the condemned inmate. The most significant finding relates to the race of the condemned. Co-victims in cases in which the condemned was Hispanic were just over half as likely to make restorative-oriented statements as those in cases with White or Black offenders ($\chi^2 = 5.75$, $p < .10$). Interestingly, no difference based on race of the condemned was found for statements with non-restorative themes. Co-victims in cases in which the condemned were foreign nationals (the large majority of whom were Hispanic) were also significantly less likely to make restorative statements ($\chi^2 = 3.32$, $p < .10$). Although it is not clear exactly what these findings indicate, it appears that cases in which the condemned is Hispanic evoke less restorative sentiments from co-victims. It is perhaps possible that in cases in which the co-victim is not him or herself Hispanic, cultural distance may play a role in the ability of co-victims to connect with the condemned and thus inhibit restorative sentiments or perspectives. With the information available, one can only speculate. More direct research on co-victims is necessary to understand this dynamic.

Finally, as can be seen in Figure 4, non-restorative statements appear to increase in likelihood as the length of time between sentencing and execution increases. More interestingly, it appears that the ratio of non-restorative to restorative statements becomes greater as the time between sentencing and execution increases. When the time on death row is less than five years, the proportion of statements with restorative and non-restorative themes is nearly equivalent. But, the gap between the two themes widens the longer the co-victims must wait for the execution to occur. This is not at all surprising given that frustration with the length of time it takes to carry out the execution is the most common non-restorative theme among co-victim statements. But, it also offers potentially strong evidence that the death penalty process, to some degree, fails the co-victims—increasingly more so as the process goes on—insofar as restorative elements equate to the meeting of their needs.

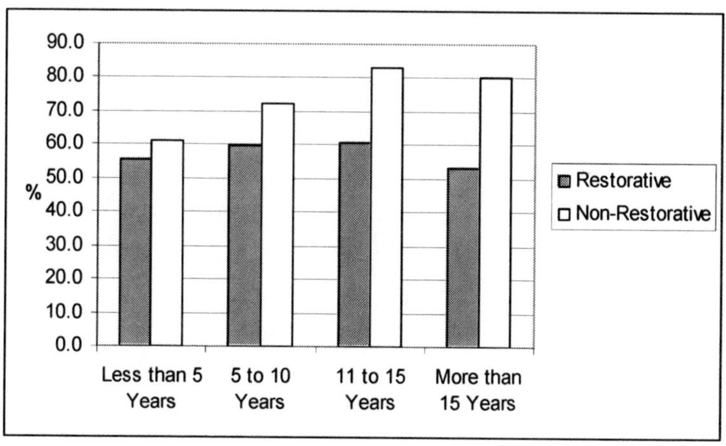

Figure 4. **Restorative and Non-Restorative Statements of Co-Victims by Length of Time between Sentencing and Execution of the Condemned.**

Table 19
Restorative and Non-Restorative Co-Victim Statement Themes by Characteristics of the Condemned

		% within Characteristic Category	
Characteristic	N	Restorative	Non-Restorative
Total Sample	159	59.1%	75.5%
Sex			
Male	157	58.6	75.2
Female	2	100.0	100.0
Race			
White	89	62.9	75.3
Black	52	61.5	75.0
Hispanic	18	33.3*	77.8
Education			
High School/GED	70	60.0	81.4
Less than High School	78	60.3	73.1
Time on Death Row			
Less than 5 Yrs.	18	55.6	61.1
5 to 10 Yrs.	72	59.7	72.2
11 to 15 Yrs.	53	60.4	83.0
More than 15 Yrs.	15	53.3	80.0
Juvenile at Time of Crime?			
Yes	4	75.0	100.0
No	155	58.7	74.8
Texas Native?			
Yes	77	63.6	75.3
No	63	57.1	77.8
Foreign National?			
Yes	5	20.0*	60.0
No	154	60.4	76.0
Prior Prison Record			
Yes	78	60.3	74.4
No	71	60.6	78.9

*Significant at $p < .10$

**Significant at $p < .05$

Table 20 presents restorative and non-restorative themes across categories of characteristics of the offense for which the condemned is being executed. Demographically, the race and gender of the victim in the offense seem to be related to the restorative nature of co-victims' statements. Although statistical significance was not determined for these variables due to their multiple response nature, substantively significant results are worth noting. First, in cases with Black victims, co-victims were much more likely to make a restorative-oriented statement (78.3% vs. 61.7% and 54.5% of cases in which there was a White or Hispanic victim, respectively). This mirrors the previous finding in regard to cases with Black victims and the major statement themes of satisfaction, sympathy and forgiveness, all elements of restorative-oriented statements. Again, because of the fact that most co-victims (family members of the victim) are the same race as the victim, this potentially indicates something about the greater likelihood of Black co-victims to make restorative statements. More research on these individuals is needed to be sure. Co-victims were also more likely to make restorative statements in cases in which the victim was a female (65.5% vs. 60.7% in cases with male victims).

As would be expected, whether or not the condemned was related to the victim seems to have some effect on the restorative nature of co-victim statements. In cases in which the victim and offender were related, co-victims were significantly less likely to express non-restorative sentiments in their statements ($\chi^2 = 4.54$, $p < .05$). Although not statistically significant, co-victims were also more likely to make a restorative statement in cases in which the victim and offender were related (66.7% vs. 58.3% in cases in which they were not related). Perhaps a bit surprisingly, co-victim statements were significantly more likely to express restorative sentiments when there were multiple victims ($\chi^2 = 10.24$, $p < .05$). Except for the fact that needs for healing and closure may potentially become compounded when the loss of more than one victim is experienced, it is unclear why there exists such a significant difference in restorative-oriented statements between co-victims in cases with only one victim and those in cases with multiple victims.

Table 20
Restorative and Non-Restorative Co-Victim Statement Themes by Characteristics of the Offense

		% within Characteristic Category	
Characteristic	N	Restorative	Non-Restorative
Total Sample	159	59.1%	75.5%
Codefendant(s)?			
Yes	63	58.7	79.4
No	91	61.5	75.8
Related to Victim?			
Yes	15	66.7	53.3**
No	144	58.3	77.8
Victim a Police Officer?			
Yes	16	56.3	68.8
No	143	59.4	76.2
Multiple Victims?			
Yes	44	79.5**	70.5
No	115	51.3	77.4
Race of Victim(s)†			
White	167	61.7	74.3
Black	23	78.3	69.6
Hispanic	11	54.5	72.7
Sex of Victim(s)†			
Male	89	60.7	73.0
Female	113	65.5	74.3
Murder in Act of a Felony?			
Yes	119	57.1	76.5
No	40	65.0	72.5
Concurrent Offense			
Yes	126	58.7	77.8
No	33	60.6	66.7

† These are multiple response variables. Due to multiple victims in some cases, their sum is larger than total number of cases.

* Significant at p < .10

** Significant at p < .05

Table 21 presents the last set of analyses of restorative and non-restorative themes among co-victim statements. In Table 21 these themes are examined in the context of characteristics of the execution. These factors include the important factors related to the presence of witnesses (on behalf of both the victim and the condemned inmate) at the execution. It is no surprise that co-victim statements were significantly more likely to express restorative sentiments in cases in which witnesses for the victim were present at the execution ($\chi^2 = 4.70$, $p < .05$). However, co-victims in such cases were also more likely to express non-restorative sentiments ($\chi^2 = 6.18$, $p < .05$). Such contradictory findings suggest that whether restorative or non-restorative, emotions potentially run higher on both ends of the spectrum when witnesses on behalf of the victim are present at the execution. Such "interaction" apparently may evoke either restorative or non-restorative sentiments, or both. Although not statistically significant, both restorative and non-restorative statements were more likely when witnesses for the condemned were present at the execution. Finally, as illustrated in Figure 5, both restorative and non-restorative statements have been more likely in the late 1990s and the early years of the new century. This is most likely also a function of the increased level of witnessing of executions, particularly on the behalf of the victim.

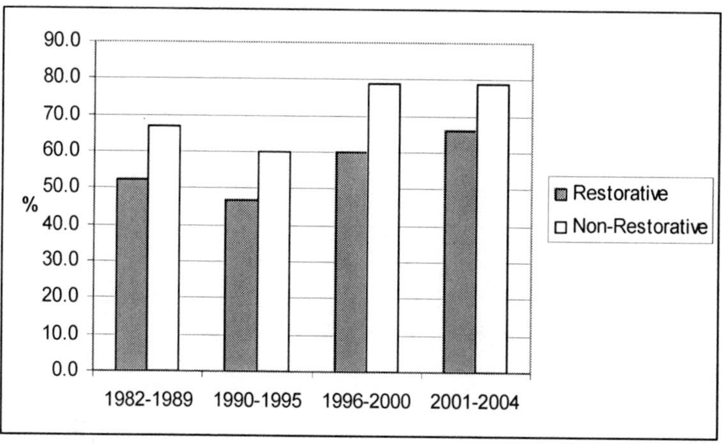

Figure 5. **Restorative and Non-Restorative Statements of Co-Victims by Time-Period in Which Execution was Carried Out.**

Table 21
Restorative and Non-Restorative Co-Victim Statement Themes by Characteristics of the Execution

		% within Characteristic Category	
Characteristic	N	Restorative	Non-Restorative
Total Sample	159	59.1%	75.5%
Witnesses for Condemned?			
Yes	125	62.4	77.6
No	26	46.2	65.4
Witnesses for Victim Allowed?			
Yes	123	61.8	78.9*
No	36	50.0	63.9
Witnesses for Victim?			
Yes	110	65.5**	80.9**
No	44	45.5	61.4
Volunteer?			
Yes	11	45.5	63.6
No	148	60.1	76.4
Victim-Offender Mediation			
Yes	3	100.0*	100.0
No	153	59.5	75.2
Requested by Co-Victim; Denied by Condemned	2	0.0	100.0
Requested by Condemned; Denied by Co-Victim or TDCJ Officials	1	0.0	0.0
Prior VIS?			
Pre-Payne	124	57.3	74.3
Post-Payne	35	65.7	75.8
Time Period of Execution			
1982-1989	21	52.4	66.7
1990-1995	15	46.7	60.0
1996-2000	85	60.0	78.8
2001-2004	38	65.8	78.9

*Significant at $p < .10$

**Significant at $p < .05$

CONCLUSION

As previously mentioned the grief of co-victims in the aftermath of murder is especially acute given the extraordinarily traumatic nature of the loss. The needs of co-victims in the weeks, months and years following the murder are many and diverse but often revolve around notions of closure and healing, of moving on with one's life in the wake of the tragedy one has experienced at the hands of a murderer. The statements of co-victims presented in this chapter reinforce the importance of these elements for co-victims. In an overwhelming majority of cases, co-victims bring up factors related to healing and closure, if not mentioning healing and closure specifically. However, there is some ambivalence in regard to whether the execution (or death penalty, generally) assists or hinders the meeting of these needs. It appears that meeting these needs in the context of the retributive punishment of death is elusive. In many cases, co-victims report finding little solace in the fact that the condemned inmate who killed their loved one will be or was killed. There seems to be a disconnect between the need and desire for healing, closure and catharsis among co-victims and the often long-awaited event held out as a response to these needs—the execution. In fact, the two single most common specific themes were expressions of dissatisfaction with the execution and/or death penalty more generally. The first was dissatisfaction with the length of time it took before the execution was finally carried out and the second was dissatisfaction with something the condemned said or did at the time of execution.

Unlike the condemned, co-victims were much more likely to make non-restorative statements than restorative ones. Expressions of justice, in contrast to healing and closure, were relatively unequivocal. In a large proportion of cases, co-victims indicated that the execution or death penalty more generally provided justice. This was expressed primarily in retributive or revenge-oriented terms. In fact, a substantial portion of co-victims indicated that the death penalty was not harsh enough and some expressed a wish to inflict harm on the condemned or see more harm done to them.

While the condemned inmates most often indicate positive expressions of reconciliation, transformation and love or concern for others in their last minutes, co-victims are much more ambivalent, often expressing anger, frustration, and dissatisfaction alongside relief that the process is over. What seem to remain elusive are the transformative elements which might bring the much needed and sought healing and closure.

CHAPTER VIII:

Discussion and Conclusion

Having examined the words of condemned inmates and their co-victims, it is clear that much can be learned about the death penalty and its often unnoticed human impact. It is also clear that these usually marginalized groups have a lot to say about the death penalty and that their voices should not be ignored or excluded from the discourse surrounding the death penalty. Indeed, these are the groups who are often symbolically at the center of the death penalty debate and the practice of state-sanctioned killing. To more fully understand the death penalty and its use, we should aspire to an understanding of their perspectives, sentiments, and attitudes, or at the least to consider them in the discourse. The results of this study offer a small window through which we get a glimpse of these things. This book sheds valuable light on the perspectives of these neglected groups and hopefully on the humanity and human feelings and sensibilities of these very damaged individuals. In this chapter, I broadly summarize and discuss the results in the context of what it tells us about the humanity of these individuals at the center of the death penalty process. I also consider the major lessons learned from this study, both in regard to the lessons learned about the death penalty and the lessons learned about researching these unique and often neglected populations. In the end, it is my hope that the reader comes away with a deeper understanding of the human side of the death penalty and of these two most central human populations swept up in the death penalty process.

HUMANITY AND THE DEATH PENALTY

At the heart of the statements of the condemned and co-victims is humanity. As Robert Johnson (1996), in his enlightening study of the death penalty and execution process, illustrates well, the death penalty strips away humanity. Both the process of the death penalty and its end result, execution, are inherently dehumanizing to the condemned. Although in a less obvious manner, this retributive process and punishment also denies victims and co-victims their humanity (Christie, 1997; Zehr, 1990) by taking away their status as "victim" and placing them outside of the process of justice. Overall, the death penalty process obscures the humanity, human needs, and human voices that lie at the center of its implementation. Often abstractly invoked but rarely personally included, the condemned and co-victims are scarcely considered as human actors in the drama of the death penalty. But they *are* human actors and their statements, in part, reflect an attempt to re-assert their humanity.

The most common themes among the last statements of the condemned revolved around human connection to others. In a majority of cases, condemned inmates expressed well-wishes and love to others including their own family and friends as well as co-victims and even society in general. Contrition and gratitude were other common themes among the last statements of the condemned. In nearly a third of the cases, condemned inmates expressed contrition for their actions, most often directed at the co-victims but also often in addressing their own family and friends. In nearly a third of all cases, condemned inmates expressed gratitude to others in their last statements. Such attempts to connect to others in their last minutes of life represent interesting assertions of humanity at the very moment when one's humanity is being taken away. As mentioned in Chapter VI, such benevolent expressions toward others may be a way to reclaim humanity as one faces the end of an otherwise dehumanizing process and at a point at which one is facing an otherwise defiled death.

Another way the condemned appear to assert their humanity is through transcendence. The second most common theme among the last statements is religion. The most common reference is to the afterlife, followed closely by proclamations of faith or of giving oneself to God. At the heart of these statements is the denial that one's humanity will end with the state-sanctioned death. In fact, some seem to express that humanity will be regained as they will be free of the judgment of this world. The condemned often express that they will live on in a spiritual sense, that their life transcends their dehumanized existence in this world and their dehumanized death. They will experience salvation of their humanity.

In over a fifth of cases, condemned inmates directly express personal reconciliation which includes personal transformation and the humanization of oneself. Although condemned inmates only rarely make direct statements humanizing themselves (4.1% of cases), the message is relatively clear throughout a large proportion of the statements. Moreover, it is very rare for the condemned to express resignation—an implicit acceptance of their dehumanized self, perhaps—in their last statements (9.2% of cases). Rather, condemned inmates take the opportunity of their last statement to re-assert their humanity and to transcend their defiled and dehumanized identity.

For co-victims, statement themes are much more conflicting and represent a much more divergent set of messages. But at the same time, they are similar to the last statements of the condemned in that they seem to also relate heavily to expressions of humanity. The three most common themes among co-victim statements relate directly to some of the predominant needs of co-victims as discussed in Chapter II. Themes of healing and closure, satisfaction or dissatisfaction, and justice and revenge—all elements of the most important human needs of co-victims—are each present in more than 60% of the cases in which statements were given. Does this mean that the death penalty adequately meets these human needs (as asked in Chapter II)? Not necessarily. The fact is that very few co-victims report that the execution brought them closure (2.5%) and that many report it brings no healing or closure (20.1%). What seems more accurate, based on the statements of co-victims, is that co-victims see the execution as a conclusion to a long process of grief and pain. This is congruent with Gross and Matheson's (2003) conclusions from their similar study of co-victim statements in newspapers across the country. Moreover, in nearly half of the cases, co-victims stated dissatisfaction with the death penalty process and/or execution itself, with the leading complaint being the length of time it took to carry out the execution. On the other hand, a substantial proportion of co-victims stated that the execution brought them satisfaction or that it brought them justice. Overall, co-victims seem to be expressing more relief that the whole ordeal is over than any kind of true catharsis or psychic closure—both essential human needs for healthy grieving and healing.

Co-victims also often made statements humanizing the deceased victim. In a third of cases, co-victims made statements memorializing or honoring the victim and in nearly a fifth of cases they made statements comparing favorably the fate (execution) of the condemned to the horrific death of the victim. These statements appear to have been asserted in a way to counteract perceived focus on the condemned. It may be an opportunity to re-establish the humanity of the victim which had been obscured in the death penalty process. Co-victims also sometimes made statements preserving their own humanity by denying any potentially perceived malevolence given their participation in the killing of another human being. This is closely related to what Klockars (1974) referred to as the "metaphor of the ledger," or a technique of neutralization by which one attempts to mitigate acts that may violate their moral sensibilities by pointing out their otherwise benevolent behavior and thus maintain their status as moral human being. At the same time, co-victims occasionally made statements specifically dehumanizing the condemned. Referring to the condemned as less than human or as some form of bug, animal, or even non-human evil entity was not uncommon, occurring in over 10% of cases. Additionally, in several cases (6.9%), co-victims express that the condemned needed to be exterminated or gotten rid of.

This last point brings up an important element of co-victim statements. It indicates a certain level of disconnection from the humanity of others in the context of the death penalty process. As Eschholz et al. (2003) point out, the death penalty process often serves to deny meaningful human connection and thus maintains or perpetuates fractures among those who may otherwise play powerful roles in the healing process for each other. There is evidence in both the statements of the condemned and of the co-victims that this connection is important and potentially transformative. Co-victims seem to indicate a strong sensitivity to the statement, demeanor, and sentiments of the condemned as evidenced by their level of frustration when the condemned does not acknowledge them or offer any kind of apology or contrition. Indeed, expressions of satisfaction and dissatisfaction are both independently more likely when there were co-victims present at the execution. Similarly, expressions of forgiveness (on both sides) and justice were also more likely when co-victims witnessed the execution. The interaction with the condemned has a clear impact on co-victims; but, more importantly, the quality of that interaction plays an important role in the outcome of the execution for the co-victims.

As previously mentioned, the connection to the humanity of others pervades the last statements of the condemned. As they assert their own humanity they inherently connect with the humanity of others. For the condemned, interaction with others appears to play a crucial role in the transformative nature of their statements. Specifically, condemned inmates are more likely to make statements expressing well-wishes, contrition, and gratitude when they have friends or family present at the execution. Also, they are more likely to express contrition when there are co-victims present at the execution.

This inter-connectivity and its apparent impact on these individuals in the death penalty process evoke the notion and principles of restorative justice. As previously discussed, restorative justice emphasizes human connections and the participation and needs of all individuals impacted by crime. Restorative justice focuses on reconciliation, healing, contrition, forgiveness, accountability of the offender, restoration of the victim, and justice for all involved. Retributive justice (of which the death penalty is the most extreme form) stands in stark contrast to restorative justice and in many people's opinions serves only to impede or inhibit these human connections and the appropriate processes necessary to meet the needs of healing and justice (Zehr, 1990; Eschholz et al., 2003; Zehr & Mika, 1998).

In regard to the restorative nature of the statements of the condemned and their co-victims, there is a notable difference between these two populations. While the condemned tend to be overwhelmingly more likely to make restorative than non-restorative statements, co-victims' statements are more likely to be non-restorative in nature. Condemned inmates were more likely to be restorative in their last statements when co-victims were present at the execution and co-victims were less likely to make non-restorative statements when the condemned was related to the victim (and, thus, potentially to the co-victims). It is not a stretch to conclude from this that restoration and its positive components are more likely when a connection between the co-victim and the offender exists or can be constructed. Unfortunately, it appears that this human connection, not to mention the many other important human connections in the death penalty process (see Arrigo & Fowler, 1998, Arrigo & Williams, 2003, and Eschholz et al., 2003), is marginalized, or perhaps even discouraged by the death penalty process.

Given the inter-connectivity mentioned above, a question that arises relates to the potential intersection of last statements and co-victim statements. In regard to restorative and non-restorative statements, as well as the general themes of statements, do the statements of the condemned and co-victims intersect in any meaningful way? Table 22 presents a cross-tabulation of restorative and non-restorative statements for these populations. Although the small number of cases in which co-victim statements were reported (N = 152) reduced the likelihood of yielding statistically significant findings, the table does indicate some interrelation between condemned inmates and co-victims in regard to whether they made restorative or non-restorative statements. The most substantial, and only statistically significant, difference was found at the intersection of non-restorative last statements of the condemned and restorative co-victim statements. In cases in which the condemned made a non-restorative last statement, co-victims were much less likely to make a restorative statement ($\chi^2 = 3.74, p < .10$). This was not supported, however, by direct relationships in regard to either restorative or non-restorative statements being given by both parties. We are left with little ability to draw solid conclusions from these findings. The lack of relationships found among restorative and non-restorative statements of the condemned and co-victims may, in fact, give us more insight than the single significant finding. It appears that there may be little connection between the restorative nature of the statements of the condemned and his co-victims.

Table 22
Co-Victim Statement Themes by Characteristics of the Condemned Offender, Percentages within Restorative Categories of Last Statements of the Condemned

	Co-Victim Statement	
Last Statement	Restorative	Non-Restorative
Restorative		
Yes	61.8	74.8
No	53.7	80.5
Non-Restorative		
Yes	40.9*	87.0
No	62.8	74.4

*Significant at p < .10

Given the limited conclusions that can be drawn from this analysis of the aggregate measures of restorative and non-restorative statements, it is potentially more elucidating to examine the more specific major statement themes across these two populations. The following table (Table 23) presents Phi correlations (correlations between binary, nominal variables) among the major themes of last statements of the condemned and statements made by co-victims. The most immediately striking finding is that there appears to be very little correlation between the statements made by these two groups. This in itself is potentially expositive of a lack of real connection between these populations. This is in spite of the fact that so much of their focus, as illustrated in their statements, is upon each other. There seems to be a psychic awareness or even construction of the other without a real attachment of humanity. Based on the prior analyses, this appears to be particularly true in regard to co-victims—those for whom reconciliation via human connection might aid in healing. The significant correlations, where they are found, seem to reinforce this notion. Some of the strongest correlations were for contradictory statements, with what might be considered negative statements made by co-victims in conjunction with positive statements made by condemned inmates. For example, condemned expressions of well-wishes and love, contrition, and gratitude were positively related to co-victims' statements indicating they do not forgive the condemned. And in cases in which the condemned made a statement related to religion, co-victims were less likely to express forgiveness. On the other hand, in cases in which the condemned expressed resignation, co-victims were more likely to report satisfaction with the execution. These findings may be explained as the co-victims reacting negatively to the condemned presenting themselves in a positive light and gaining satisfaction when the condemned shows weakness or powerlessness (a potentially important reversal from the perspective of co-victims). We should, of course, be careful in drawing too strong of conclusions from these analyses. Given that we do not know whether or not the co-victims were even aware of the condemned inmate's statement, it is only speculation to refer to such correlations as representing any form of reaction.

Table 23
Phi Correlations, Major Themes of Co-Victim Statements by Major Themes of the Last Statements of the Condemned

	Last Statements of the Condemned				
Co-Victim Statements	Well-Wishes	Religion	Contrition	Gratitude	Personal Reconciliation
Brought Healing or Closure	.116	.049	.083	-.033	-.081
Did Not Bring Healing or Closure	-.034	-.097	.072	.022	-.129
Satisfied	.024	.062	.066	-.024	.024
Dissatisfied	.069	.072	-.015	.094	-.080
Justice and Revenge	-.129	-.048	-.014	-.090	-.012
Memorialize or Honor Victim	.011	-.021	.037	-.076	-.139*
Removal of Condemned	.116	-.044	-.062	.023	-.015
Forgives	.001	-.151*	.093	.040	.059
Does Not Forgive	.226**	.106	.278**	.141*	.006
Sympathy	-.003	-.063	-.048	-.050	-.078
Rationalization	-.081	-.110	.021	-.044	.118
Religion	-.149*	-.082	.003	-.084	-.021
Support DP	.039	-.055	.015	-.013	-.010
Oppose DP	-.114	-.110	-.001	-.018	-.123

*Significant at $p < .10$

**Significant at $p < .05$

Table 23 (continued)

Co-Victim Statements	Last Statements of the Condemned: Denial of Responsibility	Criticism of Death Penalty	Anger & Resentment	Resignation	Accountability
Brought Healing or Closure	-.155*	.012	-.070	-.023	.012
Did Not Bring Healing or Closure	.093	.082	.003	.055	-.105
Satisfied	-.115	-.094	-.162**	268**	.128
Dissatisfied	.016	.032	.081	176**	-.076
Justice and Revenge	.062	-.035	.054	.103	-.026
Memorialize or Honor Victim	-.120	-.006	-.053	-.053	-.048
Removal of Condemned	.079	-.002	.084	.138*	-.023
Forgives	-.030	-.042	-.113	.033	-.093
Does Not Forgive	-.165**	-.077	-.130	-.064	-.029
Sympathy	-.063	-.046	-.105	.066	-.065
Rationalization	.046	257**	.117	.054	-.112
Religion	-.008	-.011	-.123	.081	-.020
Support DP	-.054	-.079	-.023	.056	-.084
Oppose DP	-.044	-.018	-.073	-.073	-.060

*Significant at $p < .10$

**Significant at $p < .05$

Other noteworthy findings in Table 23 indicate some interesting correlations. In cases in which the condemned criticized the death penalty, co-victims were more likely to rationalize its use or their own implicit involvement in the execution. Interestingly, co-victims were less likely to report that the execution brought them healing or closure in cases in which the condemned made a statement denying responsibility for the crime. Similarly, co-victims were less likely to express satisfaction with the execution or death penalty process when the condemned expressed anger and resentment in their last statements.

Again, conclusions made from these correlations are tentative at best. However, they do shed some light on possible interrelationships existing among the sentiments of condemned inmates and their co-victims. To the degree that we can assume some familiarity with the sentiments of the other, and that statements made at the time of execution to some degree reflect prior expressed sentiments, these correlations locate some areas of interconnection between the condemned and co-victims. They also indicate that interconnection is lacking in many regards. But, most importantly, it indicates interconnection that appears more combative and destructive than reconciliatory and healing. In regard to the elements of meaningful restoration (primarily for co-victims but also for the condemned), there is a disconnect inherent in the intersection of these statement themes. The elements of restoration and reconciliation offered by the condemned seem to evoke a lack of restoration on the part of the co-victims. This suggests to me that, in the years following the loss of their loved-one, co-victims have done little healing and instead have held on to their anger, resentment, and pain—emotions perhaps even cultivated in the lengthy death penalty process.

LESSONS LEARNED

Although the present study is limited in several ways, it sheds important light on two neglected populations by giving voice to them and allowing their perspectives to be heard. More generally, the humanity involved in the death penalty and executions is exposed and the reality of the impact of state sanctioned killing confronted. In the end, this study offers important insight and lessons both about the death penalty and about engaging in research on the death penalty and those who are most directly connected to or impacted by it.

Lessons Learned about the Death Penalty

The voices of the condemned and of the co-victims of capital crimes offer perspectives that have for too long been neglected or ignored in the discourse surrounding the death penalty. These voices reveal the humanity that too often lies just out of view in typical observations of the death penalty. Scholars philosophize about the morality of the death penalty, examine aggregate trends and patterns in its use, and analyze judicial and legal aspects of capital punishment. Politicians and policy makers consider its efficacy as a criminal punishment and whether or not the public supports or opposes it. In contrast, this study has shed light on the humanity that is often obscured by the "machinery" of the death penalty and execution processes. What we learn from this is that the death penalty has real consequences for real human beings and that these consequences are often not congruent with the intentions of capital punishment.

Condemned murderers are often depicted as evil aberrations who are irredeemable and thus need to be permanently removed from human societies (Lynch, 2002; Vollum et al., 2004). As such, the death penalty offers a way to permanently incapacitate these individuals who will always be dangerous. A recent study of public attitudes about the death penalty in Texas indicates that incapacitation or removal from society comprises the second most common rationale for death penalty support (Vollum et al., 2004). By far the most common rationale was retribution, that the death penalty was the only appropriate response to bring justice and by which to truly hold the offender accountable for his actions (Vollum et al., 2004). These are common attitudes about the death penalty but they exist in the context of a dialogue from which the voices of the condemned have been excluded, leaving a potentially important gap between perceptions and reality.

One need only examine the cases of exonerated death row inmates to realize that blanket proclamations of these individuals as inherently evil and irredeemable are misguided (Blank & Jensen, 2004). Indeed, each of the more than 120 death row inmates who have been exonerated over the last three decades (DPIC, 2007a) were at one time included among the collectively defiled "living dead." We learn further from the words of condemned inmates in the present study that such broad categorizations are overly simplistic and often misapplied. Rather, redemption and transformation resonate loudly in the words of many of these individuals. Does this mean that they are no longer dangerous, that they have truly reformed and should be free, and that we should trust their words 100 percent or that their words necessarily translate into behavior? Not necessarily. Indeed, we will never know. But, in regard to the sincerity of their words, there is little reason to lie when one is going to be killed in a matter of minutes. Regardless of what we believe in regard to the connection between their words and their potential behavior, the present study reveals that redemption and transformation are possible and expressed with regularity among these individuals. This is an astounding revelation in contrast to popular and official perceptions.

The death penalty is commonly held out as the only sure way to mete out justice for these evil killers, the only way to truly hold them accountable for their horrific crimes. And, as previously mentioned, public attitudes strongly reflect this sentiment (Vollum et al., 2004). We learn from the voices of the condemned that the death penalty fails to extract real accountability on behalf of the offender. In fact, the theme of accountability, in which the condemned overtly accepted responsibility for the crime or for other harmful acts, was the least common among the ten major themes of last statements. The condemned explicitly denied responsibility in nearly one fifth of the cases. According to those who advocate restorative justice, such accountability is central to the justice process and to the healing and reconciliation of all who are impacted by crime. Retributive justice, in spite of rhetoric about holding criminals accountable for their actions, actually discourages or impedes such accountability (Wright, 1996; Zehr, 1990; Zehr & Mika, 1998). And the death penalty, being the ultimate manifestation of retributive justice, is no different.

Co-victims' voices are also obscured in the death penalty process. From the very early stages, the victims and co-victims of capital murder are removed as meaningful subjects in the justice process, literally having their "victimhood" taken from them by the state (Christie, 1977). In spite of this apparent marginalization, the death penalty is often held out as a path toward closure and justice for victims and co-victims. In fact, victims' families are often championed by politicians and advocacy groups as the reason we need the death penalty. We learn from the words of actual co-victims that this path is rarely as clear or efficacious as many would have us believe. Rather, we find that the path is one that seems to suspend the lives and the healing and grieving processes for co-victims. Their needs for closure, healing, and justice are, in many cases, delayed.

It does seem that co-victims may obtain these things in the years during which they are awaiting the execution, but there is evidence from these statements that the death penalty process does not necessarily help this process and in many cases may impede it. In fact, the single most prevalent specific theme among co-victim statements was dissatisfaction or frustration with the delay or length of time in carrying out the execution. This was expressed by co-victims in over a quarter of the cases. Moreover, co-victims were much more likely to express that the execution represented a "conclusion" to a difficult period (22.6%) than that it brought them "closure" (2.5%). Many indicated that they had waited a long time for the execution and that they could "finally" move on with their lives. This suggests that co-victims often hold on to their grief and pain, waiting for the execution as some form of turning point for them. This is no surprise as the death penalty is often depicted as being intended for just this purpose—to provide the much needed closure and justice for co-victims. We must ask: How much sooner might these co-victims have moved through the natural grieving and healing processes had they not waited for the promised salve of the execution? Perhaps holding the execution out there as the magic point at which closure can be obtained simply leads to increased grief in the waiting. When we add to this the ambiguity of the process due to appeals, hearings, new trials, and stays as well as the often accompanying news stories and reports, the extended suffering is exacerbated even further. Co-victims must relive the traumatic events and face the unknown disposition of the person who has caused them this trauma over and over again. These realities of the death penalty are hardly conducive to healthy grieving and healing.

Finally, we learn from the voices of the co-victims that there is a lack of connection to the human "other" of the condemned. Arrigo and Williams (2003) explain the problem:

> [Co-victims] have failed to connect with the humanity of the other (i.e. the stranger unlike us) and have dismissed or repressed the realization that the constitution of one's own self-identity inexorably passes through the complexity of all social relations, including those that are devastating to accept (p. 619).

This lack of connection manifests most directly in an inability to forgive the condemned—an essential component in healing in the wake of victimization. But there is more direct evidence that this lack of connection relates to dissatisfaction with the execution and the death penalty among co-victims. The second most predominant specific theme among co-victim statements was dissatisfaction due to something about the condemned. In nearly a quarter of cases, co-victims expressed dissatisfaction in this context. Factors related to the condemned that were found to be dissatisfying were a lack of acknowledgment of the co-victim, a lack of apology, and a refusal to take responsibility for their actions. This clearly indicates an underlying need for connection to the condemned and to the damaging impact when it is not present.

Although this study was limited to two particular populations directly impacted by the death penalty process and execution, we know from the work of others that the consequences of the death penalty and executions are not limited to just these two groups of individuals. Rather, there is a whole "death row community" of individuals who are impacted by the implementation of this form of punishment (Arrigo & Fowler, 2001). There are also the broader societal impacts noted in Chapter II of this book. The impact and often unintended consequences of the death penalty reverberate throughout all of these groups. What we learn from the voices of the condemned and their co-victims is that these reverberations often produce human casualties and that we fail to leverage the inherent human connection among these groups and the potential for meaningful transformation and healing for these individual.

There is clearly a transformative process that is occurring while condemned offenders await their fate on death row. It seems that we should try to capture the factors related to this transformative process and apply it more broadly to offenders throughout the system. There is indeed something important to be learned here. Of course, we cannot know how much of the transformation is due to the condemned facing certain death, in which case such a process can not be replicated in the absence of the death penalty. We must consider the very real possibility that facing death may be a significant catalyzing force in the positive transformation and reform of condemned murderers. But the very fact that transformation and reform may be possible among a group of offenders considered beyond redemption is an important lesson. Moreover, there is clearly a need for connection and for processes that assist in healing in the wake of losing a loved-one to murder. The death penalty process clearly does not meet these needs. If we are truly seeking healing, closure, and justice for the co-victims, as advocates for the death penalty proclaim, then this is a lesson that must not be ignored.

There is a real desire among all who are touched by murder and the death penalty to assert and express their humanity and there is a need for connection to others that goes largely unmet in the death penalty process (Arrigo & Williams, 2003). The lessons we learn from the voices of the condemned and their co-victims imply that there is a need for restorative initiatives, whether they exist in the context of the death penalty or in lieu of the death penalty (the latter, many believe, is the only option if we are to have truly restorative justice). As discussed in Chapter III, restorative justice practices have begun to be employed in the context of the death penalty process with overwhelming success for both the condemned and the co-victims (Umbreit et al., 2003; Umbreit & Vos, 2000). Restorative justice offers us a paradigm in which all of these lessons may be heeded and in which the unfulilfilled needs might be more sufficiently met.

The overall lesson we learn about the death penalty from the voices of the condemned and their co-victims is that it represents missed opportunities and a failure of our responsibilities toward one another in human societies. We have missed opportunities by killing individuals who have something to offer, even if it is only their perspective and testimony to their transformation. We have missed opportunities to harness the transformative forces experienced by those on death row and offer them to offenders who will not be executed. And we have failed to offer meaningful and timely healing and justice for co-victims, instead often prolonging their pain and grief. In the end, we have surrendered to hopelessness and missed opportunities for a justice that is restorative and transformative.

Lessons Learned about Researching Condemned and Co-victim Populations

There is a richness and depth to the brief words of condemned inmates and co-victims that was, to some degree, unexpected. Although it was definitely expected that patterns, commonalities, and distinctions among the themes of these statements would be detected, the overwhelming wealth of sentiments and messages was a welcomed surprise. As pleasing as this revelation of depth and breadth was, there remained a nagging reminder that I had only scratched the surface. The wealth of information offered in the words of these individuals gave a clear indication that there existed a much greater depth of meaning, emotion, and cognition than could ever be adequately mined from these brief statements. This is one of the key lessons learned about researching these populations: They are heterogeneous groups with a diversity of thoughts, emotions, and perspectives in regard to the death penalty and that much more rigorous attempts to study them will undoubtedly continue to reveal important insights into the death penalty and the individuals most directly impacted by it.

An obvious limitation of the present study is that it relies on statements given by these populations gathered from secondary sources (in the case of the condemned, from official records and in the case of co-victims, from the local newspaper). The mediating impact of these sources can not be denied and the ability to develop a thorough and generalizable representation of the perspectives of these individuals is somewhat mitigated by these facts. Moreover, these are fairly unique statements given under extraordinary circumstances. This fact comes through loud and clear in the statements of both groups. In spite of this, however, the statements indicate that there is fertile soil in the words, emotions, sentiments, and perspectives of these individuals for cultivating a deeper understanding of the human side of the death penalty. We learn through these words, that there is much left to be learned from these individuals. Although the present study is limited in the depth of insight into the impact of executions on those involved, it does provide an important platform for further research on these groups.

As is often the case with exploratory research, one of the greatest contributions this study makes is to potentially catalyze further research on these neglected populations and the often hidden humanity that underlies the death penalty and executions. This study should encourage others to engage in other forms of research on these groups. Structured and unstructured interviews as well as longitudinal case studies are some needed methodologies if we are to better understand the dynamics of many of the factors only identified in the present study. Specifically, the ability to gather data over time on the experiences of condemned inmates may shed some light on the processes which are effecting the transformations detected in their last statements. In regard to co-victims, longitudinal research would provide some insight into the impact of the death penalty process over time and potentially identify factors related to healing and closure. From this we may find better ways to respond to the pain and suffering of homicide co-victims so that their need to grieve and heal is more adequately attended to rather than impeded and so that they may experience meaningful and restorative justice. In both cases, personal interviews would better mine the depths of these individuals and their thoughts and emotions surrounding the death penalty and execution processes—depths only speculated from the comparatively shallow waters of their statements examined in the present study. Deeper interviews will no doubt reveal a more thorough understanding of their sentiments and the meaning behind their sometimes cryptic statements. They will make their voices louder and clearer. These are sources of data that were not available for the present study but they are sorely needed, and it is my hope that this study catalyzes such research initiatives.

It would be worthwhile to also extend research, for comparative purposes, to offenders and co-victims in murder cases in which the offender is not sentenced to death. It would certainly be interesting to examine convicted murderers' attitudes and perspectives as a point of comparison to those who await their own execution. Do the same forms of transformation occur over time? Do these inmates think and feel similar things as their death row or death chamber counterparts? These are important questions. For if the answer to these questions is no, there may be something that can be learned from the transformative process that apparently occurs for those sentenced to death. Aside from the not insignificant factor of impending execution, factors serving as positively transformative forces in the lives of death row inmates may be applied more broadly to the inmate population.

It would also be interesting to examine co-victims in cases in which their offender was not sentenced to death. If the death penalty process does, indeed, extend or exacerbate the grieving and healing process, then we would expect these other populations of co-victims to exhibit signs of moving on or attaining closure or healing at earlier points than their counterparts. If we were to add to this an examination of co-victims who have taken advantage of restorative victim programs and services, we may be able to find the processes that optimize the healing and grieving process. A brighter future in the name of justice for victims may be forged from such research.

The final lesson we learn from the present study about researching the human side of the death penalty is that the human connections underlying the death penalty and all its components and processes are essential to understanding its impact on individuals and in the broader society. This is not a novel thought, as Arrigo and Fowler (2001) have already conceptualized what they refer to as the "death row community," suggesting that many diverse individuals are interconnected by the death penalty process and that these individuals have important and meaningful relationships to one another. This study has shown that such connections are wide-reaching and important but are also largely neglected in the death penalty process. Research in the future must not only consider these interconnections but also must explicitly examine them as important elements in understanding the death penalty as a social and cultural institution. In sum, research should extend beyond the condemned inmates and the co-victims to family and friends of the condemned, correctional staff, clergy and spiritual advisors, attorneys, media representatives, medical and mental health professionals, and even judges and juries if we want to understand the full human impact of the death penalty. The humanity at the center of the death penalty process lies not only in each of these individuals but in the web of interconnections spun by the machinery of death that starts with a killing and ends with a killing.

CONCLUSION

Murders and resulting death sentences leave a tumultuous wake in their path, a long path that can be both transformative and destructive for the humanity at the center of it all. As we have seen, for the condemned, statements often reflect positive transformation or at least transformative messages that reaffirm or reestablish their humanity. For co-victims, the process seems to often have a destructive effect, an effect that is evident in the non-restorative nature of their statements and the anger, pain, and revenge that are expressed repeatedly in their words and that apparently remain long after the loss of their loved one.

It was my intention in this book to "give voice" to the two populations which, although often neglected or ignored within it, are the most directly impacted by the death penalty process: those condemned to die by execution and those co-victims in whose name this brand of justice is often served. By doing this I had hoped to draw out important perspectives and attitudes that would tell us something about the human side of the use of this most extreme criminal punishment. Although not without flaws and failure, I believe I have accomplished this. By spending months poring over, thinking about, and analyzing the statements of these individuals I gained more insight into their thoughts, attitudes, and sentiments than I would have ever imagined. I have done my best to relay these findings and insights in this book and hope that the voices of these individuals resonate in the minds and hearts of the readers.

APPENDIX A

Last Statements of Condemned Inmates
CODING PROTOCOL

In applying codes to the statements of condemned inmates it is important to keep an open mind allowing the statement to speak for itself. Start by carefully reading through the statement as a whole. Then look for particular indicators (noted in more detail below with each associated code) of the specified categories and concepts. For each of the following codes, follow the researcher's description and criteria closely. The "KEY WORDS AND PHRASES" are provided as examples of words, phrases, or statements which would represent the concept. ***These are only examples***. They do not mean that the statement must be exactly like, or even substantially similar, to qualify for the associated category. They are simply provided to give you an idea of something that would qualify and to sensitize the coder to the nature of the category.

For each statement use the provided "Last Statements Code List" along with the more detailed protocol to "assign" the appropriate categories/themes. Simply write in the box below the statement the numbers for <u>all categories</u> you believe are relevant to the statement. The statements will often have multiple messages. Be sure to carefully identify all messages and their associated categories in the statement. The categories <u>are not</u> mutually exclusive and there is overlap. There may be cases in which a specific phrase or portion of the statement fits into multiple categories. Don't be afraid to be liberal in your application of categories or themes. If you are unsure, it is better to err on the side of including the category rather than not including it (i.e. err on the side of "over-coding"); and if you are unsure if it fits into one or the other or both of multiple categories, err on the side of selecting both.

<u>A BRIEF DESCRIPTION OF THE EXECUTION</u>

Executions in Texas are carried out in Huntsville, Texas at the Huntsville Unit ("Walls" Unit). Until the mid-90s, they were carried out just before midnight, but since have been carried out just after 6:00

pm. They take place in what is referred to as the "death chamber" which is a small room with a gurney and several adjoining viewing rooms for witnesses. The condemned inmate is strapped down by correctional officers and an IV line is injected through which the lethal drugs will flow. He or she is given an opportunity to speak a last statement. There is a microphone in the death chamber, but no recording is made. Instead, an administrative assistant transcribes the last statement in a remote location. Prior to 1996, co-victims were not allowed to witness an execution. Only approved family and friends of the condemned inmate were allowed in addition to state and TDCJ officials, lawyers, clergy, and media. Starting in 1996, co-victims were allowed to witness the execution. Witnesses for the condemned and co-victim witnesses watch from separate but adjacent rooms. They are all separated from the condemned by a large glass window. When the condemned inmate is finished speaking his last statement, he will often signal to the warden that he is finished by stating something like "That's it, Warden," "I'm ready," or other such phrases. When the warden gives the sign, the lethal drugs begin to flow.

CONTRITION

1. **Apology-to Co-Victim(s)** [APOL1]

DESCRIPTION/DIRECTIONS: The inmate specifically apologizes to any of the co-victims for killing their loved one. General expressions of sorrow or sympathy (e.g. "I'm sorry your son was killed") without any indication they take responsibility for that loss are not sufficient. There needs to be some direct apology on behalf of the inmate toward the co-victim(s). Stating something like "I would like to apologize to the Smith family" would be sufficient to code this category. Simply asking forgiveness is not sufficient to code this category (there is a separate category for that). If they say they are sorry for the co-victim's loss or pain but don't specify their responsibility, *consider* coding #44: "Wish Co-Victims Peace or Closure." Finally, if the inmate names people when apologizing and you're not sure they are co-victims (you may be able to infer this from what is stated even if it's not specific), contact the researcher and he can tell you whether or not those named are co-victims.

NOTE: Simply being regretful is not the same as apologizing. They must be sorry for what they did. Regret may simply mean they regret their own personal situation.

KEY WORDS AND PHRASES: "I *apologize* to Mrs. X's family for the pain I have caused you;" "I'm *sorry* for taking your loved one away from you;" "I would like to say I'm sorry to the X family."

2. **Apology to Own Family/Friends** [APOL2]

DESCRIPTION/DIRECTIONS: The inmate makes a direct apology to his or her loved ones including family and friends. This apology may come in a very general form or may be more specific to certain actions.

KEY WORDS AND PHRASES: "I'm sorry for the trouble I've caused my family;" "I'd like to apologize to my friends and family;" "Momma, I'm sorry I put you through this."

3. **Apology to God or Other Deity** [APOL3]

DESCRIPTION/DIRECTIONS: The inmate specifically apologizes to God (or other religious deity or figure).

KEY WORDS AND PHRASES: "I'm sorry for offending Allah;" "I apologize for defying God."

4. **Asks for Forgiveness from Co-Victim(s)** [FORGV1]

DESCRIPTION/DIRECTIONS: The inmate specifically asks the co-victims to forgive him. Simply saying he's sorry is not sufficient. The presence of the word "forgive" or any variation of it is critical here. (See description/directions for #1 for further guidance).

KEY WORDS AND PHRASES: Directed to co-victims: "I hope you can find it in your heart to someday *forgive* me for what I've done."

5. **Ask for Forgiveness from Own Family/Friends** [FORGV2]

DESCRIPTION/DIRECTIONS: The inmate specifically asks his family and/or friends to forgive him (no particular reason is necessary).

The presence of the word "forgive" or any variation of it is critical here.

KEY WORDS AND PHRASES: Directed to family or friends: "Please *forgive* me for all the grief I have caused you."

6. **Ask for Forgiveness from God or Other Deity** [FORGV3]

DESCRIPTION/DIRECTIONS: The inmate specifically asks for forgiveness from God or another religious figure or deity *in regard to the capital murder*. This is not the same as asking God for general forgiveness for "sins" or anything else—it should be specific to the capital offense.

KEY WORDS AND PHRASES: "God, please *forgive* me for what I done to those innocent girls."

7. **Wish to Turn Back Time** [TIME]

DESCRIPTION/DIRECTIONS: The inmate expresses a wish to take back or undo what they did (the capital murder). May also be expressed as a wish they could bring back the co-victims' loved ones.

KEY WORDS AND PHRASES: "If I could go back and change what I did, I would;" "I wish I could bring back your children, but I can't."

8. Apology/Ask for Forgiveness-Unspecified or Other [APOL4]

DESCRIPTION/DIRECTIONS: If the inmate either apologizes or asks for forgiveness without specifying to whom he is directing the apology. Or, if there is no specification of for what he is asking forgiveness.

KEY WORDS AND PHRASES: "I'm so sorry. I hope I can be forgiven for what I did (with no further specification offered);" "I'm sorry for everything I put y'all through."

RELIGION/SPIRITUALITY

9. **Prayer for Self** [PRAY1]

DESCRIPTION/DIRECTIONS: The inmate prays to God (or other religious deity) for themselves (e.g. prays to Jesus to save his soul; prays to God to accept him into heaven). Also, if the inmate asks others to pray for him.

KEY WORDS AND PHRASES: "I just pray to the Lord Jesus Christ that he will wash away my sins;" "Please God, grant me mercy and accept me into your kingdom, Amen;" "Please pray for me so that I may be saved."

10. **Prayer for Others** [PRAY2]

DESCRIPTION/DIRECTIONS: The inmate specifically prays to God (or other religious deity) on behalf of others (e.g. prays to God to watch over his family; prays to God to forgive those who are responsible for executing him). The inmate may simply ask God to bless others: "God bless each of you."

KEY WORDS AND PHRASES: "Forgive these people, Jesus, for they know not what they do;" "Allah, watch over my family and the brothers on death row."

11. **Prayer-Unspecified** [PRAY3]

DESCRIPTION/DIRECTIONS: Usually this will be in the form of a general **recital** of a prayer (e.g. The Lord's Prayer).

12. **Preaching** [PREACH]

DESCRIPTION/DIRECTIONS: This is most likely in the form of telling others to pray, accept the word of God (or other deity) or accept God into their lives. It may also be a more general statement about the greatness or power of God or a particular faith or deity.

KEY WORDS AND PHRASES: "Y'all better get right with God;" "God is fixin' to do some righteous things;" "God is the answer;" "I hope you all put your faith in God as I have."

13. **Proclamation of Faith/Giving Self over to God** [FAITH]

DESCRIPTION/DIRECTIONS: The inmate makes a statement proclaiming his faith, belief or devotion to God. He may also make a statement about giving himself over to God or putting his fate/soul/destiny in God's hands. General praising of God would also fit in this category.

KEY WORDS AND PHRASES: "Praise be to Allah;" "I accept Jesus Christ as my savior and I put my soul into his hands."

14. **Afterlife** [AFTERL]

DESCRIPTION/DIRECTIONS: The inmate makes a reference to the afterlife. This may come in the form of stating that he expects to see loved ones who are already dead. This does not have to be specifically religious (i.e. it doesn't have to refer to heaven specifically). [Do not check this category for phrases which are just simple figures of speech such as "see y'all later." These are often simply ways of saying goodbye or concluding a statement]. Any indication of believed existence after death fits into this category. But, simply stating that he will be with his family (in their hearts, memories, etc.) is not sufficient.

KEY WORDS AND PHRASES: "See you on the other side when you get there;" "I know my Grandma will be waiting for me to guide me into the hereafter;" "I'm going to a better place;" "I'm ready to go home."

GRATITUDE/THANKS

15. **To Family & Friends for Support** [THANK1]

DESCRIPTION/DIRECTIONS: The inmate thanks his family or friends for their support, love, devotion, kindness, assistance, etc. Often this will be stated in regard to support while they have been on death row, but it isn't restricted to that. If it is unclear who they are thanking, it will usually be safe to assume that those individuals qualify as friends. General expressions of appreciation (even if not explicitly thanking) are appropriate for this category.

KEY WORDS AND PHRASES: "Thank you all for sticking with me through all of this."

16. **To Criminal Justice Staff** [THANK2]

DESCRIPTION/DIRECTIONS: The inmate thanks criminal justice staff (correctional staff, wardens, police officers, judges, prosecutors). The thanks must be explicit (i.e. not just a simple "Thanks, warden" at the beginning of the statement—which would be in response to the warden asking him if he'd like to give a last statement).

KEY WORDS AND PHRASES: "I would like to thank the warden and the officers on death row for treating me so well over the last 10 years."

17. **To Lawyers** [THANK3]

DESCRIPTION/DIRECTIONS: The inmate specifically expresses gratitude or appreciation to his lawyers. This may be his trial lawyers or may be lawyers who worked his appeals. He may thank them for their legal work on his behalf or he may thank them for their general support, believing in him, or friendship.

18. **To Chaplain/Spiritual Advisor** [THANK4]

DESCRIPTION/DIRECTIONS: The inmate specifically expresses gratitude or appreciation to any spiritual advisor or religious figure (except a god or deity).

19. **To Media** [THANK5]

DESCRIPTION/DIRECTIONS: The inmate expresses gratitude or appreciation to the media.

20. **To God or other Deity** [THANK6]

DESCRIPTION/DIRECTIONS: The inmate specifically thanks God or other religious deities. The thanks need not be in reference to anything specific.

ACCEPTANCE OF RESPONSIBILITY

21. **For Specific Capital Murder** [ACCPT1]

DESCRIPTION/DIRECTIONS: The inmate owns up to their guilt in regard to the specific capital murder(s) for which they are being executed. They may state this very clearly (e.g. "I am guilty of killing those people") or in a more roundabout way (e.g. "I am here today because of what I did."). The key distinction here is that they are owning up to the capital murder(s) for which they are being executed and not just generally bad things they have done in their lives. Check this even if they own up to only one of several of the specific murders or if they own up to one or more (of the specific capital murders) while denying responsibility for others.

KEY WORDS AND PHRASES: "I killed that couple and I deserve what I'm getting;" "I would like to say that I am guilty for killing those girls."

22. **Taking Responsibility for Other Bad Acts or Crimes** [ACCPT2]

DESCRIPTION/DIRECTIONS: This may occur in addition to accepting responsibility to the specific capital murder or in place of it. The inmate may own up to the specific capital murder and also confess to other murders or crimes. The inmate may also make a statement of guilt or responsibility for other crimes without owning up to the specific murder for which they are being executed. This may also be a general expression of wrong-doing or confession of sins.

KEY WORDS AND PHRASES: "I killed those people. I would also like to clear a few things up. I also killed Mr. X in October of 1993;" "I have done plenty of bad things and am guilty of committing horrible crimes, but I didn't kill those kids."

DENIAL OF RESPONSIBILITY

23. **Minimize/Rationalize** [DENY1]

DESCRIPTION/DIRECTIONS: The inmate either downplays or rationalizes their act. Minimization would include things like claiming it was just a big mistake or accident. Rationalization would include things like claiming he was just trying to make a living, was under a lot of pressure

KEY WORDS AND PHRASES: "It was all just a big *mistake*." "I didn't intend to kill anyone. It was an *accident*."

24. **Externalize Blame** [DENY2]

DESCRIPTION/DIRECTIONS: The inmate places a portion or all of the blame for his actions on something or someone else. It doesn't have to be a complete denial of personal agency or responsibility—it may simply be an offer of an excuse. Some potential excuses offered may be self-defense or necessity. This is not the same as a claim of innocence and doesn't require that the inmate claim he didn't do the crime. It is simply an attempt to place part or all of the blame on other things or offer an excuse for his actions. Also included in this category would be any attempt to blame behavior on alcohol/drugs, sickness, or bad influences.

KEY WORDS AND PHRASES: "That bastard pulled a gun on me, so I shot him. What else was I supposed to do?" "I was under the influence of a lot of drugs. I didn't know what I was doing." "Those guys told me it was just going to be a robbery. They didn't say we were going to kill anyone."

25. **Claim of Innocence** [INNOC]

DESCRIPTION/DIRECTIONS: There are two primary forms of claims of innocence: 1) denial of any involvement or any wrongdoing in regard to the capital murder at issue; 2) acknowledgement of involvement or wrongdoing in regard to the capital murder by denial of actually committing the capital murder. The first is usually something like: "I did not kill those people; I had nothing to do with their deaths."

The second may be something like: “I robbed and beat that store clerk but I didn’t kill anyone,” or may be in the form of blaming a co-defendant for doing the actual killings.

KEY WORDS AND PHRASES: “I am *innocent*;” “I *did not kill* those people;” “You are killing an innocent man;” “I’ve done plenty of bad things in my time, but I *did not kill* anyone.”

PHILOSOPHIZE

26. **Death Penalty or Execution is Hypocritical/Killing is Wrong** [PHIL1]

DESCRIPTION/DIRECTIONS: The inmate points out the hypocrisy of the death penalty or criticizes the state for doing to him what they are condemning him for. The inmate may be more general in arguing that killing is wrong, doesn’t solve anything, or is just as bad as his actions (murders). Simply stating that the death penalty is murder is appropriate for this category.

KEY WORDS AND PHRASES: “Two wrongs don’t make a right;” “Killing me for killing is just doing the same thing you are saying is so wrong;” “This execution is just a legal murder. The state is committing murder.”

27. **Death Penalty or Execution Does Not Bring Peace or Closure** [PHIL2]

DESCRIPTION/DIRECTIONS: The inmate argues that their execution will not provide the co-victims with peace and/or closure. He may state that it won’t bring their loved-one(s) back. Statements that the execution (or death penalty, in general) doesn’t solve anything are sufficient for this category.

KEY WORDS AND PHRASES: “Killing me is not going to bring those people back;” “This execution will not bring you peace and closure (directed to co-victims).”

28. **Death Penalty or Execution is Not Justice** [PHIL3]

DESCRIPTION/DIRECTIONS: The inmate claims that his execution will not bring justice, is not right, will not bring order or make the world better, etc.

KEY WORDS AND PHRASES: "Killing me is not going to make things right, it just adds another death."

29. **Death Penalty or Execution is Inhumane** [PHIL4]

DESCRIPTION/DIRECTIONS: The inmate argues that the death penalty is inhumane. He may mention that it is barbaric or torture. The inmate may specifically refer to the Constitution or to the prohibition of cruel and unusual punishment. He may also refer to that fact that it is condemned as inhumane by other countries.

KEY WORDS AND PHRASES: "What you are doing to me today is *inhumane*. This is state sponsored *torture*."

30. **Death Penalty or Execution is Not a Deterrent** [PHIL5]

DESCRIPTION/DIRECTIONS: Inmate argues that by executing him, the state is not accomplishing anything in the way of stopping others from killing. He may also refer to his own case arguing that it didn't deter him or offering other alternatives that may have been a deterrent or have helped him before he came to commit the murders. The inmate may even go to the length of suggesting that the death penalty just creates more violence.

KEY WORDS AND PHRASES: "The death penalty does not stop people from murdering. It didn't stop me and it won't stop others."

31. **Death Penalty or Execution Only Creates More Victims** [PHIL6]

DESCRIPTION/DIRECTIONS: The inmate may refer to the death penalty and/or his execution as only creating more victims or more harm. For example, he may state that by executing him, you are only leaving another mother without a son or another X children without a father. The statement may be more general than that, however.

KEY WORDS AND PHRASES: "By executing me, you are creating one more mourning mother and denying two children their father;" "With this execution, you are only committing one more act of violence and creating more suffering."

32. **Death Penalty or Execution is Wrong (General)** [PHIL7]

DESCRIPTION/DIRECTIONS: The inmate makes a general statement about how the death penalty is wrong, needs to be abolished, etc. Include here general statements about executions of innocent people, calls for moratoriums, etc.

CONDEMNATION OF CONDEMNERS

33. **Condemns Police/CJ Officials** [CONDM1]

DESCRIPTION/DIRECTIONS: The inmate condemns criminal justice officials (police, prosecutors, wardens, correctional staff, judges) as being the ones committing the harms. It may be a straight accusation of wrongdoing or a comparison of "evil" acts, suggesting that they are no better than him and that their actions are worse (or no better) than what he has done.

KEY WORDS AND PHRASES: "The police set me up;" "The warden, by carrying out this execution, is murdering me as sure as I murdered those two women."

34. **Condemns CJ System or Government, in General** [CONDM2]

DESCRIPTION/DIRECTIONS: This is a more general statement of condemnation of the criminal justice system, state or government, in general. The inmate may condemn the system as being corrupt.

KEY WORDS AND PHRASES: "The criminal justice system, by killing me, is no better than I am;" "The whole criminal justice system is corrupt—they should be the ones on trial."

35. **Condemns Co-Victim(s)/Victim(s)** [CONDM3]

DESCRIPTION/DIRECTIONS: The inmate may condemn co-victims in a variety of ways. He may condemn them for calling for, taking a part in, or witnessing his execution, often accusing them of being murderers or being complicit in state sanctioned murder. He may also condemn them for being responsible for his execution (i.e. making initial accusations against him, testifying against him, asking for the death penalty) or for gaining satisfaction from his execution. It may accompany a claim of innocence or argument that the execution will not provide closure or bring back their loved-one.

KEY WORDS AND PHRASES: "You all know what is happening here is wrong. I didn't kill your brother and now you are guilty of killing me."

ANGER & RESENTMENT

36. **Toward Own Lawyers** [ANGER1]

DESCRIPTION/DIRECTIONS: General expression of anger toward the inmate's own attorneys. May be directed at either trial or appeal attorneys. May be in reference to their lack of effort, incompetence, or what the inmate perceives to be misconduct or wrongdoing in the course of defending him.

37. **Toward Witnesses at Trial** [ANGER2]

DESCRIPTION/DIRECTIONS: The inmate may direct anger at witnesses who testified against him. He may specifically express anger or resentment in the context of accusing them of lying or providing false statements against him. Be careful to distinguish from witnesses at the execution.

38. **Toward CJ Officials/CJ System** [ANGER3]

DESCRIPTION/DIRECTIONS: General expression of anger or resentment at either criminal justice officials (police, prosecutor, judge, warden, correctional staff) or the criminal justice system (courts, correctional system), as a whole.

39. **Toward Co-Victims** [ANGER4]

DESCRIPTION/DIRECTIONS: The inmate may express anger, resentment or hostility toward co-victims specifically. This may overlap with anger/resentment toward witnesses at trial (as some co-victims may have testified) or may be more general or un-specified. Be sure the anger, resentment or hostility is specifically directed at co-victims. See description/directions for code #1 for further directions about recognizing statements directed at co-victims.

PERSONAL RECONCILIATION/TRANSFORMATION

40. **Forgives Others** [RECON1]

DESCRIPTION/DIRECTIONS: The inmate forgives others for whatever reason. It may be a general forgiveness, be forgiveness for executing him or taking part in his execution, forgiveness for past treatment, etc. It may also be a broader reference to not having animosity/hatred/ill-feelings toward others.

KEY WORDS AND PHRASES: "Brother, I forgive you for what you said about me at trial;" "I forgive all of you for what you are about to do;" "I have found it in my heart to forgive everybody;" "I don't blame anyone for doing this to me;" "I don't have no animosity toward y'all."

41. **At Peace** [RECON2]

DESCRIPTION/DIRECTIONS: The inmate indicates that they have found peace or come to a peaceful place. The word peace is not necessary. Some inmates may use other similar words and phrases to express the same thing. Inmates may also express that they have "come to peace" with others or about circumstances or events.

KEY WORDS AND PHRASES: "It's okay everyone, I am at peace with things."

42. **Personal Transformation** [RECON3]

DESCRIPTION/DIRECTIONS: The inmate indicates a personal transformation has occurred in their lives. The inmate may directly reference his years on death row or the transformation that has occurred in the years awaiting death. In this case, religious references are acceptable. The inmate may refer to a transformation that has occurred within them or in their lives due to finding God, for example.

43. **Humanize** [HUMAN]

DESCRIPTION/DIRECTIONS: The inmate makes a statement about his own humanity. He may state that he is not a monster, is really not a bad person, is a good person, etc. He may state that he has changed and is not the person today he was then. This latter statement would qualify under both this category and the personal transformation category. For it to qualify for this category, it must go beyond the transformation statement and indicate some humanizing element in making the comparison of now with then (e.g. "I'm no longer the bad person I was then").

KEY WORDS AND PHRASES: "I just want everyone to know that I am *not a monster*;" "I am *not evil*, I am a *good person* who made a mistake;" "When I committed those acts, I was a ruthless criminal—I am no longer that evil person today."

WELL-WISHES

44. **Wish Co-Victims Peace or Closure** [WISH1]

DESCRIPTION/DIRECTIONS: The inmate directly addresses the co-victims, wishing they find peace, closure, or other similar outcomes. For direction about identifying statements made to co-victims see the description/directions for code #1.

KEY WORDS AND PHRASES: "To the parents of X, I really hope that my death helps you find peace and closure and move on in a positive direction with your lives."

45. **Wish that Execution Brings Justice** [WISH2]

DESCRIPTION/DIRECTIONS: The inmate expresses a general hope/wish that his execution provides justice (not necessarily for anyone in particular). He may refer to it as a balancing/equalizing action or state that he hopes it will make thing right.

KEY WORDS AND PHRASES: "I now give my life for taking a life. I hope that brings a sense of justice."

46. **Well-Wishes and/or Love to Family/Friends** [LOVE1]

DESCRIPTION/DIRECTIONS: The inmate expresses general well-wishes or words of love to his family and/or friends. This may come in a variety of forms. Some may be simple statements such as "I love you all. Tell Momma I love her," or "I hope that life treats you well," or "you all take care of yourselves now."

47. **General Expression of Love** [LOVE2]

DESCRIPTION/DIRECTIONS: The inmate may make a really general expression of love such as "I just want to say that I love everyone."

48. **Words of Encouragement to Family/Friends** [ENCR1]

DESCRIPTION/DIRECTIONS: The inmate may specifically address his family and/or friends with words of encouragement or words of support.

KEY WORDS AND PHRASES: "You all hang in there;" "You all keep your heads up;" "Be strong for the kids;" "I'm alright, don't cry for me."

49. **Words of Encouragement to Others on Death Row** [ENCR2]

DESCRIPTION/DIRECTIONS: The inmate may make similar words of encouragement (see Code #45) specifically to the other inmates on death row. This may be a simple expression of solidarity.

KEY WORDS AND PHRASES: "To the brothers on death row: Hang in there and keep on fighting for your lives."

RESIGNATION

50. **Fate** [RESN1]

DESCRIPTION/DIRECTIONS: The inmate may express a fatalistic attitude. This may includes statements that indicate a level of resignation because it is "just the way it is."

KEY WORDS AND PHRASES: "This is the hand I was dealt;" "I've accepted my fate."

51. **Helplessness** [RESN2]

DESCRIPTION/DIRECTIONS: The inmate may express a sense of helplessness. This will be similar to Fate but with a more depressed tone. It may be accompanied by an expression of wishing he could do something to stay alive.

KEY WORDS AND PHRASES: "I wish I didn't have to go, but there's nothing I can do about it."

52. **Release** [RESN3]

DESCRIPTION/DIRECTIONS: The inmate makes a statement indicating he is ready for release or to leave this world.

KEY WORDS AND PHRASES: "I am ready to be released;" "I am ready for the pain of this life to end."

OTHER

53. **Filibuster** [FILI]

DESCRIPTION/DIRECTIONS: This is a situation in which the inmate is attempting to speak on and on in an attempt to run the death warrant out. It is usually characterized by repetition and rambling.

54. **Recital of Song or Poem** [RECITE]

DESCRIPTION/DIRECTIONS: The inmate recites a song or poem or other type of previously written artistic expression. This may be written by someone else or by the inmate himself. The key is that he is *reciting* it.

55. **Cheer for Sport's Team** [SPORT]

DESCRIPTION/DIRECTIONS: The inmate may cheer, give praise, or thank a sports team.

KEY WORDS AND PHRASES: "How 'bout them Cowboys!?" "The Vikings are going all the way this year!"

56. **Statement or Act of Defiance** [DEFY]

DESCRIPTION/DIRECTIONS: The inmate may make a statement of defiance (toward anyone, but usually toward the CJ system, state or government). This may simply be indicated by a noted act.

KEY WORDS AND PHRASES: "You can all kiss my Black ass;" "I don't got nothing to say to the lot of you."

APPENDIX B

Co-Victim Statements
CODING PROTOCOL

In applying codes to the statements of co-victims (a co-victim is a relative or friend of the actual homicide victim) it is important to keep an open mind allowing the statement to speak for itself. Start by carefully reading through the statement as a whole. Then look for particular indicators (noted in more detail below with each associated code) of the specified categories and concepts. For each of the following codes, follow the researcher's description and criteria closely. The "KEY WORDS AND PHRASES" are provided as examples of words, phrases, or statements which would represent the concept. ***These are only examples***. They do not mean that the statement must be exactly like, or even substantially similar, to qualify for the associated category. They are simply provided to give you an idea of something that would qualify and to sensitize the coder to the nature of the category.

For each statement use the provided "Co-Victim Statements Code List" along with the more detailed protocol to "assign" the appropriate categories/themes. Simply write in the box below the statement the numbers for <u>all categories</u> you believe are relevant to the statement. The statements will often have multiple messages. Be sure to carefully identify all messages and their associated categories in the statement. The categories <u>are not</u> mutually exclusive and there is overlap. There may be cases in which a specific phrase or portion of the statement fits into multiple categories. Don't be afraid to be liberal in your application of categories or themes. If you are unsure, it is better to err on the side of including the category rather than not including it (i.e. err on the side of "over-coding."

<u>A NOTE ON REPORTERS' WORDS</u>

The objective in analyzing these statements is to analyze the actual words of the co-victims. Generally, the quoted statements are what should be relied on for the message. However, the qualifying words of the reporter may be used in identifying categories when those words refer to an associated co-victim quote. Use your discretion on this, but be aware that reporters may state things never explicitly stated by the co-victims. If you feel that the reporter's characterizations are supported by quotes, then go ahead and code accordingly.

A BRIEF DESCRIPTION OF THE EXECUTION

Executions in Texas are carried out in Huntsville, Texas at the Huntsville Unit ("Walls" Unit). Until the mid-90s, they were carried out just before midnight, but since have been carried out just after 6:00 pm. They take place in what is referred to as the "death chamber" which is a small room with a gurney and several adjoining viewing rooms for witnesses. The condemned inmate is strapped down by correctional officers and an IV line is injected through which the lethal drugs will flow. He or she is given an opportunity to speak a last statement. There is a microphone in the death chamber, but no recording is made. Instead, an administrative assistant transcribes the last statement in a remote location. Prior to 1996, co-victims were not allowed to witness an execution. Only approved family and friends of the condemned inmate were allowed in addition to state and TDCJ officials, lawyers, clergy, and media. Starting in 1996, co-victims were allowed to witness the execution. Witnesses for the condemned and co-victim witnesses watch from separate but adjacent rooms. They are all separated from the condemned by a large glass window.

SATISFACTION

1. **Looking Forward to Execution** [SATIS1]

DESCRIPTION/DIRECTIONS: Any indication that the co-victim was looking forward to or positively anticipating the execution. This is not the same as being upset or frustrated that it took so long or being glad that it's over with, although it may overlap with such sentiments.

KEY WORDS AND PHRASES: "I've been looking forward to this day for a long time."

2. **Satisfaction with Death** [SATIS2]

DESCRIPTION/DIRECTIONS: A statement simply indicating that the co-victim is glad that the condemned is dead. Only select this category if the statement is *without* any specified utility or reason other than simple satisfaction with the death. For example, "I'm glad he's dead so he can't hurt anyone else" would not be appropriate for this category. The thrust of this category is to capture statements which indicate some level of happiness deriving simply from the fact the condemned inmate is dead or that the execution was carried out.

KEY WORDS AND PHRASES: "I'm just glad he's gone;" "I'm just happy that he has taken his last breath on this earth;" "I feel satisfied that the killer of my sister is no longer living."

3. **Happy to be Present at Execution** [SATIS3]

DESCRIPTION/DIRECTIONS: The co-victim indicates that he or she is glad they could be present at or see the execution.

KEY WORDS AND PHRASES: "I'm so glad I could be here to witness the death of the man who killed my parents."

4. **Gratitude to State of Texas/CJ System** [SATIS4]

DESCRIPTION/DIRECTIONS: A statement of thanks or gratitude directed toward the State of Texas or criminal justice system and/or personnel (including juries, judges, police, Governor, prosecutor, etc.).

KEY WORDS AND PHRASES: "I just thank every one of those twelve jurors who gave us this justice;" "I'm so glad to live in Texas where real justice is possible."

5. **Grateful for Apology or Remorse** [SATIS5]

DESCRIPTION/DIRECTIONS: A statement of gratitude for an apology or other expression of remorse by the condemned inmate.

KEY WORDS AND PHRASES: "I'm really thankful that he apologized to us;" "He apologized, and it really helped. I have to at least give him credit for that."

6. **General Satisfaction with Last Statement of Condemned** [SATIS6]

DESCRIPTION/DIRECTIONS: A general statement indicating satisfaction with the last statement of the condemned inmate. This will usually be a non-specific reference to the statement.

KEY WORDS AND PHRASES: "It was good to hear what he had to say;" "His last statement brought some comfort to us."

DISSATISFACTION/FRUSTRATION

7. **Lack of Apology or Remorse** [FRUST1]

DESCRIPTION/DIRECTIONS: The co-victim expresses disappointment or frustration with the fact that the condemned did not apologize or indicate that he was sorry in any way.

KEY WORDS AND PHRASES: "I really thought he'd apologize;" "I was really hoping he would have apologized."

8. **Lack of Acknowledgement** [FRUST2]

DESCRIPTION/DIRECTIONS: The co-victim expresses disappointment or frustration with the fact that the condemned did not acknowledge them at the execution.

KEY WORDS AND PHRASES: "The coward wouldn't even look at us;" "I was really hoping to look him in the eye one last time, but he just pretended like we wasn't even there."

9. **Claim of Innocence** [FRUST3]

DESCRIPTION/DIRECTIONS: The co-victim expresses frustration or anger that the condemned proclaimed his innocence during his last statement.

KEY WORDS AND PHRASES: "I can't believe he had the audacity to sit there and say he didn't kill our daughter when we all know darn well that he did!"

10. **Lack of Claim of Responsibility** [FRUST4]

DESCRIPTION/DIRECTIONS: The co-victim expresses disappointment or frustration that the condemned, in his last words, refused to take responsibility for what he did. This is not the same as an outright claim to innocence—this simply represents a neglect to own up to the fact that the condemned committed the crime.

KEY WORDS AND PHRASES: "He wouldn't even acknowledge that he took our son away from us;" "I was hoping he would finally come clean and tell the truth, but he wouldn't say a word."

11. **Statement/Demeanor** [FRUST5]

DESCRIPTION/DIRECTIONS: The co-victim expresses a general frustration with the condemned's statement and/or demeanor in the death chamber. This would be coded in cases in which the co-victim doesn't direct their frustration at any of the particular issues indicated in the above codes, but rather shows generalized disdain, anger or frustration with the inmate's words, actions or demeanor in the death chamber.

KEY WORDS AND PHRASES: "It just made me sick that that smug ***hole could sit there and smile and joke;" "For him to be able to say he is ready to die makes me angry; our daughter wasn't ready."

12. **CJ System/Delay** [DELAY]

DESCRIPTION/DIRECTIONS: The co-victim expresses frustration or dissatisfaction with the criminal justice system or process. This is particularly likely to come in the form of frustration with the lengthy amount of time it took to execute the condemned and/or the numerous hearings, appeals, stays, and other system delays.

KEY WORDS AND PHRASES: "As far as I'm concerned this is coming 13 years too late!" "It's ridiculous that it should take 15 years to executed a guilty murderer—the system needs to be changed."

13. **Media** [MEDIA]

DESCRIPTION/DIRECTIONS: The co-victim expresses frustration or anger toward the media (news and other) for their coverage of the crime, death penalty, execution, or other aspect related to the case.

KEY WORDS AND PHRASES: "The media made this guy out to be the victim. We are the victims!" "Until now, the media has made this all about this man who killed our grandmother. Today was about her."

14. **Question the Truthfulness of Statement** [XTRUTH]

DESCRIPTION/DIRECTIONS: A statement indicating that the co-victim questions, contends with, or rejects the general truthfulness of the condemned inmate's last statement.

KEY WORDS AND PHRASES: "I don't believe a word that came out of his mouth."

15. **Dismisses Condemned's Words/Sentiments** [XWORDS]

DESCRIPTION/DIRECTIONS: A statement indicating an outright dismissal or rejection of anything the condemned inmate has or had to say. This is different than a question of truthfulness in that the truthfulness doesn't really matter—either way the co-victim is not going to consider or doesn't care about anything the inmate has to say.

KEY WORDS AND PHRASES: "Anything that man has to say to us doesn't mean a thing."

16. **No Happiness/Joy/Satisfaction from Execution** [XSATIS]

DESCRIPTION/DIRECTIONS: The co-victim indicates that the execution brought them no joy, satisfaction, or happiness.

KEY WORDS AND PHRASES: "Killing this man is not a joyous event for any of us."

DEATH PENALTY SUPPORT

17. **Personalized Death Penalty Support** [SUPP1]

DESCRIPTION/DIRECTIONS: The co-victim proclaims support for the death penalty and/or executions via a personal statement. For example, the co-victim may state that anyone who has experienced what they have would know that the death penalty is the right thing. They may state this as a counterpoint to those who oppose the death penalty or to their own prior opposition to or ambivalence about the death penalty.

KEY WORDS AND PHRASES: "I was never sure what I thought about the death penalty, but I now support it wholeheartedly."

18. **Abstract Death Penalty Support** [SUPP2]

DESCRIPTION/DIRECTIONS: The co-victim expresses more general support for the death penalty without personalized rationale. Again, this may come as a counterpoint to those who oppose the death penalty. This statement will likely be a proclamation of general agreement with the death penalty, a celebration of the fact that we have the death penalty, or some more specific rationale for the death penalty (e.g. deterrence, incapacitation, justice, retribution).

KEY WORDS AND PHRASES: "Sometimes the death penalty is the only appropriate punishment for evil people like him;" "The death penalty is necessary for real justice to be served;" "I support the death penalty because some people just don't deserve to be on this earth."

19. **Criticism of Protestors** [SUPP3]

DESCRIPTION/DIRECTIONS: The co-victim makes reference to death penalty protestors, criticizing them for opposing the death penalty and/or actively protesting the execution.

KEY WORDS AND PHRASES: "These people out here with their candles and signs don't have a clue what it's like to go through what we've gone through;" "Those who make a scene protesting the death penalty are no better than these murderers."

20. **Death Penalty or Execution Opposition** [SUPP4]

DESCRIPTION/DIRECTIONS: The co-victim expresses any form of opposition to either the death penalty in general or the specific execution.

KEY WORDS AND PHRASES: "I really don't agree with the death penalty;" "I don't think that by killing another person, we've accomplished anything."

21. **Death Penalty Doesn't Solve Anything** [SUPP5]

DESCRIPTION/DIRECTIONS: Regardless of whether or not indicating support or opposition to the death penalty, the co-victim states that the death penalty or executions don't really solve anything.

KEY WORDS AND PHRASES: "What we're doing here tonight really doesn't solve the problems."

RATIONALIZATION

22. **Dehumanization** [RATN1]

DESCRIPTION/DIRECTIONS: The co-victim makes dehumanizing remarks about the condemned. The condemned may be equated to an animal, monster, or inanimate object or just simply be referred to as evil. The co-victim may also explicitly avoid referring to the condemned as a human being.

KEY WORDS AND PHRASES: "That man—and I am reluctant to even refer to him as a man—needed to die;" "He's no better than a rat which needed to be exterminated."

23. **Denial of Malevolence** [RATN2]

DESCRIPTION/DIRECTIONS: The co-victim makes a statement to deny/diminish/rationalize any potential malevolence on his or her part. This may be expressed in a way that externalizes responsibility for the positive feelings a co-victim may have about executing the condemned.

KEY WORDS AND PHRASES: "I am not a hateful or evil person, but I wanted justice for my mother." "I really don't like to see another person killed, but it had to be done."

24. **Demeans/Maligns Character of Condemned** [RATN3]

DESCRIPTION/DIRECTIONS: A statement describing the condemned inmate in a way that depicts him in a negative light (beyond simple reference to the murder). This is broader than the dehumanization above and is intended to be selected for general statements about the negative aspects of the condemned.

KEY WORDS AND PHRASES: "He is a horrible person who doesn't care about anyone but himself."

RELIGION

25. **Prayer for Victim/Co-Victims** [RELIG1]

DESCRIPTION/DIRECTIONS: The co-victim indicates that she has prayed or is praying on behalf of the deceased victim, herself, or other co-victims.

26. **Prayer for Condemned** [RELIG2]

DESCRIPTION/DIRECTIONS: The co-victim indicates that he has prayed or is praying for the condemned and/or his soul, salvation, etc.

KEY WORDS AND PHRASES: "I pray that he has accepted Jesus Christ as his savior and finds salvation;" "I asked God to forgive him."

27. **Prayer for Family of Condemned** [RELIG3]

DESCRIPTION/DIRECTIONS: The co-victim indicates that he has prayed or is praying for the family or any family members of the condemned.

KEY WORDS AND PHRASES: "I just pray for his Mother because I know what she is going through."

28. **God's Judgment** [RELIG4]

DESCRIPTION/DIRECTIONS: The co-victim refers to the role that God's (or other religious deity) judgment will have for the condemned. This will often be in the context of what will happen to the condemned after death.

KEY WORDS AND PHRASES: "His fate is in God's hands now—God will judge him."

29. **Proclamation of Faith** [RELIG5]

DESCRIPTION/DIRECTIONS: The co-victim makes a general proclamation of his or her faith in God or other religious deity.

KEY WORDS AND PHRASES: "Jesus is my Lord…" "I just praise Jesus for helping us through this difficult time;" "It is my faith in God…"

30. **Death Penalty in the Bible** [RELIG6]

DESCRIPTION/DIRECTIONS: The co-victim refers to the Bible's representation or depiction of the death penalty.

KEY WORDS AND PHRASES: "The Bible says an eye for an eye and that is what we got tonight."

HEALING AND CLOSURE

31. **Execution brings Healing and/or Closure** [CLOSUR]

DESCRIPTION/DIRECTIONS: The co-victim states that the execution brings healing or closure. Don't get this confused with statements regarding peace or relief (see next code). The co-victim must specifically refer to the broader notion of closure or healing (as opposed to peace and relief, which may be partial).

KEY WORDS AND PHRASES: "I feel a sense of closure from the execution;" "I think this really helped me and my whole family in our healing from our tragic loss."

32. **Execution brings Peace &/or Relief** [PEACE]

DESCRIPTION/DIRECTIONS: The co-victim states that the execution brought them a sense of peace, some peace, or some relief. This relates to the more immediate feeling obtained from the execution.

KEY WORDS AND PHRASES: "It really feels like a load has been lifted from me, it's quite a relief;" "Right after the execution, I felt a great sense of peace."

33. **Conclusion** [CONCL1]

DESCRIPTION/DIRECTIONS: The co-victim indicates that the execution is a form of conclusion or end of something in his or her life. This is in reference to *personal* conclusion on behalf of the co-victim(s). This <u>does not</u> include references to the end of an external process such as trials and appeals. It also does not include references to the end of the condemned's life as in expressions of relief that he is dead and can't hurt anyone again.

KEY WORDS AND PHRASES: "This is the *end* of a really difficult *chapter* in our lives;" "It's finally *over* and *done* with;" "We're looking forward to having this all *behind us*;" "Now we can finally move on."

34. **No More Appeals, Trials, or Hearings** [CONCL2]

DESCRIPTION/DIRECTIONS: The co-victim expresses relief or satisfaction that the execution has brought an end to the criminal justice process (specifically, the appeals, trials, and hearings).

KEY WORDS AND PHRASES: "I'm just glad that it's all over with—we won't have to worry about any more appeals."

35. **Beginning** [BEGIN]

DESCRIPTION/DIRECTIONS: The co-victim refers to the execution as the beginning of a personal process or time period.

KEY WORDS AND PHRASES: "Now the real healing process can begin;" "Maybe now we can finally start to search for closure;" "…a new chapter begins."

36. **Won't Bring Them Back** [XCLOS1]

DESCRIPTION/DIRECTIONS: The co-victim makes a statement about how the death of the condemned will not bring back the victim. This does not necessarily accompany a statement against the death penalty or negative statements about the execution.

KEY WORDS AND PHRASES: "He's dead, but that doesn't bring back my sister."

37. **No Healing or Closure** [XCLO2]

DESCRIPTION/DIRECTIONS: The co-victim states that the execution does not bring him or her healing or closure. This does not necessarily accompany negative statements about the death penalty or execution.

KEY WORDS AND PHRASES: "I'm glad he's gone, but killing him will not bring me closure."

38. **Prior Reconciliation** [PRECON]

DESCRIPTION/DIRECTIONS: The co-victim makes a statement that she has already found reconciliation with the crime/condemned/execution. She may state it in terms such as making peace.

KEY WORDS AND PHRASES: "I've been at peace with him and what he did for some time now;" "I've already made my peace with what has happened."

39. **Execution was Traumatizing** [TRAUMA]

DESCRIPTION/DIRECTIONS: The statement indicates that the co-victim found the execution in some way traumatizing.

KEY WORDS AND PHRASES: "It was horrible. I'll never get that image out of my mind."

JUSTICE AND REVENGE

40. **Justice for Victim** [JUST1]

DESCRIPTION/DIRECTIONS: The co-victim states that the execution is or brings justice for the deceased victim. To code this category, the co-victim must specify the deceased victim as the recipient of the justice.

41. **Justice for Society** [JUST2]

DESCRIPTION/DIRECTIONS: The co-victim states that the execution is justice for society at large or generally serves justice for the community, state, etc. Code this for non-specified references to justice such as "justice was served" with no reference to a specific recipients of that justice.

KEY WORDS AND PHRASES: "Tonight, justice was served;" "This execution brings justice for Texans."

42. **Desire to See or Inflict Harm or Suffering** [JUST3]

DESCRIPTION/DIRECTIONS: The co-victim indicates that he either wishes he could have inflicted harm on the condemned or to have seen more extensive harm and suffering come to the victim. The first aspect may be expressed as a desire to have been the one to kill the condemned or to have been allowed "some time alone" with the condemned. The second is more likely to be expressed in explicit terms about how the condemned should have been treated, killed, tortured, etc. Also, any specified desire to see him suffer fits within this category.

KEY WORDS AND PHRASES: "I wish I could have had just five minutes alone with him—I would have taken care of him good;" "They should have taken him out and dragged him slowly through the streets;" "If I had ever gotten my hands on him, he would have suffered like my brother suffered."

43. **Not Harsh Enough** [JUST4]

DESCRIPTION/DIRECTIONS: The co-victim states that the execution was not harsh enough or "too easy." This statement may come in the context of a comparison between the way the victim died and the nature of the execution.

KEY WORDS AND PHRASES: "My sister suffered for hours before she died; he got off easy;" "It was much too easy—I wish he had suffered more."

44. **Just Deserts** [JUST5]

DESCRIPTION/DIRECTIONS: The statement indicates that execution or the death penalty was the appropriate punishment deserved. This may be indicated with such phrases, as "the punishment fit the crime," "a death for a death," "eye for an eye" and "paying the price."

KEY WORDS AND PHRASES: "He took a life and so he must pay with his own."

45. **Comparison of Suffering of Victim & Condemned** [COMPAR]

DESCRIPTION/DIRECTIONS: The co-victim makes a comparison between the suffering or manner of death of the victim and that of the condemned inmate being executed. This will often accompany a statement about the execution being too easy or not harsh enough.

KEY WORDS AND PHRASES: "His death was certainly much less painful than my sister's;" "After the horrible way in which he killed my daughter, he sure had a luxury to be killed so humanely."

FORGIVENESS

46. **Forgive** [FORG]

DESCRIPTION/DIRECTIONS: The co-victim states that she forgives or has forgiven the condemned.

47. **Don't Forgive** [XFORG]

DESCRIPTION/DIRECTIONS: The co-victim specifically states that he does not forgive the condemned. Do not code this simply because the co-victim fails to make any statement indicating they do forgive the condemned.

KEY WORDS AND PHRASES: "I don't forgive him for what he did, I don't know how I could;" "I will never forgive him for taking my child away from me."

48. **Reject Apology** [XAPOL]

DESCRIPTION/DIRECTIONS: The co-victim explicitly rejects an apology offered by the condemned. This may be expressed as or accompany a statement regarding a belief that the apology was not sincere.

KEY WORDS AND PHRASES: "He said he was sorry, but I don't believe he really is;" "He apologized but it doesn't make up for what he did;" "His apology is way too late;" "He should have thought about how sorry he would be before he killed my aunt."

SYMPATHY

49. **For Condemned** [SYMP1]

DESCRIPTION/DIRECTIONS: The co-victim expresses sympathy or compassion for the condemned. This can be sympathy or compassion for any reason (e.g. the hard life they had, the fact that they are being executed, etc.).

KEY WORDS AND PHRASES: "I feel bad for him—I'm sure he is suffering." "I don't like to see another human being go through what he has to go through, but he put himself into this situation."

50. **For Condemned's Family** [SYMP2]

DESCRIPTION/DIRECTIONS: The co-victim expresses sympathy or compassion for the family or family members of the condemned.

KEY WORDS AND PHRASES: "I just feel really bad for his mother. She has lost a child and I know her pain must be great." "I feel sorry for his family."

REMOVAL/EXTERMINATION

51. **No Longer Presents a Threat to Co-Victim(s)** [REMOV1]

DESCRIPTION/DIRECTIONS: The co-victim states that he is glad that the condemned is gone and no longer presents a threat or source of fear for the co-victim(s). This will often be expressed as a relief from fear that existed as long as the condemned was still living. Sometimes it will be more symbolic than real, although it may be expressed as a very real fear that the condemned would escape or get out and come after them.

KEY WORDS AND PHRASES: "I'm just so glad that he's no longer around and can no longer pose a threat to my family."

52. **No Longer Presents Threat to Others/Society** [REMOV2]

DESCRIPTION/DIRECTIONS: The co-victim states that she is glad that the condemned can no longer hurt anyone (other than co-victims). This may also be a general statement about safety for the general public (in light of or due to the execution).

KEY WORDS AND PHRASES: "I'm just relieved that he will never be able to hurt anyone else like he did my grandmother;" "He's gone and the world is a safer place because of it."

53. **Extermination** [EXTERM]

DESCRIPTION/DIRECTIONS: The co-victim expresses the general sentiment that the inmate needed to be killed or gotten rid of (not necessarily for any utilitarian reason). The co-victim may also claim something along the lines of the world needing to be rid of people like the condemned or being a better place (without stating a safer place) without him. Such a statement may accompany a dehumanizing statement.

KEY WORDS AND PHRASES: "He needed to die;" "We don't need people like him breathing our air;" "The world is a better place without him;" "Anyone who can do what he did doesn't deserve to be alive."

HONOR/LEGACY

54. **Speaks to Qualities of Victim** [HONOR1]

DESCRIPTION/DIRECTIONS: The co-victim relays specific qualities of the victim.

KEY WORDS AND PHRASES: "He was a great father and a wonderful man who would give you the shirt off of his back;" "She was so beautiful and had so much going for her. She was going to be a doctor and help people."

55. **Memorializes or Honors Victim** [HONOR2]

DESCRIPTION/DIRECTIONS: The co-victim speaks of honoring the victim or speaks in memory of the victim. This may be expressed by an action such as holding up a picture of the victim.

KEY WORDS AND PHRASES: "This is a moment to remember the grandmother we lost;" "On this occasion, we shouldn't forget the wonderful little girl who was taken from us."

56. **Wishes for Peace/Release for Victim** [RIP]

DESCRIPTION/DIRECTIONS: This will often be expressed as a wish or hope that the deceased victim can now be at peace or now rest in peace.

KEY WORDS AND PHRASES: "My daughter can now finally be at rest."

57. **Refers to Specifics of Victim's Murder** [MURDER]

DESCRIPTION/DIRECTIONS: The co-victim refers to the specific nature of the murder or gives details about it.

KEY WORDS AND PHRASES: "He tortured her for two hours before finally choking her to death with a telephone cord."

58. **Wished to Witness Execution** [WIT]

DESCRIPTION/DIRECTIONS: The co-victim states that they wished they could have been present at or witnessed the execution. This is primarily relevant to pre-1996 executions which co-victims were not allowed to witness.

KEY WORDS AND PHRASES: "I would have liked to have seen him die;" "They should really let the families of the victims witness the execution."

References

Abramson, L. Y., Alloy, L. B., & Metalsky, G. I. (1989). Hopelessness depression: A theory-based subtype of depression. *Psychological Review, 96*, 358-372.

Abramson, L. Y., Seligman, M. E. P., & Teasdale, J. D. (1978). Learned helplessness in humans: Critique and reformulation. *Journal of Abnormal Psychology, 87*, 49-74.

Abu-Jamal, M. (1995). *Live from death row*. New York: Addison-Wesley.

Acker, J. R., Bohm, R. M., & Lanier, C. S. (1998). *America's experiment with capital punishment: Reflections on the past, present, and future of the ultimate penal sanction*. Durham, NC: Carolina Academic Press.

ACLU of Virginia. (2003). *Broken justice: The death penalty in Virginia*. Richmond: ACLU of Virginia, Capital Punishment Project.

Aguirre, A., Davin, R. P., Baker, D. V., & Lee, K. (1999). Sentencing outcomes, race, and victim impact evidence in California: A pre- and post-Payne comparison. *The Justice Professional, 11*, 297-310.

Albert, C. J. (1999). Challenging deterrence: New insights on capital punishment derived from panel data. *University of Pittsburgh Law Review, 60*(2), 321-371.

Alexander, E. K., & Lord, J. H. (1994). *Impact statements: A victim's right to speak...a nation's responsibility to listen*. Arlington, VA: National Victim Center.

American Civil Liberties Union. (2004). *How the death penalty weakens U.S. international interests*. New York: Author.

American Psychiatric Association. (1994). *Diagnostic and statistical manual of mental disorders* (4th ed.). Washington, DC: Author.

Arriens, J. (1997). *Welcome to hell: Letters and writings from death row*. Boston: Northeastern University Press.

Arrigo, B. A., & Fowler, C. R. (2001). The "death row community": A community psychology perspective. *Deviant Behavior, 22*, 43-71.

Arrigo, B. A., & Williams, C. R. (2003). Victim vices, victim voices, and impact statements: On the place of emotion and the role of restorative justice in capital sentencing. *Crime & Delinquency, 49*(4), 603-626.

Atkins v. Virginia, 536 U.S. 304 (2002).

Bailey, W. C. (1998). Deterrence, brutalization, and the death penalty: Another examination of Oklahoma's return to capital punishment. *Criminology, 36*(4), 711-733.

Baldus, D. C., Pulaski, C., & Woodworth, G. (1983). Comparative review of death sentences: An empirical study of the Georgia experience. *Journal of Criminal Law and Criminology, 74*, 661-753.

Baldus, D. C., Pulaski, C., & Woodworth, G. (1986). Arbitrariness and discrimination in the administration of the death penalty: A challenge to state supreme courts. *Stetson Law Review, 15*, 133-261.

Baldus, D. C., Woodworth, G., Zuckerman, D., Weiner, N. A., & Broffitt, B. (1998). Racial discrimination and the death penalty in the post-Furman era: An empirical and legal overview, with recent findings from Philadelphia. *Cornell Law Review, 83*, 1638-1770.

Bandura, A. (1990). Selective activation and disengagement of moral control. *Journal of Social Issues, 46*(1), 27-46.

Bandura, A. (1999). Moral disengagement in the perpetration of inhumanities. *Personality and Social Psychology Review, 3*(3), 193-209.

Beck, E., Blackwell, B. S., Leonard, P. B., & Mears, M. (2003). Seeking sanctuary: Interviews with family members of capital defendants. *Cornell Law Review, 88*, 382-418.

Beck, E., Britto, S., & Andrews, A. (2007). *In the shadow of death: Restorative justice and death row families.* New York: Oxford University Press.

Bedau, H. A., & Cassell, P. G. (2004). *Debating the death penalty: Should America have capital punishment?* New York: Oxford University Press.

Belknap, J. (1996). *The invisible woman: Gender, crime, and justice.* Belmont, CA: Wadsworth Publishing Company.

Belknap, K. L. (1992). The death penalty and victim impact evidence: Payne v. Tennessee, 111 S. Ct. 2597. *Harvard Journal of Law & Public Policy, 15*(1), 275-284.

Beloof, D. E. (2003). Constitutional implications of crime victims as participants. *Cornell Law Review, 88*(2), 282-305.

Berg, B. L. (2004). *Qualitative research methods for the social sciences.* Boston: Pearson Education, Inc.

Berns, W. (1982). The morality of anger. In H. A. Bedau (Ed.), *The death penalty in America* (3rd ed., pp. 333-341). New York: Oxford University Press.

Bessler, J. D. (2003). *Kiss of death: America's love affair with the death penalty.* Boston: Northeastern University Press.

Bianchi, H. (1994). *Justice as sanctuary: Toward a new system of crime control*. Bloomington: Indiana University Press.

Blank, J., & Jensen, E. (2004). *The exonerated.* New York: Faber & Faber, Inc.

Bluestone, H., & McGahee, C. L. (1962). Reaction to extreme stress. *American Journal of Psychiatry, 119*, 393-396.

Blume, J. H. (2003). Ten years of *Payne*: Victim impact evidence in capital cases. *Cornell Law Review, 88*(2), 257-281.

Bohm, R. M. (2007). *Deathquest III: An introduction to the theory and practice of capital punishment in the United States*. Newark, NJ: LexisNexis.

Bohm, R. M., Clark, L. J., & Aveni, A. F. (1991). Knowledge and death penalty opinion: A test of the Marshall Hypotheses. *Journal of Research in Crime and Delinquency, 28*(3), 360-387.

Booth v. Maryland, 482 U.S. 496 (1987).

Boudreaux, P. (1989). *Booth v. Maryland* and the individual vengeance rationale for criminal punishment. *The Journal of Criminal Law and Criminology, 80*(1), 177-196.

Bowers, W. J., & Pierce, G. L. (1980). Deterrence or brutalization: What is the effect of executions? *Crime and Delinquency, 26*(4), 453-484.

Braithwaite, J. (1989). *Crime, shame, and reintegration.* Cambridge: Cambridge University Press.

Braithwaite, J. (1999). A future where punishment is marginalized: Realistic or utopian? *UCLA Law Review, 46*, 1727-1750.

Braswell, M., Fuller, J., & Lozoff, B. (2001). *Corrections, peacemaking, and restorative justice*. Cincinnati, OH: Anderson Publishing Co.

Brown, S. L. (1991). *Counseling victims of violence*. Alexandria, VA: American Association for Counseling and Development.

Buffington-Vollum, J. K. (2005). *The utility of the Sorensen and Pilgrim actuarial model in predicting institutional violence among death row inmates*. Unpublished doctoral dissertation, Sam Houston State University, Huntsville, TX.

Bureau of Justice Statistics. (2002). *Capital punishment, 2002.* Washington, DC: U.S. Department of Justice, Office of Justice Programs.

Bursik, R. J. (1988). Social disorganization and theories of crime and delinquency: Problems and prospects. *Criminology, 26*(4), 519-551.

Callihan, J. M. (2003). Victim impact statements in capital trials: A selected bibliography. *Cornell Law Review, 88*(2), 569-581.

Camus, A. (1960). *Resistance, rebellion, and death.* New York: Alfred Knopf, Inc.

Cerney, M. S. (1999). Healing the wounds of sibling survivors of violence. In H. V. Hall (Ed.), *Lethal violence: A sourcebook on fatal domestic, acquaintance and stranger violence* (pp. 527-541). Boca Raton, FL: CRC Press.

Christie, N. (1977). Conflicts as property. *The British Journal of Criminology, 17*, 1-15.

Cloninger, D. O., & Marchesini, R. (2001). Execution and deterrence: A quasi-controlled group experiment. *Applied Economics, 33*(3), 569-576.

Coates, R. B., & Gehm, J. (1989). An empirical assessment. In M. Wright, & B. Galaway (Eds.), *Mediation and criminal justice: Victims, offenders and community* (pp. 251-263). Newbury Park, CA: Sage Publications.

Cochran, J. K., Boots, D. P., & Heide, K. M. (2003). Attribution styles and attitudes toward capital punishment for juveniles, the mentally incompetent, and the mentally retarded. *Justice Quarterly, 20*(1), 65-93.

Cochran, J. K., & Chamlin, M. B. (2000). Deterrence and brutalization: The dual effects of executions. *Justice Quarterly, 17*(4), 685-706.

Cose, E. (2004). *Bone to pick: Of forgiveness, reconciliation, reparation, and revenge*. New York: Atria Books.

Daly, K. (1999, September). *Does punishment have a place in restorative justice?* Paper presented at the Australia and New Zealand Society of Criminology Annual Conference, Perth, Australia.

Daly, K., & Immarigeon, R. (1998). The past, present, and future of restorative justice: Some critical reflections. *Contemporary Justice Review, 1*(1), 21-45.

Darrow, C. (1957). *Attorney for the damned.* New York: Simon and Schuster.

Davis, R. C., & Smith, B. E. (1994a). The effects of victim impact statements on sentencing decisions: A test in an urban setting. *Justice Quarterly, 11*(3), 453-469.

Davis, R. C., & Smith, B. E. (1994b). Victim impact statements and victim satisfaction: An unfulfilled promise? *Journal of Criminal Justice, 22*(1), 1-12.

Death Penalty Information Center. (2007a). Retrieved July 25, 2007, from http://www.deathpenaltyinfo.org/

Death Penalty Information Center. (2007b). Victims and the death penalty. Retrieved July 25, 2007, from http://www.deathpenaltyinfo.org/article.php?did=573&scid=62

Death Penalty Information Center. (2007c). Victims News and Developments, 2003-1998. Retrieved July 25, 2007, from http://www.deathpenaltyinfo.org/article.php?&did=2087

del Carmen, R. V., Vollum, S., Cheeseman, K., Frantzen, D., & San Miguel, C. (2005). *The death penalty: Constitutional issues, commentaries and case briefs*. Cincinnati, OH: Anderson Publishing.

Dickey, W. J. (1998). Forgiveness and crime: The possibilities of restorative justice. In R. D. Enright, & J. North (Eds.), *Exploring forgiveness* (pp. 106-120). Madison: University of Wisconsin Press.

Dicks, S. (1991). *Victims of crime and punishment: Interviews with victims, convicts, their families, and support groups*. Jefferson, NC: McFarland & Company, Inc.

Dicks, S. (2000). *Death row: Interviews with inmates, their families and opponents of capital punishment.* San Jose, CA: iUniverse.com, Inc.

Domino, M. L., & Boccaccini, M. T. (2000). Doubting Thomas: Should family members of victims watch executions? *Law and Psychology Review, 24*, 59-75.

Dostoevsky, F. (1958). *The idiot.* New York: Bantam Books.

Doyle, P. (1980). *Grief counseling and sudden death.* Springfield, IL: Charles C. Thomas.

Durham, A. M., Elrod, H. P., & Kinkade, P. T. (1996). Public support for the death penalty: Beyond Gallup. *Justice Quarterly, 13*(4), 705-736.

Dzur, A. W., & Wertheimer, A. (2002). Forgiveness and public deliberation: The practice of restorative justice. *Criminal Justice Ethics, 21*(1), 3-30.

Ehrlich, I. (1975). The deterrent effect of capital punishment: A question of life and death. *American Economic Review, 65*, 397-417.

Ehrlich, I. (1977). Capital punishment and deterrence. *Journal of Political Economy, 85*, 741-788.

Eisenberg, T., Garvey, S. P., & Wells, M. T. (2003). Victim characteristics and victim impact evidence in South Carolina capital cases. *Cornell Law Review, 88*(2), 306-342.

Ekland-Olson, S. (1988). Structured discretion, racial bias and the death penalty: The first decade after *Furman* in Texas. *Social Science Quarterly, 69*, 853-873.

Enright, R. D. (2001). *Forgiveness is a choice: A step-by-step process for resolving anger and restoring hope.* Washington, DC: American Psychological Association.

Enright, R. D., & North, J. (1998). *Exploring forgiveness*. Madison: The University of Wisconsin Press.

Erez, E. (1994). Victim participation in sentencing: And the debate goes on... *International Review of Victimology, 3*, 17-32.

Erez, E., & Roeger, L. (1995). The effect of victim impact statements on sentencing patterns and outcomes: The Australian experience. *Journal of Criminal Justice, 23*(4), 363-375.

Erez, E., Roeger, L., & Morgan, F. (1997). Victim harm, impact statements and victim satisfaction with justice: An Australian Experience. *International Review of Victimology, 5*, 37-60.

Erez, E., & Rogers, L. (1999). Victim impact statements and sentencing outcomes and processes. *British Journal of Criminology, 39*(2), 216-239.

Eschholz, S., Reed, M. D., Beck, E., & Leonard, P. B. (2003). Offenders' family members' responses to capital crimes: The need for restorative justice initiatives. *Homicide Studies, 7*(2), 154-181.

Espy, M. W. (1980). Capital punishment and deterrence: What the statistics cannot show. *Crime and Delinquency, 26*, 537-544.

Espy, W. (1989). Facing the death penalty. In M. L. Radelet (Ed.), *Facing the death penalty: Essays on a cruel and unusual punishment* (pp. 27-37). Philadelphia: Temple University Press.

Estrada-Hollenbeck, M. (1996). Forgiving in the face of injustice: Victims' and perpetrators' perspectives. In B. Galaway, & J. Hudson (Eds.), *Restorative justice: International perspectives* (pp. 303-313). Monsey, NY: Criminal Justice Press.

Ewing, C. P. (1998). "Above all, do no harm": The role of health and mental health professionals in the capital punishment process. In J. R. Acker, R. M. Bohm, & C. S. Lanier (Eds.), *America's experiment with capital punishment: Reflections on the past, present, and future of the ultimate penal sanction* (pp. 461-476). Durham, NC: Carolina Academic Press.

Fagan, J. (2005, January). *Deterrence and the death penalty: A critical review of new evidence.* Report presented at the Hearings on the Future of Capital Punishment in the State of New York, Assembly Standing Committee on Codes, Assembly Standing Committee on Judiciary and Assembly Standing Committee on Correction, Albany, NY.

Ferrell, J. (1998). Honesty, secrecy, and deception in the sociology of crime: Confessions and reflections from the backstage. In J. Ferrell & M.S. Hamm (Eds.), *Criminological verstehen: Inside the immediacy of crime* (pp. 20-42). Boston: Northeastern University Press.

Fitzgibbons, R. (1998). Anger and the healing power of forgiveness: A psychiatrist's view. In R. D. Enright, & J. North (Eds.), *Exploring forgiveness* (pp. 63-74). Madison: University of Wisconsin Press.

Flack, K. (1993). A look at day-to-day death row operations. *Corrections Today, 55*(4), 74-76.

Flaten, C. L. (1996). Victim-offender mediation: Application with serious offenses committed by juveniles. In B. Galaway, & J. Hudson (Eds.), *Restorative justice: International perspectives* (pp. 387-401). Monsey, NY: Criminal Justice Press.

Fleury-Steiner, B. (2004). *Jurors' stories of death: How America's death penalty invests in inequality*. Ann Arbor: The University of Michigan Press.

Ford v. State, 919 S.W. 2nd 107 (Tex. Cr. App. 1996).

Foucault, M. (1975). *Discipline and punish: The birth of the prison*. New York: Vintage Books.

Freedy, J. R., Resnick, H. S., Kilpatrick, D. G., Dansky, B. S., & Tidwell, R. P. (1994). The psychological adjustment of recent crime victims in the criminal justice system. *Journal of Interpersonal Violence, 9*(4), 450-468.

Freeman, L. N., Shaffer, D., & Smith, H. (1996). Neglected victims of homicide: The needs of young siblings of murder victims. *American Journal of Orthopsychiatry, 66*(3), 337-345.

Garland, D. (1990). *Punishment and modern society: A study in social theory*. Chicago: The University of Chicago Press.

Garvey, S. P. (1999). Punishment as atonement. *UCLA Law Review, 46*, 1801-1858.

Geberth, V. J. (1992). Secondary victims of homicide. *Law and Order, 40*(9), 91-96.

Gehm, J. R. (1992). The function of forgiveness in the criminal justice system. In H. Messmer, & H. U. Otto (Eds.), *Restorative justice on trial* (pp. 541-550). Netherlands: Kluwer Academic Publishers.

Gehm, J. R. (1998). Victim-offender mediation programs: An exploration of practice and theoretical frameworks. *Western Criminology Review, 1*(1). Retrieved October 31, 2005, from http://wcr.sonoma.edu/v1n1/gehm.html

Giarratano, J. M. (1989). The pains of life. In M. L. Radelet (Ed.), *Facing the death penalty: Essays on a cruel and unusual punishment* (pp. 193-197). Philadelphia: Temple University Press.

Gillespie, L. K. (2003). *Inside the death chamber: Exploring executions.* Boston: Allyn & Bacon.

Goffman, E. (1959). *The presentation of self in everyday life.* Garden City, NY: Doubleday.

Goffman, E. (1967). *Interaction ritual.* Garden City, NY: Doubleday.

Goffman, E. (1974). *Frame analysis: An essay on the organization of experience.* Cambridge, MA: Harvard University Press.

Greene, E. (1999). The many guises of victim impact evidence and effects on jurors' judgments. *Psychology, Crime and Law, 5*, 331-348.

Greene, E., Koehring, H., & Quiat, M. (1998). Victim impact evidence in capital cases: Does the victim's character matter? *Journal of Applied Social Psychology, 28*, 145-156.

Gross, S. R., & Matheson, D. J. (2003). What they say at the end: Capital victims' families and the press. *Cornell Law Review, 88*(2), 486-516.

Haley, J. O. (1989). Confession, repentance and absolution. In M. Wright, & B. Galaway (Eds.), *Mediation and criminal justice: Victims, offenders and community* (pp. 195-211). Newbury Park, CA: Sage Publications.

Halmari, H. (1998, July). *Discourse of death: The function of the local newspaper coverage of Huntsville, Texas executions.* Paper submitted to the Proceedings of the 6th International Pragmatics Conference, Reims, France.

Heflick, N. A. (2005). Sentenced to die: Last statements and dying on death row. *OMEGA: Journal of Death & Dying, 51*(4), 323-336.

Hochstetler, A. (2001). Reporting of executions in U.S. newspapers. *Journal of Crime and Justice, 24*(1), 1-13.

Hood, R. (2002). *The death penalty: A worldwide perspective.* New York: Oxford University Press.

Immarigeon, R. (1996). Prison-based victim-offender reconciliation programs. In B. Galaway, & J. Hudson (Eds.), *Restorative justice: International perspectives* (pp. 463-476). Monsey, NY: Criminal Justice Press.

Ingle, J. B. (1989). Ministering to the condemned: A case study. In M. L. Radelet (Ed.), *Facing the death penalty: Essays on a cruel and unusual punishment* (pp. 112-122). Philadelphia: Temple University Press.

Johnson, R. (1981). *Condemned to die: Life under sentence of death.* New York: Elsevier.

Johnson, R. (1998). *Death work: A study of the modern execution process.* Belmont, CA: West/Wadsworth.

Kane, K. (1986). Forgotten families of death row. *The Defender, 8*, 33-35.

Keil, J., & Vito, G. (1995). Race and the death penalty in Kentucky murder trials: 1971-1991. *The Advocate, 17*, 5-15.

King, K. (2004). It hurts so bad: Comparing grieving patterns of the families of murder victims with those of families of death row inmates. *Criminal Justice Policy Review, 15*(2), 193-211.

King, R. (2003). *Don't kill in our names: Families of murder victims speak out against the death penalty*. New Brunswick, NJ: Rutgers University Press.

King, R. (2005). *Capital consequences: Families of the condemned tell their stories*. New Brunswick, NJ: Rutgers University Press.

Kirchmeier, J. L. (2002). Another place beyond here: The death penalty moratorium movement in the United States. *University of Colorado Law Review, 73*, 1-116.

Klockars, C. (1974). *The Professional Fence*. New York: Free Press.

Kobil, D. T. (1998). The evolving role of clemency in capital cases. In J. R. Acker, R. M. Bohm, & C. S. Lanier (Eds.), *America's experiment with capital punishment: Reflections on the past, present, and future of the ultimate penal sanction* (pp. 531-546). Durham, NC: Carolina Academic Press.

Kubler-Ross, E. (1969). *On death and dying*. New York: Simon & Schuster.

Latimer, J., Dowden, C., & Muise, D. (2001). *The effectiveness of restorative practice: A meta-analysis*. Ottawa, Canada: Department of Justice, Research and Statistics Division Methodological Series.

Lifton, R. J., & Mitchell, G. (2000). *Who owns death? Capital punishment, the American conscience, and the end of executions*. New York: William Morrow.

Llewellyn, J. J., & Howse, R. (1999). *Restorative justice: A conceptual framework*. Toronto: Law Commission of Canada.

Luginbuhl, J., & Burkhead, M. (1995). Victim impact evidence in a capital trial: Encouraging votes for death. *American Journal of Criminal Justice, 20*(1), 1-16.

Lynch, M. (2002). Capital punishment as moral imperative: Pro-death penalty discourse on the internet. *Punishment and Society, 4*(2), 213-236.

Magee, D. (1983). *What murder leaves behind: The victim's family*. New York: Dodd, Mead & Company.

Martin, G. N. (1993). Enforcing the death penalty with competence, compassion. *Corrections Today, 55*(4), 60-62.

McCullough, M. E., Pargament, K. I., & Thoresen, C. E. (2000). *Forgiveness: Theory, research and practice*. New York: Guilford Press.

Meek, E. A. (1992). Victim impact evidence and capital sentencing: A casenote on Payne v. Tennessee. *Louisiana Law Review, 52*, 1299-1310.

Mello, M. (1989). Another Attorney for Life. In M. L. Radelet (Ed.), *Facing the death penalty: Essays on a cruel and unusual punishment* (pp. 81-91). Philadelphia: Temple University Press.

Miller, K. S., & Radelet, M. L. (1993). *Executing the mentally ill: The criminal justice system and the case of Alvin Ford*. Newbury Park, CA: Sage Publications.

Moore, D. B., & O'Connell, T. A. (1994). Family conferencing in Wagga Wagga: A communitarian model of justice. In C. Alder, & J. Wundersitz (Eds.), *Family conferencing and juvenile justice: The way forward or misplaced optimism?* (pp. 45-86). Canberra: Australian Institute of Criminology.

Morris, A., & Maxwell, G. (1998, June 1). Restorative justice in New Zealand: Family group conferences as a case study. *Western Criminology Review, 1*(1). Retrieved October 31, 2005, from http://wcr.sonoma.edu/v1n1/morris.html

Mosley v. State, 983 S.W. 2nd 249 (Tx Crim. App. 1998).

Murder Victims' Families for Reconciliation. (2005). Retrieved November 7, 2005 at http://www.mvfr.org/

Myers, B., & Arbuthnot, J. (1999). The effects of victim impact evidence on the verdicts and sentencing judgments of mock jurors. *Journal of Offender Rehabilitation, 29*(3/4), 95-112.

Myers, B., & Greene, E. (2004). The prejudicial nature of victim impact statements: Implications for capital sentencing policy. *Psychology, Public Policy, and Law, 10*(4), 492-515.

Niven, D. (2004). Southern newspaper coverage of exonerations from death row. *Journal of Criminal Justice and Popular Culture, 11*(1), 20-31.

Nugent, W. R., Umbreit, M. S., Wiinamaki, L., & Paddock, J. (2001). Participation in victim-offender mediation and reoffense: Successful replication? *Journal of Research on Social Work Practice, 11*(1), 5-23.

Obold-Eshleman, C. (2004). Victims' rights and the danger of domestication of the restorative justice paradigm. *Notre Dame Journal of Law, Ethics & Public Policy, 18*, 571-603.

Osofsky, M. J., Bandura, A. & Zimbardo, P. G. (2005). The role of moral disengagement in the execution process. *Law and Human Behavior, 29*(4), 371-393.

Panetti v. Quartermain, No. 06-6407 (2007).

Parkes, C. M. (1993). Psychiatric problems following bereavement by murder or manslaughter. *British Journal of Psychiatry, 162*, 49-54.

Payne v. Tennessee, 501 U.S. 808 (1991).

Phillips, A. K. (1997). Thou shalt not kill any nice people: The problem of victim impact statements in capital sentencing. *American Criminal Law Review, 35*, 93-118.

Physicians for Human Rights. (1994). *Breach of trust: Physician participation in executions in the United States*. New York: Human Rights Watch.

Pickett, C., & Stowers, C. (2002). *Within these walls: Memoirs of a death house chaplain.* New York: St. Martin's Press.

Posner, A. K. (1984). Victim impact statements and restitution: Making the punishment fit the victim. *Brooklyn Law Review , 50*, 301-338.

Potter, J. (2004). Discourse analysis as a way of analysing naturally occurring talk. In D. Silverman (Ed.), *Qualitative research: Theory, method and practice* (pp. 200-221). Thousand Oaks, CA: Sage Publications.

Prejean, H. (1993). *Dead man walking*. New York: Vintage Books.

Purdum, E. D., & Paredes, J. A. (1989). Rituals of death: Capital punishment and human sacrifice. In M. L. Radelet (Ed.), *Facing the death penalty: Essays on a cruel and unusual punishment* (pp. 139-155). Philadelphia: Temple University Press.

Radelet, M. L. (1989). *Facing the death penalty: Essays on a cruel and unusual punishment*. Philadelphia: Temple University Press.

Radelet, M. L., & Akers, R. L. (1996). Deterrence and the death penalty: The views of the experts. *The Journal of Criminal Law & Criminology, 87*(1), 1-16.

Radelet, M. L., & Borg, M. J. (2000a). The changing nature of death penalty debates. *Annual Review of Sociology, 26*, 43-61.

Radelet, M. L., & Borg, M. J. (2000b). Comment on Umbreit and Vos: Retributive versus restorative justice. *Homicide Studies, 4*(1), 88-92.

Radelet, M. L., Vandiver, M., & Berardo, F. M. (1983). Families, prisons, and men with death sentences: The human impact of structured uncertainty. *Journal of Family Issues, 4*, 593-612.

Ragin, C. C. (1994). *Constructing social research.* Thousand Oaks, CA: Pine Forge Press.

Ransley, C., & Spy, T. (2004). *Forgiveness and the healing process: A central therapeutic concern.* New York: Brunner-Routledge.

Reid, D., & Gurwell, J. (2001). *Have a seat, please*. Huntsville: Texas Review Press.

Riffe, D., Lacy, S., & Fico, F. G. (1998). *Analyzing media messages: Using quantitative content analysis in research.* Mahwah, NJ: Lawrence Erlbaum Associates, Publishers.

Ring v. Arizona, 536 U.S. 584 (2002).

Robertson, D. (2002). *Tears from heaven, voices from hell: The pros and cons of the death penalty as seen through the eyes of the victims of violent crime and death row inmates throughout America.* New York: Writers Club Press.

Robinson, M. B. (2008). *Death nation: The experts explain American capital punishment.* Upper Saddle River, NJ: Pearson Prentice Hall.

Rock, P. (1998). Murderers, victims and 'survivors'. *The British Journal of Criminology, 38*(2), 185-200.

Roper v. Simmons, 125 S. Ct. 1183 (2005).

Rossi, R. M. (2004). *Waiting to die: Life on death row*. New York: Vision Paperbacks.

Sampson, R. J., & Groves, W. B. (1989). Community structure and crime: Testing social disorganization theory. *American Journal of Sociology, 94*(4), 774-802.

Sarat, A. (1997). Vengeance, victims and the identities of law. *Social & Legal Studies, 6*(2), 163-189.

Sarat, A. (2001). *When the state kills: Capital punishment and the American condition.* Princeton, NJ: Princeton University Press.

Savage, J., & Kanazawa, S. (2002). Social capital, crime, and human nature. *Journal of Contemporary Criminal Justice, 18*(2), 188-211.

Schneider, G. B. (1992). Victim impact statements: A victim's steam valve. *Criminal Justice Journal, 14*(2), 407-424.

Schutt, R. K. (2004). *Investigating the social world: The process and practice of research* (4th ed.). Thousand Oaks, CA: Pine Forge Press.

Shepherd, J. M. (2004). *Deterrence versus brutalization: Capital punishment's differing impacts among states.* Unpublished manuscript.

Slone, N., Barrile, L., Donovan, P., Cotterman, N., & Smith, A. (2002, November). *Their dying words: Analyzing the last statements of executed offenders.* Paper presented at the annual meetings of the American Society of Criminology, Chicago, IL.

Smith v. State, 919 S.W. 2nd 96 (Tx. Crim. App. 1996).

Smykla, J. O. (1987). The human impact of capital punishment: Interviews with families of persons on death row. *Journal of Criminal Justice, 15*, 331-347.

Sorensen, J., Wrinkle, R., Brewer, V., & Marquart, J. (1999). Capital punishment and deterrence: Examining the effect of executions on murder in Texas. *Crime & Delinquency, 45*(4), 481-493.

South Carolina v. Gathers, 490 U.S. 805 (1989).

Sprang, M. V., McNeil, J. S., & Wright, R. (1989). Psychological changes after the murder of a significant other. *Social Casework: The Journal of Contemporary Social Work, 70*(3), 159-164.

Steffen, L. (1998). *Executing justice: The moral meaning of the death penalty.* Cleveland, OH: The Pilgrim Press.

Stolzenberg, L., & D'Alessio, S. J. (2004). Capital punishment, execution publicity and murder in Houston, Texas. *The Journal of Criminal Law and Criminology, 94*(2), 351-379.

Strauss, A., & Corbin, J. (1990). *Basics of qualitative research: grounded theory procedures and techniques*. Newbury Park, CA: Sage Publications.

Sunriver Cartel. (2000). *Texas death row: Executions in the modern era.* Atlanta, GA: Longstreet Press.

Szmania, S. J. (2005). Victim offender mediation media coverage has both potential and pitfalls. *VOMA Connections, 19*, 6-10.

Tavuchis, N. (1991). *Mea culpa: A sociology of apology and reconciliation.* Stanford, CA: Stanford University Press.

Texas Department of Criminal Justice. (2005a). *Death row facts.* Retrieved November 7, 2005, from http://www.tdcj.state.tx.us/stat/drowfacts.htm

Texas Department of Criminal Justice. (2005b). *Executed offenders.* Retrieved November 7, 2005, from http://www.tdcj.state.tx.us/stat/executedoffenders.htm

Texas Department of Criminal Justice. (2005c). *Viewing executions*. Retrieved November 7, 2005, from http://www.tdcj.state.tx.us/victim/victim-viewexec.htm

Thigpen, M. L. (1993). A tough assignment (managing death row). *Corrections Today, 55*(4), 56-57.

Tonry, M. (2004). *Thinking about crime: Sense and sensibility in American penal culture*. New York: Oxford University Press.

Trail, R. (2002). The future of capital punishment in the United States: Effects of the international trend towards abolition of the death penalty. *Suffolk Transnational Law Review, 26*, 105-131.

Trochim, W. M. K. (2001). *The research methods knowledge base* (2nd ed.). Cincinnati, OH: Atomic Dog Publishing.

Tunnell, K. D. (1998). Honesty, secrecy, and deception in the sociology of crime: Confessions and reflections from the backstage. In J. Ferrell, & M.S. Hamm (Eds.), *Ethnography at the edge: Crime, deviance, and field research* (pp. 206-220). Boston: Northeastern University Press.

Turow, S. (2003). *Ultimate punishment: A lawyer's reflection on dealing with the death penalty*. New York: Farrar, Straus and Giroux.

Umbreit, M. S. (1989a). Crime victims seeking fairness, not revenge: Toward restorative justice. *Federal Probation, 53*, 52-57.

Umbreit, M. S. (1989b). Violent offenders and their victims. In M. Wright, & B. Galaway (Eds.), *Mediation and criminal justice: Victims, offenders and community* (pp. 99-112). Newbury Park, CA: Sage Publications.

Umbreit, M. S. (1996). Restorative justice through mediation: The impact of programs in four Canadian provinces. In B. Galaway, & J. Hudson (Eds.), *Restorative justice: international perspectives* (pp. 373-385). Monsey, NY: Criminal Justice Press.

Umbreit, M. S. (1998). Restorative justice through victim-offender mediation: A multi-site assessment. *Western Criminology Review, 1*(1). Retrieved October 31, 2005, from http://wcr.sonoma.edu/v1n1/umbreit.html

Umbreit, M. S., Coates, R. B., & Vos, B. (2001a). The impact of victim-offender mediation: Two decades of research. *Federal Probation, 65*(3), 29-35.

Umbreit, M. S., Coates, R. B., & Vos, B. (2001b). *Victim offender mediation & dialogue in crimes of severe violence*. St. Paul, MN: Center for Restorative Justice & Peacemaking.

Umbreit, M. S., & Vos, B. (2000). Homicide survivors meet the offender prior to execution: Restorative justice through dialogue. *Homicide Studies, 4*(1), 63-87.

Umbreit, M. S., Vos, B., Coates, R. B., & Brown, K. A. (2003). *Facing violence: The path of restorative justice and dialogue*. Monsey, NY: Criminal Justice Press.

Van Ness, D., & Strong, K. H. (1997). *Restoring justice*. Cincinnati, OH: Anderson Publishing Co.

Van Stokkom, B. (2002). Moral emotions in restorative justice conferences: Managing shame, designing empathy. *Theoretical Criminology, 6*(3), 339-360.

Vandiver, M. (1989). Coping with death: Families of the terminally ill, homicide victims, and condemned prisoners. In M. L. Radelet (Ed.), *Facing the death penalty: Essays on a cruel and unusual punishment* (pp. 123-138). Philadelphia: Temple University Press.

Vandiver, M. (1998). The impact of the death penalty on the families of homicide victims and of condemned prisoners. In J. R. Acker , R. M. Bohm, & C. S. Lanier (Eds.), *America's experiment with capital punishment: Reflections on the past, present, and future of the ultimate penal sanction* (pp. 477-505). Durham, NC: Carolina Academic Press.

Vandiver, M., Giacopassi, D. J., & Gathje, P. R. (2002). "I hope someone murders your mother!": An exploration of extreme support for the death penalty. *Deviant Behavior: An Interdisciplinary Journal, 23*, 385-415.

Vasquez, D. B. (1993). Helping prison staff handle the stress of an execution. *Corrections Today, 55*(4), 70-71.

Vollum, S. (2005, March). *An examination of Supreme Court death penalty jurisprudence: The (de)evolution of the "death is different" doctrine*. Paper presented at the annual meetings of the Academy of Criminal Justice Sciences, Chicago, IL.

Vollum, S., Kubena, J., & Buffington-Vollum, J. (2004, March). *Attitudes about the death penalty: An examination of underlying bases of support for the "ultimate punishment."* Paper presented at the annual meetings of the Academy of Criminal Justice Sciences, Las Vegas, NV.

Vollum, S. & Longmire, D. R. (2007). Covictims of capital murder: Statements of victims' family members and friends made at the time of execution. *Violence and Victims, 22*(5), 599-617.

Vollum, S. & Longmire, D. R. (Forthcoming). Giving voice to the dead: The last statements of condemned inmates. *Contemporary Justice Review*.

Vollum, S., Longmire, D. R., & Buffington-Vollum, J. (2004). Confidence in the death penalty and support for its use: Exploring the value-expressive dimension of death penalty attitudes. *Justice Quarterly, 21*(3), 521-546.

Weber, R. P. (1985). *Basic content analysis*. Beverly Hills, CA: Sage Publications.

Webster's new world dictionary of the American language (2nd College ed.). (1976). Cleveland, OH: William Collins World Publishing Co., Inc.

West, L. J. (1975). Psychiatric reflections on the death penalty. *American Journal of Orthopsychiatry, 45*, 689-700.

Westberg, G. E. (1962). *Good grief.* Philadelphia: Fortress Press.

Wimmer, R. D., & Dominick, J. R. (2000). *Mass media research: An introduction.* Belmont, CA: Wadsworth Publishing Company.

Wolfgang, M. E. (1958). *Patterns of criminal homicide*. Philadelphia: University of Pennsylvania Press.

Wollan, L. A. (1989). Representing the death row inmate: The ethics of advocacy, collateral style. In M. L. Radelet (Ed.), *Facing the death penalty: Essays on a cruel and unusual punishment* (pp. 92-111). Philadelphia: Temple University Press.

Wright, M. (1996). *Justice for victims and offenders: A restorative response to crime* (2nd ed.). Winchester, UK: Waterside Press.

Zehr, H. (1990). *Changing lenses*. Scottsdale, PA: Herald Press.

Zehr, H., & Mika, H. (1998). Fundamental concepts of restorative justice. *Contemporary Justice Review, 1*(1), 47-55.

Zimring, F. E. (2003). *The contradictions of American capital punishment.* New York: Oxford University Press.

Index

M

O

P

R

S

T

V

W

Z

CPSIA information can be obtained at www.ICGtesting.com
265310BV00001B/2/P

9 781593 324360